Johann Bernhard Basedow and the Transformation of Modern Education

Also Available From Bloomsbury

Emotion, Reason, and Action in Kant, Maria Borges
Intellectual Agency and Virtue Epistemology, Patrick Frierson
Kant's Transition Project and Late Philosophy, Oliver Thorndike
The Philosophy of Anne Conway, Jonathan Head

Johann Bernhard Basedow and the Transformation of Modern Education

Educational Reform in the German Enlightenment

Robert B. Louden

BLOOMSBURY ACADEMIC
LONDON • NEW YORK • OXFORD • NEW DELHI • SYDNEY

BLOOMSBURY ACADEMIC
Bloomsbury Publishing Plc
50 Bedford Square, London, WC1B 3DP, UK
1385 Broadway, New York, NY 10018, USA
29 Earlsfort Terrace, Dublin 2, Ireland

BLOOMSBURY, BLOOMSBURY ACADEMIC and the Diana logo are trademarks of
Bloomsbury Publishing Plc

First published in Great Britain 2021
This paperback edition published in 2022

Copyright © Robert B. Louden, 2021

Robert B. Louden has asserted his right under the Copyright, Designs and Patents Act, 1988, to be identified as Author of this work.

For legal purposes the Acknowledgments on p. ix constitute an extension of this copyright page.

Cover design by Charlotte Daniels
Cover image © Quagga Media / Alamy Stock Photo

All rights reserved. No part of this publication may be reproduced or transmitted in any form or by any means, electronic or mechanical, including photocopying, recording, or any information storage or retrieval system, without prior permission in writing from the publishers.

Bloomsbury Publishing Plc does not have any control over, or responsibility for, any third-party websites referred to or in this book. All internet addresses given in this book were correct at the time of going to press. The author and publisher regret any inconvenience caused if addresses have changed or sites have ceased to exist, but can accept no responsibility for any such changes.

A catalogue record for this book is available from the British Library.

Library of Congress Cataloging-in-Publication Data

Names: Louden, Robert B., 1953- author.
Title: Johann Bernhard Basedow and the transformation of modern education: educational reform in the German Enlightenment / Robert B. Louden.
Description: London; New York: Bloomsbury Academic, 2020. | Includes bibliographical references and index.
Identifiers: LCCN 2020033923 (print) | LCCN 2020033924 (ebook) | ISBN 9781350163669 (hardback) | ISBN 9781350194090 (paperback) | ISBN 9781350163676 (ebook) | ISBN 9781350163683 (epub)
Subjects: LCSH: Basedow, Johann Bernhard, 1724-1790. | Education–Germany–History–18th century. | Enlightenment–Germany. | Educators–Germany–Biography.
Classification: LCC LB575.B4 L68 2020 (print) | LCC LB575.B4 (ebook) | DDC 370.92 [B]–dc23
LC record available at https://lccn.loc.gov/2020033923
LC ebook record available at https://lccn.loc.gov/2020033924

ISBN: HB: 978-1-35016-366-9
PB: 978-1-3501-9409-0
ePDF: 978-1-3501-6367-6
eBook: 978-1-3501-6368-3

Typeset by RefineCatch Limited, Bungay, Suffolk

To find out more about our authors and books visit www.bloomsbury.com
and sign up for our newsletters.

For Hiroko

Contents

List of Illustrations		viii
Acknowledgments		ix
Abbreviations		xi
	Introduction	1
1	A New School for a New Age	9
2	Blame It on the Parents?	29
3	College Days	45
4	A New Way of Teaching	53
5	The Professor	63
6	That Old-Time Religion	79
7	"For Fathers and Mothers of Families and Nations:" The *Methodenbuch*	95
8	"A Well-Ordered Stock of All Necessary Knowledge:" The *Elementarwerk*	129
9	Back to School	149
10	After School	167
11	"The Mother of All Good Schools in the World"	175
Notes		185
References		211
Index		223

Illustrations

1. Portrait of Basedow by Daniel Chodowiecki, 1769. (By permission of the Graphische Sammlung, Fach Kunstgeschichte der Universität Trier.) — 8
2. The original title page of Basedow's *Methodenbuch*, 1770. (By permission of the Universitäts- und Landesbibliothek Sachsen-Anhalt, Halle (Saale).) — 94
3. The original title page of Basedow's *Elementarwerk*, 1774. (By permission of the Staatsbibliothek Berlin: PK: https://digital.staatsbibliothek-berlin.de/werkansicht/?PPN=PPN1016516983.) — 128
4. The first Philanthropin building in Dessau (on the right—destroyed in the Second World War). (By permission of the Stadtarchiv Dessau-Roßlau.) — 148
5. The second Philanthropin building in Dessau (Palais Dietrich). (By permission of the Stadtarchiv Dessau-Roßlau.) — 154
6. Robert B. Louden at the new Basedow Memorial in Magdeburg, July 2018. (By permission of Hiroko Fogarty.) — 176

Acknowledgments

Much of the research for and writing of this book was done in Halle, Germany in 2018, where I was a guest of the Philosophy Seminar and IZEA (Interdizplinäres Zentrum für die Erforschung der Europäischen Aufklärung) at Martin-Luther-Universität. My work in Halle was supported by research grants from both the Fulbright and Alexander von Humboldt Foundations, and I am very grateful to each of these groups for making my extended visit to Germany possible. I am also indebted to Heiner Klemme, my host in Halle, as well as to Allen Wood, Manfred Kuehn, and the late Michael Bachem, for their letters in support of my Fulbright application.

The library at IZEA—the best research library for work on the Enlightenment that I have ever had the pleasure of visiting—was always one of my favorite places to visit in Halle. Special thanks here to Andrea Thiele, IZEA's Research Coordinator, and to Director Daniel Fulda, both of whom helped me to feel at home there.

Sigrun Rößler, Secretary of the Philosophy Seminar, and Antonino Falduto, Lecturer in Philosophy, were both extremely generous with their time in helping me to become acclimated to the city of Halle as well as the university.

During my stay in Halle I lived at the Georg Forster Haus, a new university guest house for visiting scholars just down the street from the Philosophy Seminar. The opportunity it afforded me to interact with fellow researchers from a number of different countries and academic disciplines was another highlight of my visit. The university's *Sprachenzentrum* was also near the Forster Haus, and I would like to thank Frank Schulze for allowing me to sit in on several of the German courses for foreign students that he taught there.

Thanks also to Eckhard Zilm, former principal of the Philanthropinum Gymnasium in Dessau, as well as Ralf Schüler, assistant for twin-town partnerships in Dessau-Roßlau, for their informative tour of Dessau as well as the field trip they organized to the Salzmann Schule in Schnepfenthal—and to Daniel Franch, a fellow US Fulbrighter who was working as an English instructor at the Philanthropinum in 2018, for putting me in touch with Zilm and Schüler.

I finished a draft of the manuscript in late spring 2019, while I was working in Honolulu, Hawaii. This extended visit was made possible by a leave of absence from my home institution, the University of Southern Maine. While I was in Honolulu I enjoyed the hospitality of the Philosophy Department at the University of Hawaii at Mānoa as well as the resources of the University's Hamilton Library.

My work on the manuscript in both Germany and Hawaii was continually enlivened by music. In Halle I was fortunate to play with the university's *Akademisches Orchester*, conducted by Mattias Erben. An invitation from Adam Jones and Mariko Mitsuyu to participate in several *Hauskonzerte* in Polenz (near Leipzig) was also a thrill. And my weekly sonata sessions with pianist Irene Lau, who lives just around the corner from the Forster Haus with her husband Andreas, were another high point of my stay in Halle. In Hawaii I enjoyed playing with the University of Hawaii Symphony Orchestra, conducted by Joseph Stepec.

For help, advice, and suggestions on the manuscript I would like to thank Lucinda Baker, Sarah Louden, Robert McCauley, Pablo Muchnik, and Sharon Smith, as well as the four anonymous readers chosen by Bloomsbury to review the text.

Extra thanks to Andrea Thiele and Sarah Louden, for their help with the illustrations and permissions.

Finally, thanks to the staff at Bloomsbury for their help in getting the book into print—particularly my editor, Colleen Coalter; Becky Holland, Editorial Assistant for Philosophy; Ian Howe, copy-editor; and Merv Honeywood, project manager.

Abbreviations

The following books by and about Johann Bernhard Basedow are cited in the body of the text by page number (except where noted) and are abbreviated as follows:

MB   Basedow, Johann Bernhard ([1770] 1979), *Das Methodenbuch für Väter und Mütter der Familien und Völker*. Introduction by M. P. Krause. Vaduz: Topos Verlag. (Cited by Chapter and Section number.)

E   Basedow, Johann Bernhard ([1909, 1774] 1972], *Elementarwerk mit dem Kupfertafeln Chodowieckis u.a.*, ed. Theodor Fritzsch, 3 vols., Hildesheim: Georg Olms.

R   Basedow, Johann Bernhard (1965), *Ausgewählte Pädagogische Schriften*, ed. Albert Reble, Paderborn: Ferdinand Schöningh.

VM   Basedow, Johann Bernhard ([1768] 1901), *Vorstellung an Menschenfreunde und vermögenden Manner über Schulen und Studien und ihren Einfluß in die öffentliche Wohlfahrt. Mit einen Plane eines Elementarbuchs der menschlichen Erkenntnis*, ed. Theodor Fritzsch, Leipzig: Philipp Reclam. (Cited by Section number.)

G   Basedow, Johann Bernhard (1880), *Basedow's ausgewählte Schriften. Mit Basedow's Biographie, Einleitungen und Anmerkungen*, ed. Hugo Göring, Langensalza: Hermann Beyer & Söhne.

ES   Basedow, Johann Bernhard (1776), *Erstes Stück des philanthropischen Archivs, Mitgeteilt von verbrüderten Jugendfreunden an Vormunder der Menschheit, besonders welche eine Schulverbesserung wünschen und beginnen; auch an Väter und Mütter, welche Kinder ins Dessauische Philanthropin senden wollen*, Dessau: Siegfried Lebrecht Crusius.

DEP	Basedow, Johann Bernhard (1774), *Das in Dessau errichtete Philanthropinum, eine Schule der Menschenfreundschaft und guter Kentnisse für Lernende und junge Lehrer, Arme und Reiche; ein Fidei-Kommiß der Publikums, zur Vervollkommung des Erziehungswesens aller Orten nach dem Plane des Elementarwerks. Den Erforschen und Thätern des Guten und Fürsten, menschenfreundlichen Gesellschaften und Privatpersonen empfohlen von J. B. Basedow*, Leipzig: Siegfried Lebrecht Crusius.
AB	Basedow, Armin (1924), *Johann Bernhard Basedow (1724–1790): Neue Beiträge, Ergänzungen und Berichtungen, zu seiner Lebensgeschichte*, Langensalza: Hermann Beyer & Söhne.
M	Meier, Johann Christian (1791–2), *Johann Bernhard Basedows Leben, Charakter und Schriften unparteisich dargestellt und beurtheilt*, 2 vols., Hamburg: Benj. Gottlob Hoffmann.
Ra	Rathmann, Heinrich (1791), *Beiträge zur Lebensgeschichte Joh. Bernh. Basedows: aus seinen Schriften und anderen ächten Quellen gesammelt*, Magdeburg: Verlag der Pansaischen Buchdruckerey.

Immanuel Kant's writings are also cited in the body of the text according to volume and page number in Kant, Immanuel (1900–), *Kants gesammelte Schriften*, ed. Berlin-Brandenburg Academy of Sciences, 29 vols., Berlin: Walter de Gruyter (traditionally referred to as the "Academy Edition"). The following traditional German abbreviations and shortened titles are used to refer to specific works of Kant:

Anth	*Anthropologie in pragmatischer Hinsicht*, 7: 107–333.
AP	*Aufsätze, das Philanthropin betrffend*, 2: 445–52.
Br	*Briefe*, vols. 10–13.
EACG	*Entwurf und Ankündigung eines Collegii der physischen Geographie*, 2: 1–12.
GMS	*Grundlegung der Metaphysik der Sitten*, 4: 385–463.
KpV	*Kritik der praktischen Vernunft*, 5: 1–163.

KrV	*Kritik der reinen Vernunft*. References to this work are cited by the customary use of the pagination from its first (A) and second (B) editions.
NEV	*Nachricht von der Einrichtung seiner Vorlesungen in dem Winterhalbenjahre von 1765–1766*, 2: 303–13.
Päd	*Pädagogik*, ed. Friedrich Theodor Rink, 9: 437–99.
SF	*Der Streit der Fakultäten*, 7: 1–116.
V-Anth/Fried	*Vorlesungen Wintersemester 1775–1776 Friedländer*, 25: 465–728.
V-Mo/Collins	*Moralphilosophie Collins*, 27: 237–473.
V-PP/Herder	*Praktische Philosophie Herder*, 27: 1–89.
WA	*Beantwortung der Frage: Was ist Aufklärung?* 8: 33–42.

Translations from all of these texts are my own.

Introduction

Johann Bernhard Basedow (1724–90) is incontestably one of the leading figures in German pedagogy of the eighteenth century—indeed, the influence of his writings and projects (particularly his experimental school, the Philanthropin) extends far beyond Germany.[1] Accordingly, since his death in 1790 a substantial body of German-language literature about his life and work has developed. But in English-speaking countries, the story is quite different—at present, very few people even know his name, much less his significant and influential body of work. There are no English-language monographs on Basedow,[2] none of his books have been translated into English, and, while he is often granted at least a short section in English-language works on the history of education (especially those published during the late nineteenth and early twentieth centuries),[3] these books no longer have the readership that they once enjoyed.

Johann Bernhard Basedow and the Transformation of Modern Education: Educational Reform in the German Enlightenment is an attempt to remedy this sorry situation. Basedow was and is a major voice in the German Enlightenment, and more people should have the opportunity to hear his voice. A prolific and influential author (he published well over 100 works, ranging from short manifestos to multi-volume treatises, on a wide variety of topics, not only within the field of education but also in philosophy and theology), Basedow was, among other things, the rare theorist who ventured into the real world in an attempt to actualize his ideals through concrete institutional transformation. Although his immediate success in this area was limited (due in large part to his lack of administrative skill as well as his cranky and unsociable character, both of which were fuelled by excessive alcohol consumption), many younger teachers who moved to Dessau to work with Basedow and teach at the Philanthropin later established their own experimental schools elsewhere in Germany and beyond. An extremely influential Philanthropinist reform movement thus literally sprang up out of Basedow's tiny school.

I first became curious about Basedow in 1992, when I began translating Immanuel Kant's two short *Essays Regarding the Philanthropinum* (1776–7; see Louden 2007b: 98–104) for the *Cambridge Edition of the Works of Immanuel Kant*. In these essays and elsewhere, Kant—not generally viewed as a writer who expressed strong emotions about anyone or anything—is extremely effusive in his praise for both Basedow and the school he founded in Dessau in 1774. For instance, echoing Basedow's earlier call for the *"necessity … of the total transformation of schools and instruction"* (VM § 24; reprinted in R: 28), in his second Philanthropinum essay Kant tells readers that all schools "must be transformed if something good is to come out of them because they are defective in their original organization … Not a slow *reform*, but a swift *revolution* can bring this about" (AP 2: 449). And in a 1776 classroom lecture to his students in Königsberg, he refers to the Philanthropin as "the greatest phenomenon which has appeared in this century for the improvement of the perfection of humanity" (V-Anth/Fried 25: 722). I have explored various aspects of the relationship between Basedow and Kant in several earlier essays (see, e.g., Louden 2016a, 2012). But in the present study I focus on Basedow. Who was Basedow, and what was his school all about? How and why could someone whose name few English speakers even recognize lead not only the emotionally reticent Kant but also scores of other liberal Enlightenment intellectuals to sing his praises so unreservedly? Answering these questions has been a quiet obsession of mine since 1992, and the present book is the result.

Because so few people in the English-speaking world are even familiar with Basedow's name, the main questions addressed in what follows are the straightforward ones mentioned above. (Who was Basedow? What was so special about the Philanthropin? Why did so many Enlightenment intellectuals support his educational reform projects with such enthusiasm?) But I am also trying to set the record straight on several contested issues regarding Basedow's life and work. First, many previous biographers claim that he is merely "a relatively mediocre thinker" (Chester 1912: 216) whose "root ideas … are those of Rousseau" (Quick 1896: 279)[4]—a German Rousseau, so to speak. But while it is true that Basedow and Rousseau both advocate child-centered, naturalistic theories of education, Basedow arrived at his core position long before the publication of *Émile* in 1762—viz., in 1749, while he was employed as a tutor for the von Qualen family in Borghorst. Basedow is a much more original and independent thinker than he is often given credit for. Second, although Basedow's place in the history of education is generally acknowledged, the impact of his ideas and theories on subsequent educational reform movements is seldom accurately assessed. In this study I demonstrate that Basedow is in fact the unacknowledged father of the progressive education movement. Third, I unravel several paradoxes surrounding the Philanthropin. Throughout its brief and stormy existence (the school closed in 1793, and from the start was marked by unsteady leadership), the Philanthropin was plagued by low enrollment and insufficient funding. How could "the greatest phenomenon which has appeared in this century for the perfection of humanity" sink so quickly? And how could a school with such low enrollment and funding merit such a designation in the first place? Fourth, while Basedow's personal eccentricities and character flaws have long served as cheap fodder for commentators, my study offers a positive reassessment of the significance of his difficult personality. Far from detracting from the value of his work, Basedow's multiple personal demons (a painful childhood, alcoholism, depression, unsociability, congenitally weak eyesight that grew worse over the years) in fact served as spurs for his intellectual work. Without the former, the latter probably would not have been possible.

In preparing this intellectual biography—a contribution to the history of education and Enlightenment studies, with occasional excursions into philosophy and theology—I have been guided primarily by the extensive German literature on Basedow (both the earliest biographies as well as more recent assessments), in addition to his own profuse (and often repetitious) writings. Divided into eleven chapters, *Johann Bernhard Basedow and the Transformation of Modern Education* follows the arc of Basedow's personal life as well as his professional successes and setbacks, paying particular attention to the Philanthropin and its impact on educational reform as well as to Basedow's place within the larger sphere of the German Enlightenment.

Chapter 1 ("A New School for a New Age") focuses on the famous public examination of the Philanthropin held on May 13-15, 1776—Basedow's open invitation to intellectuals, teachers, clergymen, and financial supporters to visit his new school in Dessau and witness firsthand (and hopefully spread the word about) the kind of institution he was trying to build. This opening chapter also highlights some of the unique features of the school (for instance, its nondenominational orientation and core message of religious tolerance, its emphasis on learning through play,[5] and its inclusion of sex education within the curriculum)—features that drew extravagant praise from many liberal Enlightenment authors, but also strong criticism from their conservative opponents.

In Chapter 2 ("Blame It on the Parents?") I turn to Basedow's birth and turbulent early home environment in Hamburg. Ever since Goethe first recorded his musings about Basedow's personal eccentricities in Book 14 of his *Dichtung und Wahrheit* (Goethe's recollections here are based on a trip that he, Lavater, and Basedow took together in summer 1774 along the Rhine river), commentators have speculated about the causes behind Basedow's complex personality. Son of an overbearing and financially pressed wigmaker and "a mother who was increasingly melancholic to the point of insanity" (Basedow 1783a: 67–8; cf. Raumer 1857: 262)—but some of whose ancestors were also, for a short time, quite wealthy—daily life in the family home was so painful that Basedow ran away from home at age sixteen, eventually finding work as a servant at the home of a country physician in Denmark. But after returning home, he nevertheless managed to graduate with distinction from Hamburg's oldest and most distinguished gymnasium, where his teachers included Hermann Samuel Reimarus, one of the German Enlightenment's most prominent and controversial philosophers of religion.

Chapter 3 ("College Days") tracks Basedow's university studies at both the University of Leipzig, where he studied briefly with Christian August Crusius, who served as an important counterweight to Reimarus's more radical deism; and the University of Kiel, from which he finally received his *Magister* degree in 1752. Although not a good student when judged by conventional standards (by his own admission, he rarely attended class), Basedow read voraciously on his own during this period of his life, and it was here that several of his key intellectual positions (particularly in theology) first took shape.

Chapter 4 ("A New Way of Teaching") recounts a crucial turning point in Basedow's life—his three-year stint (1749–52) as a private tutor in the family home of Josias von Qualen in Borghorst, a small town north of Kiel. Like many Enlightenment intellectuals from working-class backgrounds (Kant and Fichte are two other prominent examples), Basedow first found employment as a tutor in a wealthy family's home. But in his own case, this also proved to be a life-altering experience. For as a result of his work in Borghorst, Basedow decides not to pursue further his father's wish that he become a member of the clergy and discovers his own vocation as an educational reformer and author. His Kiel dissertation—*An Unused, and also the Best Method of Instructing Distinguished Youth, Not Only in all Scholastic Pursuits, but Especially in the Latin Language* (written in Latin; see Basedow 1752a)—is essentially an extended write-up of his tutoring experience in Borghorst, and also contains the seeds of many themes developed at greater length in later publications (in particular, his advocacy of a conversation-based approach to foreign language instruction, and his emphasis on learning through play). In Borghorst Basedow also meets his future wife

Emilie Dumas, who was employed as a governess at the von Qualen home. Sadly, she died in childbirth on August 1, 1753, only ten months after they were married.

Chapter 5 ("The Professor"), which opens with a discussion of the Kiel dissertation, focuses on Basedow's first academic appointment as Professor of Rhetoric and Moral Philosophy at the *Ritterakademie* in Sorø, Denmark. Although an extremely popular teacher and lecturer from the moment he arrived on campus, Basedow's later decision to discuss theological topics (more specifically, his own liberal interpretations of theological topics) in his lectures eventually proved to be his undoing. "The entire orthodox tribe rose up with outrage, in order to hand over the bold one to the severity of the government" (Pinloche 1896: 35), and as a result Basedow was dismissed from his position in early 1761. During his tenure at Sorø Basedow also meets his second wife, Gertrude Elisabeth Hammer, daughter of a minister. Together they have four children—three sons (two of whom died in early childhood) as well as a daughter, Emilie (named after Basedow's first wife, and not, as some have surmised, after Rousseau's *Émile*), who would later become one of the star students at the Philanthropin.

In Chapter 6 ("That Old-Time Religion") I follow Basedow through his next significant life episode after being removed from the Sorø *Ritterakademie*; viz., his transfer to the Gymnasium Christianeum in Altona, not far from his birthplace in Hamburg. Basdow's ten-year residency in Altona definitely marks the stormiest period of his life—for several years, his books were banned, his family was excommunicated from the Lutheran Church, and conservative ministers publically encouraged their parishioners to stone him in their weekly sermons (see Overhoff 2004: 166). But there was also an unexpected upside to his exile in Altona: out of fear of arousing the local townspeople, the authorities severely curtailed his teaching and public lecture duties, while still allowing him to retain his full salary. As a result Basedow was able to devote much more time to his writing. As he notes later in a 1774 publication, "due to a special favor, I became a paid writer" (DEP: 24). Many earlier Basedow biographies exclude discussion of his extensive (and often polemical) theological writings, preferring to focus exclusively on his more accessible pedagogical works. In my view, this is a mistake, for Basedow's pedagogy is, to a large extent, informed by his theology and philosophy of religion—in particular, his desire to overcome religious sectarianism.

Chapters 7 ("'For Fathers and Mothers of Families and Nations': The *Methodenbuch*") and 8 ("'A Well-Ordered Stock of All Necessary Knowledge':

The *Elementarwerk'*") together focus on Basedow's two most popular and influential books: the *Method Book* (MB—see Basedow 1979) and the four-volume *Elementary Work* (E—see Basedow 1972). This latter work also includes nearly 100 copper engravings by Polish artist Daniel Chodowiecki. Basedow's extensive list of publications poses a formidable challenge to everyone, and even those who are fortunate in being fluent in German cannot easily navigate his idiosyncratic writing style. However, as critics often point out, his "countless writings" are marked by "frequent repetitions and extensions" (Reble 1965: 253), and thus the hope behind each of these chapters is that by examining in some detail the contents of two of his most important books, we can more easily gain a solid sense of his overall position.

In Chapter 9 ("Back to School") I return to the Philanthropin in Dessau; where, largely as a result of the growing influence of his many publications, Basedow had been invited by Prince Leopold Friedrich Franz to move in order to bring his ideals into reality by establishing a new kind of school. In this chapter, however, I focus not on the public examination of the school held on May 13–15, 1776 discussed earlier in Chapter 1, but instead survey the Philanthropin's rocky development from its official opening on December 27, 1774 (when only three students were enrolled, two of whom were Basedow's own children) up to its final closing in 1793. What was daily life like for students enrolled at the school? What texts did teachers use for the different grades, and what were the school's curricular policies and rules of conduct? Why were there so many personnel changes in the directorship of the institute, and what were the chief causes behind the school's closing?

Chapter 10 ("After School") examines Basedow's final decade, after he leaves Dessau and the Philanthropin in 1780 up until his death in 1790. Highlights here include his continued productivity as an author (Basedow published twenty-two books during the last decade of his life), his volunteer work as a teacher at Frau Kalisky's school for young girls in Magdeburg (a city about thirty-eight miles northeast from Dessau), his unsuccessful plans to move to Magdeburg with his son Ludwig after his wife's demise in 1788, and several controversies surrounding his own death.

Finally, in Chapter 11 ("'The Mother of All Good Schools in the World'"), I briefly examine Basedow's intellectual legacy. Here I argue that he is not only the unacknowledged father of the progressive education movement, but that there is also much truth in Kant's bolder claim (in a letter to Pastor Wilhelm Crichton of July 29, 1778, in which Kant extricates himself from his uncomfortable role as unofficial fundraiser and recruiting agent for the school) that the Philanthropin is "the mother of all good schools in the world" (Br 10: 234). For in Kant's view, the Philanthropin was not only a school where education was "in touch with real life and in accordance with human nature" (Paulsen 1908: 134), but it was also a place where ideas were continually tested by experiment and practice, where young teachers came to work with veteran educators and scholars, where staff members were motivated by an unparalleled devotion to the overriding importance of education in human life, and where students of all religious, national, and economic backgrounds were welcome. And this is at least part of what good schools everywhere (whether they are labeled "progressive" or not) should aspire to.

I regret that Overhoff (2020) did not reach me until my book was already in production and that I was therefore unable to make use of it in the present study.

Figure 1 Portrait of Basedow by Daniel Chodowiecki, 1769. By permission of the Graphische Sammlung, Fach Kunstgeschichte der Universität Trier.

1

A New School for a New Age

Education is the most important thing in all of life.
          Johann Bernhard Basedow, *Das Methodenbuch*: IV.5; in G: 50

May 13, 1776. Dessau—a town of about 10,000 in present-day Sachsen-Anhalt, Germany. Johann Bernhard Basedow has invited "every expert, every reasonable world citizen in Germany and in other lands, who has the time and interest" (Ra: 101) to take part in the public examination of his new school. "Many teachers and respected clergymen, [and] also envoys of German princes presented themselves. The Prince and Princess of Dessau were likewise present."[1]

Why is a new school needed? Because although modern European society has undergone many significant changes, educational methods and institutions have for centuries remained much the same. Education is behind the times. As Basedow remarks in the opening sentence of his *Small Book for Parents and Teachers of all Classes* (1771):

> The world has become much more sophisticated [*viel klüger*] over the past few hundred years, *more sophisticated*, certainly, but also *worse* [*schlimmer*], and therefore less happy. To be sure, its worsening has many causes. But our greatest misfortune comes from the fact that education, teaching, and the schoolbooks of children have hardly become any better than they were formerly.
>   Basedow 1771a: 1

Or, as he remarks more bluntly in a 1774 publication: "I am occupied now with a matter of concern to humanity! *School dust* [*Der Schulstaub*] has lain around for centuries! Young and old, who must walk and breathe in the schools, become sick in the brain [*krank im Gehirn*]" (DEP: IX).

What is different about Basedow's school? The clearest and most controversial difference concerns religion. The Philanthropin[2] advocates a nondenominational orientation—students of all faiths are welcome:

this affair is *not Catholic, Lutheran, or Reformed; but Christian* ... We are philanthropists [friends of humanity], or Cosmopolitans. *Russia or Denmark's sovereignty* is not favored in our teachings and opinions, and is also not placed below *Switzerland's freedom*. Everything good has its time and its place. And we are world citizens.

ES: IV–V

Prior to Basedow's effort, schools in Europe, as Albert Pinloche remarks, "were, with Protestants as well as Catholics, nothing more than an appendage of the church" (Pinloche 1896: 2). But Basedow's core conviction is that modern schools must overcome the religious sectarianism that has divided Europeans from one another and seek common ground. "*The purpose* of education must be therefore to form a European, whose life shall be as safe, as useful, and as peaceful as it can be made by education" (ES: 16). And "*by a European we understand* a human being of a civilized nation, with such manners and dispositions as are, not here or there, but almost universal" (ES: 15). Consequently, all texts used in the Philanthropin (many of which were written by Basedow himself) must be

> *free from theological verdicts* for Christianity against Jews, Muslims [*Mahomedaner*], and Deists; or for this or that church against so-called Dissidents, who in some places are called *heretics* ... For *cosmopolitan education* must be universal [*allgemein*], and cannot advise against clergy of any denomination.

ES: 65

For "in the temple of the universal father, Dissident fellow citizens worship in houses with their brothers" (ES: 112).

However, "nondenominational" does not mean entirely secular and nonreligious. For Basedow, whose father had hoped he would become a pastor and who began his university studies as a theology student, religious instruction must retain an important place in modern education:

> In the Philanthropin the first beginning of instruction is to have faith in God, the creator, supporter, and lord of the world ... As we have a general, Christian, Philanthropinist liturgy, approved by persons of reputation in all Christian churches, we promise also to offer a general Christian instruction, which, by means of its omission of all points of distinction, shall offend neither Catholics, Protestants, nor Greeks, but which shall necessarily please all Christians.

ES: 39[3]

Karl von Raumer, after citing many of these same passages from Basedow's *Erstes Stück des philanthropischen Archivs* (1776), characterizes "the most general concept" in the religious orientation of Basedow's school as "the broadest deism,"[4] and F. C. Schlosser congratulates Basedow for recognizing "the necessity of a system of religion purified from the dross of the middle ages" (Schlosser 1844: II: 207). But Jürgen Overhoff offers a more positive and accurate assessment when he notes that Basedow

> established the first European school to abolish the traditional divisions of youths according to religious affiliation. In Basedow's Dessau institute the shared experience of learning among children of different confessions was one of the most important aspects of teaching. The constant reference to those principles and values common to all faiths was intended to convey to the pupils those elements of their religion that connected them, not that divided them.
>
> Overhoff 2007: 804–5

Basedow's liberal, quasi-deistic orientation clearly did strike a chord with the more tolerant segments of German Enlightenment society. For instance, Hugo Göring notes that both Freemasons and Jews generously supported the new school: "The four Hamburg lodges immediately gave 500 Thaler, the Leipzig lodge gave 100, the Göttingen lodge 25, the New Brandenburg lodge 30. At the suggestion of Mendelssohn,[5] the Berlin Jewish community sent over 500 Thaler" (Göring 1880: LXVI). The multiple contributions given by different Freemason groups is particularly noteworthy, given that Basedow himself was not a Freemason. However, as we will see later, many conservative Christians reacted vehemently against Basedow's nondenominational approach. Theological controversies followed him for much of his adult life, and at one point cost him his job, endangered his personal safety, and led to his family's excommunication from the Lutheran Church.

Joy in Learning

But what was distinctive about the educational methods employed in Basedow's school? One point he stresses emphatically is that memorization and physical punishment will be sharply curtailed:

> There will be very little *memorizing* with us ... [T]he students will *not be forced*, not even by means of *reprimands*. Yet we promise, by means of the excellence of our teaching method, ... at least *twice as much progress in study* ... as one is accustomed to in the best schools, boarding institutions, or gymnasiums. And in particular we promise great *cultivation of sound reasoning* through practice of the *true philosophical method of thinking*.
>
> ES: 39–40

This too marks a radical departure from existing pedagogical practice. For instance, Raumer, in his *History of Pedagogy*, offers the following contrast:

> Youth was, in those days, for the most part, a very tormented time. Instruction was hard and heartlessly severe. Grammar was beaten into the memory, so were portions of Scripture and hymns. A common school punishment was to memorize the 119th Psalm.[6] The schoolrooms were miserably dark. No one conceived it possible that the young child could find pleasure in any kind of work, or that they had eyes for anything besides reading and writing.
>
> Raumer 1843: 2: 278

In place of the corporal punishment and forced memorization that were standard features of eighteenth-century European schools, Basedow promised to instill a joy of learning in his students. School should be fun. And as a means of promoting this fundamental goal, he devised a number of educational games to help children learn, in some cases taking an already-existing children's game and tweaking it for pedagogical purposes. As he remarks in his 1768 book, *Vorstellung an Menschenfreunde und vermögende Männer über Schulen, Studien und ihren Einfluß in die öffentliche Wohlfahrt* [*Presentation to Friends of Humanity and Men of Means concerning Schools, Studies, and their Influence in the Public Welfare*]: "It is ... possible to make almost all of their games instructive [*lehrreich*], without taking the pleasure away from them ... As far as possible all frustration and loathing in learning must be avoided" (VM § 47; in R: 57). One of his best-known games, used in teaching foreign languages, was the "Commander Game." A demonstration of it was offered to visitors at the public examination, as recorded by Johann Gottlieb Schummel[7] in Letter VIII of *Fritzens Reise nach Dessau* (1776):

> First they played the Commander Game, all of them with each other, from eight until nine. See Karl, how it goes: first they all position themselves in a row like soldiers, and Herr Wolke[8] is the officer. He gives his commands in Latin, and then they must do what he says. For example, if he says, "*Claudite oculos*," then they all shut their eyes; or, "*Circumspicite*," then they look all around; or, "*Imitate sartorum*," then they stitch each other up like the tailor does; or, "*Imitate sutorum*," then they pull the waxed thread like the cobbler. Herr Wolke commanded thousands of funny things, but many more have occurred to me which I shall command to you when I return home.
>
> In R: 229; cf. Pinloche 1896: 218–24

But did the students actually learn anything from these games? According to Basedow, they learned a great deal; indeed, much more than students at traditional schools:

The results, which can already be shown, prove that what we promise is true ... [T]hey are *unbelievable*. Everything with us is *so pleasant, that no one wishes to be at home* ... By the age of fifteen the *necessity of a punishment* occurs only very rarely. The students learn *without sitting too much*, by various diversions and movements, and more outside of than in school-hours. Of our *method* we can say (and God knows it is with sincerity and reflection) the following. When we really have all our help and arrangements completed, a twelve-year-old boy sent to us, whose morals are not too far ruined, and who is of moderate capacity, if he knows only how to read and write in his native language, nothing else, will become with us, without compulsion or discomfort, *in four years, by all consideration one of the most competent citizens at a university to study in the higher faculties.*[9]

ES: 41

There is of course more than a bit of salesmanship in many of Basedow's pronouncements. He was after all trying both to solicit more financial support for the school among his readers as well as increase enrollment. And the promise to make learning fun has continued to haunt progressive educators for many generations afterward. For instance, John Dewey, toward the end of *School and Society*, writes:

> I am confident that the parents who have intrusted their children to us for any length of time will agree in saying that while the children like, or love, to come to school, yet work, and not amusement, has been the spirit and teaching of the school; and that this freedom has been granted under such conditions of intelligent and sympathetic oversight as to be a means of upbuilding and strengthening character.
>
> Dewey 1900a: 128–9

But Basedow, like Dewey and other progressive education theorists[10] (and one of the goals of this study is to demonstrate that Basedow's work is the true source of this movement), held on to his conviction that there should be joy in learning, despite continued opposition from conservative quarters.

Foreign-Language Instruction

One of Basedow's best-known educational innovations was his approach to teaching foreign languages. He first developed the technique in 1749 when he was taking some time off from his university studies and employed as a private tutor in the family home of Josias von Qualen in Borghorst, Holstein, and he publicly defended it several years later in his 1752 dissertation submitted to the philosophy faculty at the University of Kiel for his *Magister* degree, entitled *An Unusual and Also the Best Method of Instructing Youth, Not Only in All Scholastic Pursuits, but Especially in the Latin Language* (see Basedow 1752a). Basedow was hired by von Qualen to educate his only son, also called Josias (he also had five daughters), a boy of seven, and "on the advice of the father he began to teach the son Latin through discussions" (Swet 1898: 37).

The method of foreign-language instruction that Basedow gradually developed—in addition to incorporating his ground rule that learning should be fun—was a conversation-based approach that, at least at the beginning stages, deemphasized formal grammar and syntax. In daily walks with his pupil, Basedow would teach the child Latin words for actual objects with which he was already familiar. "That is a tree, *arbor*. That is a horse, *equus*. That is a wheel, *rota*," etc. (see Landschoof 1933: 60).

While Basedow cannot claim to be literal inventor of the conversation-based approach to foreign-language instruction (it has been informally employed for centuries by parents and tutors),[11] he certainly did develop and apply it much more extensively than previous educators had done. And he writes about it in great detail in many of his publications. For instance, Book VI of his influential *Methodenbuch für Väter und Mütter der Familien und Völker* (1st edition: 1770, 2nd ed.: 1771, 3rd ed.: 1773)[12] is entitled "Particularly Concerning Instruction in Languages." In Section 2, he responds to the objection that it is hard to find qualified language teachers by stating: "I answer that in a seminary not a small number of such teachers must be educated" (MB VI.2; in G: 110). (Here he is alluding to the future Philanthropin—see "A Teacher-Training Institute," below.) And in Section 7 he emphasizes that "according to my plan the teacher must for the most part instruct the students through conversation [*durch Unterredung*]," that students "should be encouraged early on to have an actual exchange of letters with parents, teachers, friends, and their playmates; that is, they must set down in writing carefully much which they were otherwise accustomed to say only with haste," and recommends that "practice in composition or style and an orderly recitation of rhetoric or poetry is unnecessary before the age of fifteen" (MB VI.7; in G: 121).

Vocational and Physical Education

Another significant departure from existing educational practice was Basedow's emphasis on both vocational and physical education. The focus of the

Philanthropin was not merely confined to academic subjects; rather, the goal was to educate the whole person and to help prepare students for life in the real world. (Here too, one sees a strong similarity with one of the later tenets of progressive education.) In a section from his *Elementarwerk* (1774) entitled "Exercises of a Future Man in High-Ranking Classes of the tenth to the sixteenth Year" he writes:

> Such a boy has at least sixteen hours. Six hours for book study [*Bücherfliess*], four for meals and an instructive walk. Gradually two hours may be spent with the dance teacher, the music teacher, and the drawing teacher, but none at all with the hairdresser and only minutes for dressing.
>
> 1) Now we still have four hours for exercises in genuine adult living. To some degree a boy needs to learn the tools of the tradesman, the cabinet-maker, the woodworker, the smith, the mason, and the gardener, some small use for which any household has need. For in an emergency he must help himself and give his house-servants proper instruction.
>
> E I.i.4; in G: 277

Additional recommended exercises are then added to this list, including the following:

> 2) He must ... learn about the simplest machines and tools ...
>
> 3) From an experienced and prudent man he must learn *the movements, skill in which may save ourselves and others from danger* ... *Hunting* and *fishing* in these circumstances must also not be forgotten.
>
> 4) He must ... know how to cook common food, how to start a fire correctly, ... how to heat a room, how to kill snakes, [and] how to bandage wounds in an emergency ...
>
> 5) From the sixteenth year, in each of the four seasons, he must spend fourteen days with a farmer, accompanied by his proctor ... And during this time he must ... study nothing except agriculture.
>
> E I.i.4; in G: 277–78

Although it is not clear whether all of these recommendations became official school policy at the Philanthropin, most of them did. For instance, in an Appendix to Pinloche's *History of Philanthropinism* entitled "Regulations and Study Plan of the Philanthropinum in Dessau," we learn that students in the upper classes received instruction in dancing and riding from 9 to 10 am, "moderate exercise, such as threshing, planning, and cabinet-making" from 1 to 2 pm, and that younger students had lessons in music from 1 to 2 pm, drawing from 2 to 3 pm, practice in dancing from 3 to 4 pm, and "a free hour for walking under supervision" (Pinloche 1896: 465–7) from one of the instructors.

In his *Methodenbuch* Basedow also stresses the benefits of physical activity and exercise, recommending at one point that teachers

> accustom boys, for example, to swimming, walking over a narrow footbridge,[13] climbing ropes, sitting on a horse, or guiding it and stopping it on a walk, going down hills and scrambling up them, jumping over small ditches and fences, using the pogo stick [*Springstock*], dodging thrown balls, bringing an escaped hunting dog back, walking over slippery ice, and so forth. You may judge for yourselves, how many of these exercises would also be beneficial for girls. Through such means confidence is increased, and bravery, when it is necessary, facilitated.
>
> MB IV.6; in G: 56–7[14]

Realia

Although this next educational innovation did not actually begin with Basedow, he stresses it a great deal in his writings. In the Philanthropin curriculum a strong emphasis was placed on "realia"—pictures, maps, charts, natural history collections, or what today might simply be called "visual aids." In his *Methodenbuch* he writes:

> I must say a bit more about the use of paintings and copperplates in the teaching of children. 1) Experience shows how much everything that resembles a picture pleases children, even if only mundane matters are depicted, or things to which they are accustomed. 2) The views and customs which are presented by such figures are livelier than others, last longer, and are shared and repeated from one child to another. 3) During class hours one can give no conception of many sensory things without pictures, because they are in foreign lands [*ausländisch*], or at least absent. 4) Through the help of pictures, the teacher is more readily understood when he repeats known facts in a foreign or dead language … through this natural teaching the children most easily and most quickly become skillful.
>
> MB V.8; in G: 107

And a few pages earlier he also notes: "At different times I have suggested a *cabinet of natural objects* and *models* which would be far more useful than copperplates in instruction as well as in teaching languages" (MB V.4; in G: 100). But in fact Basedow makes very heavy use of copperplates in the earlier-mentioned *Elementarwerk* (*The Elementary Work*), whose full title is: *An Orderly-Arranged Encyclopedia of all Necessary Knowledge for the Instruction of Youth from the Beginning up to the University Level, for the Guidance of Parents and School Teachers, and Tutors, for the Needs of Every Reader, to Perfect His Knowledge—in Combination with a Collection of Copper Engravings*. Weighing in at over 1,600 pages divided into four volumes, it was a very expensive book. And both Basedow's text and illustrator Daniel Chodowiecki's copperplates certainly have their critics. Meier, for instance, in volume two of his 1791 biography of Basedow, writes: "In this entire precious and expensive work, which is a tumbled-together chaos, I find nothing new, nothing unusual, nothing remarkable, and nothing exceptional. Most of it has been far better stated before" (M: II: 301). And Goethe, in Book XIV of *Dichtung und Wahrheit*, remarks:

> it displeased me that the drawings of the *Elementarwerk* ... do not represent actual life conditions ... In nature all things, in spite of their many-sidedness and apparent disorder, always have something orderly and settled. This *Elementarwerk*, however, is so divided and disarranged, that things never found together in actual experience are, for the sake of the relationship of concepts, placed in juxtaposition.
>
> In R: 239–240

Göring, while acknowledging that the *Elementarwerk* "as a first attempt at a detailed pedagogy for its time is epoch-making, indeed, superb," also complains that "in many cases the copperplates are concerned with astonishing trivialities" (G: 242). But a more influential and characteristic response is the following remark from a speech made by Prussian Minister Karl Abraham von Zedlitz in 1776: "The Basedowian engravings for the *Elementarwerk* ought to be the first handbook of all educators. They present a true picture gallery, and teach children the clearest concepts in the matter of education" (in G: 242).

However, as Basedow himself acknowledged, the real founder of this now-popular teaching method was in fact Czech pedagogue John Amos Comenius (1592–1671). In his *Orbis Pictus* (1657), the first children's picture book, Comenius sought to offer readers "a Nomenclature, and Pictures OF ALL THE CHIEF THINGS that are in the WORLD, and of MENS EMPLOYMENT therein; In above 150 COPPER CUTS"—in effect, "a brief of the whole world" (Comenius 1887: title page, xiv). But there is one fundamental difference between Comenius's and Basedow's use of pictures as an educational tool. As Otto Friedrich Bollnow notes:

While Comenius begins with God and from there unfolded the world in great objective order, in which the human being is also put in his place, and in the Last Judgment (in the absolute sense) receives a final settlement [*letzten Abschluß*], Basedow enters in with the children's environment: the family at the dinner table, food, clothing, and the home, and expands from here outward slowly to the surrounding vicinity in ever-expanding regions. It is thus the change in emphasis in the frame of reference from the objective order of the world to the subjective order of the human being. In the field of pedagogy this is the same turn that Kant described with his "Copernican Turn."[15]

In short, Comenius's pictorial account of the world is God-centered; Basedow's, human-centered.

Clothing

Prior to the founding of the Philanthropin, students were expected to dress in extremely formal and uncomfortable clothes, the apparent goal being to make them look like miniature versions of men at court. As Raumer notes: "the pernicious age of Louis XIV also inflicted on the poor children of the upper class hair frizzled with powder and smeared with pomade, embroidered coats, knee breeches, silk stockings, and a dagger at their sides; for active, lively children the severest torture" (Raumer 1843: II: 278). But at Basedow's school, students dressed in a radically different manner. The most famous description comes from Letter IV of *Fritzens Reise nach Dessau*:

> I must first briefly describe to you how they look. All of them have their hair cut short, and no one needs a wig-maker. They go around without a necktie, with the neck of their shirts open, and the collar rolled back over their little coats: it really looks very sweet! And papa also says this would be much healthier than the warm, thick scarves that are in fashion now.
>
> In R: 228

On this point too, the Philanthropin represents a step into the modern age.

Rich and Poor

Basedow's school, as emphasized in the title of one of his 1774 publications, welcomed both "poor and rich" students: "*The Philanthropinum established at*

Dessau, a school of human friendship and good knowledge for pupils and young teachers, poor and rich ..." (DEP: title page). This too was something new in the era before public education, and stems in part from Basedow's own working-class background. The Philanthropin enrolled two groups of students: "*Pensionisten*," or boarding pupils who paid full tuition, and "*Famulanten*," who were charged a reduced fee. The former came from wealthier families, and were charged a yearly fee of 250 *Reichsthalers* (200, if another family member also enrolled); the latter were charged 100 *Reichsthalers* annually (which included the price of the school uniform) (see ES: 38, 43). However, in the end Basedow's idealistic goal of creating a school open to students of all economic backgrounds was forced to bow to financial pressures. In reality, most of the students enrolled at the Philanthropin were *Pensionisten*:

> of the approximately 150 students (from, among other places, Holland, Denmark, France, Portugal, Poland, Vienna, Prague, and Riga) who attended the school during its existence, 60 had aristocratic origins, and the remaining students were sons of businesspeople, wealthy farmers, and scholars. This was allowed, although the school was originally intended to be a school for poor and rich students.
>
> Schmitt 2008: 176–7

Gender

The issue of gender is much more ambiguous. On the one hand, Basedow's own daughter Emilie (b. 1769) was often singled out as evidence of the superiority of her father's teaching methods, for she was herself one of the star pupils at the Philanthropin and featured prominently in the public examination of the school:

> We have a girl, Basedow's daughter, seven years old, who ... has more knowledge ... than well-informed and much older children. She understands, speaks, and reads with understanding as much Latin as German, and only a little more than both of French ... In arithmetic she has come so far, that she understands fours ways of counting.
>
> ES: 54–5

Christian Heinrich Wolke, the first assistant teacher hired by Basedow, describes in detail how he applied Basedow's teaching methods to Emilie and the results obtained:

I taught her, for example, after a certain order and selection, about all kinds of things and their qualities, by showing them to her, or by clear and accurate descriptions of them; further the art of how to stand up, how to fall down judiciously, how to avoid falling down by catching hold of something, and so forth ... When she was a year and a half old, she could not only speak much more clearly and more correctly than other children of such an age, but also (by means of our special method of teaching spelling before the knowledge of letters), already understand sentences.

DEP: 44–5

And when Emilie was only four years old, Wolke continues, he began to teach her French, "a language of which she had not before heard a word ... In three and a half months, she could speak of her wants and things about her in French, so well that the mixing of German words in the instruction was no longer needed" (DEP: 46). Furthermore, he emphasized, "all of this knowledge was learned through play, that is, without strain or harmful sitting still" (DEP: 47), and "she never memorized a word" (DEP: 51).

On the other hand, in his *Methodenbuch*, Basedow defends a very traditional and extremely gendered view of education. He opens Chapter VIII ("Of the Different Education of Sons and Daughters") with the following pronouncement:

> The *male sex* is by nature and through our customs [*von Natur und durch unsre Sitten*] more skilled, to work a great deal, to take in experiences from a distance, to learn skills, arts, business or sciences; as a result to acquire needs [*Bedürfnisse*], to hold offices, and to be able to use his superior strength to care for the family. All of this, and in many religions it is a divine command, gives man the decisive rule [*die entscheidende Herrschaft*] in the family ... On the other hand, a *person of the other sex* is the most skilled [*am geschicktesten*] to please man through her charm ... She is under the rule, as a result she must know how to bear this; however, she has a part of the rule over children, tenants, and servants; she must therefore also possess the gifts and virtues of a domestic sovereign [*häuslichen Regentin*]. She must also understand every small family concern better than the man. Therefore it follows, that [in] the education of a daughter, the performance of all these duties which are in store for her must be made easier.
>
> MB VIII.1; in G: 159

As a result, "one must educate daughters for the prospect of a happy marriage" (MB VIII.11; in G: 184). But why then did Basedow and Wolke devote so much effort (in a manner eerily similar to John Stuart Mill's later home-schooling experience)[16] to teaching the young Emilie Latin and mathematics? A future housewife, as Basedow explicitly points out, has no need of languages "other than the customary one and French;" and as for mathematics, "one must arrange for some practice in counting" (MB VIII.11; in G: 182), but nothing more. A generation later, Amalia Holst, in her *Über die Bestimmung des Weibes zur höhern Geistesbildung* (1802—*On the Destiny of Woman for Higher Education*)—apparently unaware of the extensive education that Emilie received under her father's tutelage—would take Basedow and fellow Philanthropinist Joachim Heinrich Campe (1746-1818) to task for their unenlightened views about women's education. "Are we here only for the sake of men?"[17] she pointedly asks. But while Basedow's remarks in the *Methodenbuch* clearly present readers with a slightly less than progressive and enlightened account of girls' education, the education that his own daughter Emilie received stands in stark contrast with this account. When it came to his daughter, Basedow did not follow his own advice concerning *Mädchenerziehung*.

A Teaching-Training Institute

The Philanthropin was not just a new kind of school for students, but also a teacher-training institute. This important point is also indicated in the title of one of Basedow's 1774 publications: "*The Philanthropinum Established at Dessau, a School of Human Friendship and Good Knowledge, for Pupils and Young Teachers [junge Lehrer]* ..." (DEP: title page). Later in the Preface to this same publication he describes the Philanthropin as a "*mother school*" and the "planting center [*Pflanzort*] of teachers for everyone" (DEP: XVI). Most teachers in Basedow's day received no formal training. There were no Schools of Education at universities (the first university chair in pedagogy was not established until 1779, at the University of Halle, and its first occupant was Ernst Christian Trapp (1745-1818), who taught briefly at the Philanthropin from 1778 to 1779). And those who became teachers often fell into this line of work after becoming unsatisfied with (or being shown to be unsuited for) their chosen career in, e.g., the ministry. Basedow's hope was that young teachers would also come to Dessau, learn better teaching methods, and then take their newly acquired skills with them to found new Philanthropin-oriented schools elsewhere.

This particular aspect of the Philanthropin experiment was a solid success. As Henry Barnard notes:

> From the Dessau Philanthropinum a great pedagogical excitement and agitation spread over Germany and Switzerland, and, indeed, over a great part of

Europe ... Educational institutions, on the model of the Philanthropinum, arose in all quarters. Ulysses von Salis first established one, in 1775, at Marschlins, in Switzerland ... Campe founded a third institution, in Hamburg, after leaving Dessau ... Salzmann's Institute [at Schnepfenthal], founded in 1784, existed longest, and still exists ... The Philanthropinists exerted an influence, not only through these institutions, but also through a multitude of authors, for young and old, who swarmed all over Germany. At the head of the teachers who wrote stands Campe.[18]

Indeed, according to one estimate, "by the year 1790 sixty-three other schools of this type had been founded in Germany" alone (Hertz 1962: 2: 385). The young teachers trained at Basedow's institute helped to popularize his new educational methods, and since the founding of the Philanthropin in Dessau many of them have gradually worked their way into mainstream educational curricula all over the world.

Kant, in his *Lectures on Pedagogy*, offers particularly strong praise for the teacher-training component of the Philanthropin:

> The only experimental school which to an extent made a beginning in blazing a trail was the Dessau institute. We must let it keep this glory regardless of the many mistakes of which one could accuse it ... It was in a sense the only school in which teachers had the freedom to work according to their own methods and plans, and where they were in contact with each other as well as with all scholars in Germany.
>
> Päd 9: 451; cf. 467, V-Anth/Fried 25: 723

Sex Education

Another radical feature of Basedow's school was its inclusion of sex education as part of the curriculum.[19] For the most part, students in eighteenth-century German schools did not hear a word about this topic. In some of his writings, Basedow's remarks on the subject are rather tame (though, again, his decision merely to broach the topic marks a radical departure from common practice). For instance, in Book IV.9 of the *Methodenbuch*, he offers the following list of specific instructions to parents:

> If circumstances permit, give each child not only its separate bed, but also a separate room for sleeping and dressing, which is at the same time his own special room. Children of different sex must not only not sleep together, but not

undress in one another's presence. I would recommend light nightclothes, through which nakedness would be covered with certainty. Accustom your children, when it is possible, to be alone in privies when defecating or urinating [*Entleerung des Leibes*].

MB IV.9; in G: 60

But immediately after this passage he writes:

> Of the *procreation* of animals and human beings, one must speak with veracity even to young children, at least from the tenth or twelfth year, although not elaborately, as with other natural phenomena ... so that they may be made acquainted with these matters in the right way ... If one tries to hide these natural phenomena from them, or to satisfy their thirst for knowledge through fables, then without the knowledge of the parents or guardians, in such years as the abuse of them may be quite possible, experiences of the truth will strongly lure their new desires into a harmful path.

MB IV.9; in G: 60

And in his *Elementarwerk*, Basedow offers the following recommended lecture as an accompaniment to engraver Chodowiecki's infamous Plate XXIX:

> But see, children, how many great deeds of kindness a child enjoys from both parents, of whom one is the father, and the other the mother! There sits an honorably married woman in the easy chair, a prospective mother, very pregnant [*hoch schwanger*], sickly in this pregnancy and a bit worried about the outcome. But her best friend, her faithful husband, is comforting her and assures her with tenderness and all possible assistance and anticipates with her the future enjoyment that they will have in the virtue and happiness of their future child. There is the bed where she will endure the illness after the birth. The cradle with all its accessories is already ready for their soon-to-arrive darling. At birth the child will undergo a small cut, just like the mother; therefore it must be taken care of with a bandage so that it does not bleed to death; further it will be dirty, and must be washed.

In G: 345–6

Schummel, in Letter IX of *Fritzens Reise nach Dessau*, reports that Wolke actually employed a version of Basedow's lecture during the public examination of the Philanthropin:

> Dearest, best mother,
> ...But now mama, the tears that I have shed for you! Oh, if only I could remember all of the words that the dear, very best Professor Wolke spoke. He brought out a picture, hung it up and said: "Dear children, today I am bringing

you here a picture which you have not yet seen, but I am telling you beforehand that it concerns the most serious thing in the world, therefore be serious!" And the children were. Now I must really tell you, mama, what was in the picture. First, a pregnant woman was sitting in a grandfather's chair, and next to her stood her husband, holding her hand. Nearby on the other side stood a table, on it lay two small caps, one for a girl, the other for a boy, and underneath stood a basin with water and a sponge in it.

In R: 230–1

The child's narrative continues for several more pages, and in the following passage it is clear that Wolke tried to turn the discussion into a teaching moment:

There were still many other things that Mr. Wolke said and asked, for example, concerning the basin filled with water he said that when the baby first came into the world it would suffocate immediately in its own blood if the good parents did not care for it and wash and clean it ... Consider sometime what your mother has undergone for you! She has been in danger of death, and for your sake she has suffered unspeakable pain.

R: 231

Basedow's radical departure from accepted pedagogical practice and societal norms—and his desire to replace them with an enlightened, modern pedagogy—are perhaps best illustrated in his and Wolke's remarks about Plate XXIX in the *Elementarwerk*.

Naturalism[20]

Many of the curricular innovations associated with Basedow's Philanthropin—including not only his conversation-based method of teaching foreign languages and his doctrine of learning through play, but also the introduction of both physical education and sex education into the school, the advocacy of simpler, less restrictive clothing for students, and the strong emphasis on "realia" (pictures, maps, natural history collections), have their roots in Basedow's commitment to naturalism. By "naturalism" in the present context is meant not the heavy-handed doctrine familiar to contemporary philosophers—the rejection of all supernatural entities, the view that natural science offers all the knowledge that is humanly possible, the belief that philosophical method must not differ from scientific method, etc. Rather, I mean the milder view that much that we find in nature is good, and that humans should therefore try to follow nature rather than reject it or overcome it. This is what I have elsewhere called "a species of *weak naturalism*" (Louden 2000: 145). It is not quite as gung-ho as some of the more reductive naturalisms that have been popular in recent years, but that may not be a bad thing.

Basedow repeatedly emphasizes his naturalistic teaching methods in many of his writings. For instance, the second chapter of his 1752 *Magister* thesis at the University of Kiel is entitled "The Unused and Natural Method of all Scholastic Studies, chiefly Latin." And in the Preface to his 1774 work, *Das in Dessau errichtete Philanthropinum*, Basedow writes:

> *Nature! School! Life!* Friendship is under these three; so is the human being, what he should be, but cannot immediately be; happy in childhood, lively and witty in youth, peaceful and useful when a man. But when nature is whipped out of school, and school is mocked in the life of man, then in the end the human being grows into a monster [*eine Misgebuhrt*].
>
> DEP: XIII

Similarly, in the *Elementarwerk* he expresses hope that his method of "natural education and instruction ... will be introduced in public schools" (G: 283).

As we have already seen, philosopher Immanuel Kant (1724–1804; Kant and Basedow were both born in 1724) was an enthusiastic supporter of Basedow's school. And Kant particularly praised Basedow's commitment to naturalism—in part because he had announced his own intention to find a way "to make public education more adopted to nature [*nach der Natur mehr zu bequemen*]" (NEV 2: 305) in a 1765 publication. In the second of his two short essays written in support of the Philanthropin, originally published in the *Königsbergische gelehrte und politische Zeitung* in 1777, Kant congratulates Basedow for having developed "an educational method ... wisely derived from nature itself [*aus der Natur selbst gezogen*] and not slavishly copied from old habit and inexperienced ages" (AP 2: 449). All other schools, Kant asserts, "were spoiled at the outset, ... because everything in them works against nature [*der Natur entgegen arbeitet*]" (AP 2: 449).

In Enlightenment pedagogical theory, this emphasis on naturalistic teaching methods is traditionally associated with Rousseau's *Émile* (1762). And as a result, Basedow is often dismissed as a "mediocre thinker" (Parker 1912: 216) whose "root-ideas ... are those of Rousseau" (Quick 1896: 279)– an unoriginal German Rousseau, so to speak. But while Rousseau does indeed advocate a general principle "of letting nature alone in everything" (Rousseau 1979: 131; cf. 107, 137) in *Émile*, it should be noted that this book was not published until ten years after Basedow began advocating his "natural method" of education in his 1752 *Magister* thesis. And the material in Basedow's thesis, as noted earlier, is based on his earlier experience as a *Hauslehrer* in the von Qualen family home in Borghorst from 1749 to 1752. So it is clearly not the case that Basedow's naturalistic teaching method is borrowed from Rousseau.

Broadly speaking, the positive evaluation of humans as natural creatures is a key part of modernity's break with the Middle Ages, and Basedow is a leader in this movement. And in fact the Enlightenment appeal to nature as a positive norm for human conduct extends far beyond pedagogy. For instance, Wolfgang Amadeus Mozart's father Leopold, in his famous treatise on the principles of violin playing, continually advises his readers to follow "nature herself" in determining how best to play their instrument (Mozart 1756: 193; cf. 238).

Who actually attended the Public Examination at the Philanthropin on May 13–15, 1776, and what were their reactions? Göring writes:

> When the time for the Examination arrived, the most dignified men greeted each other in the rooms of the Philanthropin. *Nicolai*[21] and *Feller* from Berlin were present; from Halberstadt, *Struensee*;[22] from Leipzig, *Platner*[23] and *Zollikofer*;[24] from Magdeburg, *Resewitz*[25] and *Schummel*;[26] from Potsdam, *Campe*;[27] from Quedlinburg, *Stroth*;[28] from Hamburg, *Bode*;[29] from Rekahn, *Rochow*.[30]
>
> Göring 1880: LXX

A more complete list of attendees is available in Letter VII of Schummel's *Fritzens Reise nach Dessau*. Some additional (and less socially prominent) guests are mentioned in the following passage:

> [Q]uite a lot have come, and right at the door lies a book which we all must sign. I have also entered my name ... From Berlin there was Provost *Teller*[31] ... Also from Berlin a nobleman, the *Baron von Rek*. From Potsdam ... a small, sweet woman ... Madame *Gilbert* ... From Brandenburg Director *Brenmann* ... and Herr *Rambacher* and *Strothen*, and also their two young wives ... Principal *Sangerhausen* ... from Dresden a young businessman, *Bassange*, with his father and mother, who either had a brother or son enrolled at the Philanthropin ... From Leipzig, a certain Count *von Schönburg* and Professor *Eck* from Hamburg.
>
> Schummel 1776: 44–50

How did the guests react to the Examination? In most cases, enthusiastically. Raumer writes: "Most of the strangers went away with a favorable impression of the Examination ... Flattering reports concerning the outcome of the Examination appeared soon afterward in the *Deutsche Merkur* and in the

Allgemeine Deutsche Bibliothek" (Raumer 1843: 2: 269). And many other testimonials soon followed. Financially pressed clergyman Johann Friedrich Oberlin[32] (1740–1826), in a famous 1777 letter to his former student Johann Friedrich Simon, now a teacher at the Philanthropin, effused enthusiastically:

> Oh, if only we had money, which is so useless in many hands! So I have thought a thousand times since I have known of the institute at Dessau, and so my wife and I had to think again, when we read the third part of your *Archives*. We considered everything, whether we had not some thing that could turn into money. I mourned, for I knew we did not. Then my wife came silently into my study, and with cheerful eyes brought me a pair of earrings, with the request that I send them to the Philanthropinum, or their monetary value, if we could sell them.[33]

But perhaps the school's most ardent supporter was Kant. In the first of his two short essays in support of the experimental school he praises the Philanthropin for the "entirely new order of human affairs" (AP 2: 447) commencing in it. Working as an unofficial fundraiser and student recruiter for the school ("Local subscriptions, against receipt, are given out at Prof. Kant's in the morning hours from 10 until ... around 1 o'clock in the afternoon"—AP 2: 452)—a job he did not relish, and from which he was able to finally free himself in 1778—he expresses still stronger admiration for the new school toward the end of his *Friedländer*[34] anthropology lecture:

> The present-day Basedowian institutes are the first that have come about according to the perfect plan of education. This is the greatest phenomenon which has appeared in this century for the improvement of the perfection of humanity. Through it all schools in the world will receive another form, and the human race will thereby be freed from the constraints of the prevailing schools.
> V-Anth/Fried 25: 722–3; cf. Päd 9: 451

What Kant and many other Enlightenment intellectuals believed they saw in Basedow's Philanthropin was the best means available to human beings for achieving their collective destiny. As he remarks in an ethics lecture delivered during the winter semester of 1775–6: "The final destiny of the human race is moral perfection ... How, then, are we to seek this perfection, and from what point is it to be hoped for? From nowhere else but education" (V-Mo/Collins 27: 470, 471). And in calling Basedow's school "the greatest phenomenon which has appeared in this century for the improvement of the perfection of humanity" he is clearly singling out the Philanthropin—among all other educational institutions of the time—as humanity's best vehicle for achieving this goal of moral perfection. Popular philosopher Christian Garve (1742–98), another major voice in the German Enlightenment, also praises Basedow's singular devotion to the perfection of humanity in a 1771 review of two of his books:

> There are perhaps many people among us who are just as profound: but people who have had this keen perception turned entirely on the improvement and happiness of human beings, on the hindrances and means of promoting moral perfection in all social classes, are much more rare; and finally, among those who have combined this insight with such a great enthusiasm, so much activity, so much hardening [*Abhärtung*] against dangers and difficulties, so much persistence against opposition and hindrances, there are perhaps none except Basedow.[35]

This theme of the destiny of humanity (*die Bestimmung des Menschens*) is a major motif in German Enlightenment thought. As Norbert Hinske rightly notes, "discussion of the late German Enlightenment is unimaginable without it, [and] there is hardly any author in the late German Enlightenment who does not call up this key term in one form or another" (Hinske 1990: 435).

However, despite the enthusiastic praise and adulation of Oberlin, Kant, Garve, and many other Enlightenment intellectuals, by the end of 1776 Basedow had already resigned from the school's directorship, and, after years of continuing financial problems, low enrollment, and administrative infighting and mismanagement, in 1793 the Philanthropin finally closed for good. How could "the greatest phenomenon which has appeared in this century for the improvement of the perfection of humanity" sink so quickly? The remaining chapters of this biography are, in part, an attempt to answer this question.[36]

2

Blame It on the Parents?

Sooner or later, everyone who writes about Basedow is forced to deal with his complex personal character. Some biographers even devote separate chapters to "Basedow's Personality."[1] By all accounts, he was not an easy person to get along with, and he possessed a higher than average number of negative character traits.[2] The closing of the Philanthropin in 1793 can be traced in part to this issue (the school was marked by continual administrative infighting and mismanagement, much of which centered around Basedow), but his personality is significant for other reasons as well.

Goethe, in Book XIV of his *Dichtung und Wahrheit* (first published in 1813; Basedow had been dead for twenty-three years), offers one of the earliest and most insightful statements regarding Basedow's personality, based on his recollections of a trip that he, Basedow, and Lavater[3] took together in the summer of 1774 along the Rhine River. The main purpose of the trip, at least as far as Basedow was concerned, was to raise funds for the Philanthropin, which officially opened in Dessau on December 27, 1774, the birthday of its chief patron, Prince Leopold III of Anhalt-Dessau. Although Goethe acknowledged that Basedow's "great intellectual gifts were admired," he quickly added that he "was not the man, either to edify souls or to lead them," noting also that while Basedow could speak "in a lofty and convincing way of his plans" for a new school, his fundraising efforts were frequently hampered by his rude manners and "the most incomprehensible way he injured the feelings of the men whose contributions he wished to gain: indeed, he offended them unnecessarily because he could not suppress his opinions and silly ideas on religious topics" (in R: 239, 240). Basedow's egotism and heavy pipe-smoking habit were additional causes of irritation:

> Basedow ... could not pay attention to anything outside himself. His ceaseless smoking of bad tobacco was extremely annoying, and the more so because his pipe was no sooner out than he brought forth a dirtily prepared kind of tinder, which lit quickly, but had a most horrid stench, and every time contaminated

the air unbearably with the first whiff. I called this preparation "Basedowian smelly fungus" [*Basedowschen Stinkschwamm*], and wanted to introduce it into natural history under this name, which greatly amused him, and to my disgust he minutely explained the revolting preparation, taking a malicious pleasure in my abhorrence of it. For it was one of the most deeply rooted, evil characteristics of this admirably gifted man that he enjoyed teasing, and loved to maliciously jab the most impartial persons. He could never leave anyone in peace; with mocking irony and a hoarse voice he provoked them, embarrassed them by an unexpected question, and laughed bitterly when he had achieved his goal; however, he was very content when the objects of his jests were quick enough to collect themselves and gave him a retort.

In R: 241

Similarly, Hamann, in a letter to Herder,[4] after confessing that he feared he could "do nothing" for his son's education, added: "I had one Sunday, the horrid idea of packing him off, neck and heels, to the *Pontifex Maximus* at Dessau," to which Herder replied: "as concerns Basedow, whom I know personally, I would not give him any calves to educate, much less human beings" (Hamann 1957: 3: 236, 251). And Kant, in a 1791–2 transcription of one of his anthropology lectures—when the Philanthropin was on its last legs, and his own early enthusiasm had waned—told his audience that "Basedow's shortcoming was that he drank too much Malaga" (25: 1538).[5] Many biographers have commented on Basedow's excessive drinking. As Lauchkard remarks: "He loved a glass of wine, and now and then drank more than was necessary—as if he didn't want to get the Philanthropin under way" (Lauchkard 1848: 99). But, to his credit, even Basedow was able to acknowledge some of his personal shortcomings. In a 1783 publication he confessed that "in *business* I am or was rash and argumentative, and in social intercourse often sorrowful and neurotic" (Basedow 1783a: 59).

Surprisingly, several of Basedow's earliest biographers are even more critical about his character flaws than Goethe, Herder, and Kant. Meier, for instance, in volume I of his *Johann Bernhard Basedows Leben, Charakter und Schriften*, writes: "As a boy he was wild and unmanageable; as a youth, boisterous and independent; and as a man ... too old to improve and to cast off deep-rooted evil habits" (M: I: 37–8). And in volume II: "in his external behavior he was rather disgusting and dirty. He spat [*sprudelte*] when he spoke, particularly when he had drunk from the *poculo hilaritatis* [cup of joy] ..." (M: II: 10). Even his own colleagues, according to another source, often called him "Mad Basedow" behind his back (Lang 1892: 8).

Reble summarizes the views of many earlier biographers when he refers to Basedow's

> restless nature and lack of moderation, his uneasy, loud, stubborn, and even quarrelsome character, his love of experimentation and agitation, his boastful and egocentric behavior and the alternation between overestimation of his abilities and depression, his pushiness and tactlessness, the constant emphasis of his ideas for improving the world and his theological controversies.
>
> Reble 1965: 254

All of this has contributed to ongoing speculation concerning the genetic and environmental factors that may have contributed to Basedow's personality. So let us turn now to some details concerning his birth, parents, family background, and early upbringing.

Basedow was born in Hamburg on September 11, 1724. Many earlier biographers—including not only Meier, Rathmann, Pinloche, and Göring, but also Basedow's great-grandson Max Müller[6]—record the birth year as 1723, but Basedow himself states clearly in the vita that he submitted with his master's thesis to the University of Kiel on June 7, 1752: "*I, Johann Bernhard Basedow, was born on September 11, the year of salvation, 1724 in Hamburg.*"[7] At present, most scholars regard the 1724 date as accurate. The original spelling of his name was "Johan Berend Bassedau" (Diestelmann 1897: 101 n. 1), a spelling that Basedow later changed when he submitted his MA thesis in 1752.[8]

Rathmann, at the beginning of his 1791 biography, describes Basedow's father, Hinrich Bassedau (1699–1782), as follows:

> His father, a citizen and wigmaker in Hamburg, was a fiery, strict, and rough man who held back, and tried to weaken and suppress, the early activity, the restless liveliness, the bold, fiery, adventurous spirit of his son, according to the usual method, more through strictness and punishment than through prudence, love, and kindness ... [Basedow] therefore found little joy in the family home.
>
> Ra: 3

Similarly, Göring portrays Hinrich Bassedau as a man who

> grew up in miserable conditions, who appears to have been of a harsh and raw character, as the force of a hard situation in life would form. He was a wigmaker. His nature is described as brusque, violent, and gloomy. It is thought that such qualities come from a total lack of education, and one can imagine that it was no easy task to live with this man ... He was a father in whom a violent temper had never been ameliorated through education ... Basedow's instability, abnormal and tormenting restlessness, frequently recurring melancholic depression,

pathologically heightened irritability, his often violent temper, even his alcoholism—all of these are phenomena in his mental life which psychiatry is only able to explain through the assumption of a hereditary strain [*hereditärer Belastung*]

Göring 1880: XX, XXI

Göring is convinced that Basedow's father is the source of much of the trouble. However, there are a few dissenting opinions regarding this dark portrayal of Hinrich Bassedau. For instance, Meier, who claims to have known Basedow's father "very well" (M: I: 161) and to have also been a frequent guest at his dinner table, describes him as "an honorable old man, a good, honest citizen . . . a good cosmopolitan and citizen, which he showed in words and judgments as well as in deeds, and that is why he was loved and respected by all acquaintances" (B: I: 162). Curt Swet, in his 1898 biography, writes: "Of Basedow's father it is almost universally accepted that he was an uneducated man, a dark and raw character who raised his son with excessive severity" (Swet 1898: 11). But two pages later he sides with Meier when he claims "that Basedow's father was not the raw and dark character he is usually described as being" (Swet 1898: 13). Most biographers, however, do describe Basedow's father as a very stern taskmaster and disciplinarian.

Basedow's mother, Anna Maria (1693–1780), was also not quite a paragon of normality. She was the widow of Hinrich Andreas Jungbluth, who ran the wig-making store before Basedow's father took it over. She and Hinrich Bassedau were married on February 21, 1724, and the birth of their son only six and a half months later has led some to speculate that Hinrich Bassedau was not in fact the biological father, and/or that she married more out of a concern for the family business rather than for love (see, e.g., Swet 1898: 12). Regardless of which (if either) of these hypotheses is correct, it was not a happy marriage, and this tension in the family home undoubtedly also contributed to the formation of Basedow's personality. But the most frequently commented-on issue concerning Basedow's mother is the state of her own mental health. Meier writes:

> Basedow's real mother, as all relatives and trustworthy witnesses affirmed, suffered frequent and very strong fits of insanity, and died in a violent convulsion of rage. This was the daily domestic affliction [*Hauskreuz*] . . . which the good and honest and industrious Basedow had to bear for so long.
>
> M: I: 164

And Basedow himself, in a short autobiographical reflection in which he attempts to explain his own melancholy and alcoholism, writes: "Perhaps it lies in a natural cause, that I was born from an extraordinarily lively *father* and a *mother* who was increasingly melancholic to the point of insanity" (Basedow 1783a: 67–8).

However, information about Basedow's earlier family history adds some unexpected complications to the speculation concerning both genetic and environmental factors in his own character development. Göring writes:

> His ancestors go back to an ancient, distinguished family on the bends of the East Sea. His great-grandfather was a rich baron who, as a result of heavy losses, had to sell the family name and estate [*das Gut*] "Basedow." A feature that made up a basic element of the grandchild, a certain restlessness, coupled with an untiring urge for activity, seems already to have been inherited from the grandfather. He was an enterprising individual, and is described as a traveler of the East Indies who acquired a considerable fortune, lost his property three times and three times worked his way up again to a considerable fortune.
>
> Göring 1880: XX[9]

But what is most extraordinary about Basedow is not his all-too-human character flaws and his many-hued family history, but the tremendous energy and devotion he brought to his project of improving humanity through an enlightened method of education against this background of a difficult family life. He published over 100 books during his lifetime[10]—an enviable record from any perspective. [As the anonymously published biography in the *Deutsche Monatschrift* puts it: "Basedow was *extremely active*: he worked a great deal and fast" ("Fragmente über Basedow" 1790: 296).] Lauchkard comes closer to the truth than most biographers in his observation that "the fire and intensity of ... [Basedow's] nature gave him the strength throughout his entire life to work and carry out as much as only a few human beings have been able to do" (Lauchkard 1848: 98). But even this remark diminishes Basedow's achievements in its suggestion that his extensive publication record is somehow a simple causal result of a genetically determined personality. How many other melancholics with drinking problems and grandfathers who lost the family fortune have managed to publish over 100 books?[11]

Given the unhappy marriage between Basedow's parents, their conflicting personalities, and the family's financially pressed circumstances, it is easy to guess what his early years were like. Göring stresses "the cruel violence with which the father mistreated the boy," adding that "such an unjust treatment naturally made the most detrimental impression on the mind of the young Basedow" (Göring 1880: XXIII), while Diestelmann notes that "in the education of his son," Basedow's father "no doubt united gloomy strictness with a lack of understanding for happy, childish enjoyment of life" (Diestelmann 1897: 8).

But there is one unexpected twist in these stereotypical descriptions. In his 1752 vita, Basedow himself writes:

> Coming from a poor family, until the eighth year of my life I was taught how to read Latin and German by my father, the use of Latin declensions and conjugations, as well as writing. Indeed, despite our poverty and despite my inherited eye weakness, which only increased over the course of time and through study at night, my father decided that I would study theology.
>
> As cited by AB: 7

This autobiographical statement should incline us to read the earlier unflattering descriptions of Basedow's father with a grain of salt. Even if Basedow's father was "a dark and raw character," he appears also to have been a highly intelligent man who did care about his son. Perhaps Meier—even if it is true that one should use his biography "only with great caution" (AB: 10)—was not far off the mark. None of the Basedows were saints, but Hinrich clearly wanted a better future for his son, and he took substantial efforts to help him achieve it. As Joachim Specht writes at the beginning of his imaginatively rendered biography of Basedow written in the first person (*Ich, Johann Bernhard Basedow*): his father's "ambitious wish was to make me a theologian, that is, a position of high standing" (Specht 1999: 7). Basedow's own statement in the vita that his father wanted him to study theology also casts doubt on the claims of several biographers that Basedow was fated to follow his father in the wig-making trade. For instance, Meier claims that "Basedow was, as he and his father often affirmed to me, destined to learn his father's trade" (M: I: 174), and Göring and Diestelmann both repeat Meier's assertion: "From the start he was destined for his father's trade and had to learn wig-making" (Göring 1880: XXII); "From his father, he was destined for the learning of the paternal trade" (Diestelmann 1897: 9). A more plausible explanation, however, is simply that the father needed help with the family business, and hiring his son was easier (and cheaper) than hiring a stranger. At any rate, while Hinrich did want his son to become a theologian, it is also the case that Basedow was already working part-time in the family business by the age of twelve:

> and soon as a budding apprentice, according to Hamburgian custom, he had to run along the streets with a long and narrow wooden box, in order to pick up and carry off wigs. For a youth of twelve and more years, who had so much conspicuous liveliness, cheerfulness ... and mischievousness, and who for his

years had too much youthful fire, and who distinguished himself from his numerous comrades through many playful pranks, such an arduous and low business was certainly not appropriate ... His rough, raw, wild, and boisterous nature ... was nurtured and increased still more by this business.

M: I: 174–5

In 1732, when he was eight years old, Basedow's father enrolled him in the famous Johanneum school in Hamburg. Founded in 1529 by Johannes Bugenhagen,[12] the Johanneum was a school whose regulations provided that not only rich but also poor students would be allowed to attend. Johann started in the eighth or lowest class, and while he made good progress—either "due to his previous knowledge, which he had acquired from his father" (AB: 23) or his own native ability—he did not enjoy his time at the school. Göring writes: "along with compulsion in the parents' home came the countless atrocities of a pedantic school despotism ... [T]he instruction in that school was worthless. Even in the lower classes he was plagued with memorizing countless things that he did not understand at all. Even in the third class ... he had to memorize the entire Dresden Catechism" (Göring 1880: XXIII). As Diestelmann notes, it was here that the first seed was planted for Basedow's later opposition to memorization and physical punishment: "From this being poured down his throat against his will at the time presumably originates his repugnance against all memorization in his later pedagogical views" (Diestelmann 1897: 10).

But at least when he was not in class or in his parents' home, Basedow did manage to occasionally free himself from this oppressive learning environment. Meier offers the following intriguing examples:

> That the young Basedow as a boy in his running around on the streets already felt he was inclined to reflect and think deeply, he explained to me in many anecdotal proofs from his boyhood years, of which I want to dig out only a pair. While he reflected on the words of the Bible, "who seizes the wind in his hand?" he would often run, without paying any attention to his heavy box, against the wind with hand uplifted and fingers outstretched, and then suddenly clench them together to see whether one could not seize the wind. The spectators and observers, who in large cities are always very numerous regarding the slightest insignificant things, asked him if he were really clever [recht klug], and he answered, "I want to seize the wind with my hand; but I see indeed that the Bible is correct." From this some people decided that more than a wigmaker must be hiding in him. Another time, in order to test whether money placed under the earth continued to move, or whether there are people who can sniff and smell it out, he buried some collected coins in the earth in a secret spot on the street, and

then in a few days he rejoiced warmly when he recovered the pennies that he had regarded as lost.

M: I: 176–7

According to Rathmann, of his teachers at the Johanneum Basedow "remembered even in his old age with thankfulness and reverence the former Rector there, Müller,[13] the well-known translator of Tacitus, and a Herr Hake"[14] (Ra: 6). And Müller, according to another account, was also an outstanding teacher:

> In order to instill joy and love of the sciences in his students, he broke with the then-existing system of one-sided emphasis on classical language education and in the first class lectured on logic, the history of Roman and Greek literature, and German art. Additionally, he gave instruction in composing verses and competed with the students to see who could write the most beautiful rhymes.

Specht 1999: 7

Müller's more flexible and student-friendly style of teaching spurred Basedow's imagination (were his rhyming competitions perhaps the source of Basedow's later views about learning as play?), but it also set the stage for a remunerative sideline of composing verses for birthdays, weddings, etc. And this activity in a sense marks the real beginning of Basedow's life as an author. Although it is not clear how much income he actually earned from writing these poems for special occasions, Basedow later claimed to have achieved financial independence from his parents by the age of sixteen: "More than once he boasted in his writings that from his sixteenth year he did not cost his parents a penny more, and he explained that a young man with sixteen years should have come so far that he can stand on his own feet" (AB: 29). Additionally, the adolescent Basedow somehow managed to squirrel away enough income to run away from home and self-finance a trip to Amsterdam when he was sixteen.

What led Basedow to run away is not entirely clear. One would think that it was due to ongoing tensions with his "fiery, strict, and rough" father as well as domestic quarrels between his mismatched parents, but this is not the way Basedow himself describes the situation. He had also progressed well in school and was now in the upper class of the Johanneum. But in his 1752 vita he implies that he was tired of school and wanted to devote himself "to some trade:"

> During this time I was discouraged over further progress in my studies, and because my father would not permit me to exchange this for any kind of business, I traveled to Amsterdam without knowledge of my parents in order to devote myself to some trade. For I lived with the definite conviction that I could find a favorable opportunity there. But I was deceived in my expectation. And as the

small savings that I had were now exhausted, I tried to go to India. However, because I was too short, the commissioners would accept me neither as a soldier nor as a sailor. Finally, a merchant from Copenhagen, who stopped there for business and had learned of my distress, engaged me out of pity as his traveling companion to Denmark, and promised that he would find an appropriate position for me there that fit my abilities. But this hope was also dashed, for we suffered a shipwreck near the North Shore Island, and the merchant who had taken me under his protection was barely able to take care of himself. From there, for nine months, I earned my living by acting as a servant in Flensburg in the house of Boessel, a doctor and physician of the province.

As cited by AB: 7–8

Dr. Boessel, who studied medicine at the University of Halle from 1723 to 1726 under Professors Bey and Bassino and later lived in Berlin, Paris, and Copenhagen before settling down in Flensburg, was a well-educated man who had seen a bit of the world and could open new doors for Basedow. As Armin Basedow notes:

> He was the right man, not only to employ his servant, but also to support him and expand his horizons. Basedow enjoyed reading many books from his library, which stimulated the world of ideas in the sixteen-year-old, and caused his hitherto reliable, pious childish beliefs to totter: he later noted repeatedly that the great change in his life was in his sixteenth year.
>
> AB: 28

Rathmann and Meier also describe Basedow's stay with Boessel in extremely positive terms. In Boessel's home Basedow "was very well provided for, and he often said in his later years that it was there that he spent the most enjoyable time of his life and first learned love of humanity [*Menschenliebe*]" (Ra: 4). Basedow soon "believed a special power of God brought him there," for Boessel "regarded him more as his son than his servant" (M: I: 180).

But Boessel also eventually notified Basedow's father of his son's whereabouts; in addition, he was later able to partially heal the rift between father and son. As a result, after nine months in Flensburg Basedow returned to Hamburg, where—after apologizing to Rector Müller, who, needless to say, had not been happy with his student's unexpected departure from his classes—he was allowed to reenroll at the Johanneum. And this time things went better at school. Basedow was not as bored with the instruction in the upper classes as he had been earlier when he first enrolled in the school's lowest class. Göring writes:

> With his return to Hamburg Basedow reentered the Johanneum. As much as he also later complained of the important loss of time and mental power in public

schools, he nevertheless liked being in the higher classes which he had now entered, having found sufficient nourishment and stimulation for his lively spirit. He soon distinguished himself over his classmates through his many-sided talents as much as through his industry and persistence.

Göring 1880: XXVI

Although Basedow continued to be a source of irritation to some of his teachers, his last two years at the Johanneum went fairly smoothly. According to the "new school ordinance of 1732" that was in effect at the time, students who wanted to be admitted for further study at a gymnasium "'should be properly prepared by having had eight classes at the Johanneum in the Christian religion, the Latin and Greek languages, arithmetic, logic, and rhetoric', and be examined by the Director in the presence of a professor, and be found worthy" (AB: 32). And, as Basedow himself writes in his vita, "I remained for two years now under the discipline of the Rector with best success" (AB: 32; cf. 9). However, his claim of having achieved the "best success" in his studies at the Johanneum is predictably challenged by Meier, who claims that Basedow

> took little and very shallow preparatory knowledge for continuation of the study of theology from the school to the university ... He could read no Hebrew, in the Greek language his knowledge was so weak and superficial that he could read and understand only the easiest parts of the New Testament; although at the same time he used so many Greek words in the editions of his writings ... that one should have assumed he was a great authority in this language.

M: I: 191, 191 n.

Nevertheless, "according to the matriculation register of the academic gymnasium that was closely connected to the Johanneum, Johan Bernhard Bassedau was a graduate of the Johanneum and was admitted as a theology student there on May 13, 1743" (AB: 32). And so Basedow successfully reached the next step in the educational ladder, and was able to spend the following three years at "the Hamburg Gymnasium, an academic school that differed from other institutions ... in that it allowed students a certain freedom in the choice of teachers and subjects" (Diestelmann 1897: 11). In his vita, Basedow singles out three teachers at this well-known school, founded in 1613, under whom he studied:

> Afterward I transferred to the Gymnasium, where I was especially loved by Richey. I enjoyed the instruction of this famous man, in public and in private lectures, in universal history and the Greek language. At the same time I heard the expositions of preacher and Professor Reimarus on Wolffian philosophy and

Jewish antiquity. Professor Dornemann[15] taught pure mathematics. Above all, I occupied myself with poetry and modern literature, through which I both earned my living and also won friends.

AB: 9

Michael Richey (1678–1761), who, in addition to teaching at the gymnasium was also a published poet and translator of Latin poetry, financially supported and encouraged Basedow in an almost paternal manner after his former student left Hamburg. Richey also nurtured Basedow's own talent for poetry, which had first been awakened in Müller's classes at the Johanneum. According to Göring, during his three years at the Hamburg Gymnasium "Basedow wrote many occasional poems which, especially when they were ordered by others, provided him with a not inconsiderable part of his income" (Göring 1880: XXVII). Indeed, Basedow dedicated his first publication to Richey, a poem of one hundred stanzas entitled *The Necessity of a Science of History* (see Basedow 1746). As he notes in the Preface: "For over two years it has been my intention, according to my weak ability, to offer a sign of my strong respect and gratitude to Herr Professor Richey, to whom I owe almost everything in my present condition that can be regarded as happy" (Basedow 1746; as cited by AB: 39). In the body of the poem Basedow offers even stronger testimony of his debt to Richey: "Oh dear man, I shall always / honor that day as the happiest one / when I obtained my foremost desire / to hear you, my great Richey."[16] Similarly, in a second poem written in Latin and first published in 1750—*Epistolae ad Michaelem Richeum*—Basedow continues his praise of Richey by drawing attention to "the weight of his reputation in the scholarly world."[17] And over a decade later, when Basedow the university graduate was teaching at the Gymnasium in Altona (near Hamburg, the city of his birth) he offered the following remarks in his public inaugural speech—delivered in Latin—regarding his recently deceased friend and teacher Richey:

> Oh how gladly, blessed Richey, would I publicly offer my thanks to you, if you had not already been summoned from earth to heaven as the reward for your devotion (faith), all your toil and charity. I cannot find words that sufficiently praise your great deeds. I can only express in all simplicity, what my grateful heart urges. You have not only given me your instruction with the same generosity as my other teachers, without allowing remuneration, for which no price would be adequate, but also, which almost goes beyond human kindness, many other good deeds, for no other reason than that you saw that they bore good fruits. As a student at the Hamburg Gymnasium you often saved me from dire circumstances, through your influence and generosity, by paying my debts,

by aiding me when I was sick with medicine and healthy food, by offering frequent gifts, by defending me against those who wanted to harm me without just cause, and finally by paying a considerable part of the expenses incurred for living and studying at the University of Leipzig [when I was a student there]. Without doubt our heavenly father is now rewarding you deservedly for your good deeds.[18]

Clearly, Basedow and Richey enjoyed something much stronger than a typical student-teacher relationship. In addition to cultivating Basedow's interest in writing poetry, Richey also provided a great deal of financial and emotional support to the impoverished son of a wigmaker. But the bigger question, at least from the perspective of Basedow's later theological and philosophical writings, is the extent of the influence of the second gymnasium teacher mentioned in his vita, Hermann Samuel Reimarus (1694–1768). Professor of Hebrew and Oriental Languages at the Hamburg Gymnasium, Reimarus would later be viewed as "the most important philosopher of religion between Leibniz and Lessing and also 'the great systematizer of deism during the German Enlightenment'" (Raupp 2016: 611). His *Wolfenbüttel Fragmente*, first published only in parts by Gotthold Ephraim Lessing (1729–1781) after Reimarus's death under the title *Fragments of an Anonymous Author*, inaugurated "the most explosive religious debate in eighteenth-century Germany" (Raupp 2016: 614). Armin Basedow claims that "since Reimarus was an enthusiastic Wolffian, it is understandable [*erklärlich*] that he familiarized his young students with this philosophy above all" (AB: 34). But it might not be this simple. Wolff's rationalistic interpretation of religion was very controversial, and promulgating this radical outlook on young students would not be a prudent choice for a gymnasium teacher to make. Furthermore, Basedow's statement in his vita that he heard Professor Reimarus's expositions "on Wolffian philosophy" do not indicate to what extent (if any) philosophy of religion was one of the topics discussed.

Basedow and Reimarus definitely had very favorable opinions of each other. For instance, Meier notes that in a review of Rathmann's biography (*Beiträge zur Lebensgeschichte Joh. Bernh. Basedows*) published in the June 11, 1791 issue of the *Hamburgischer Korrespondent*, both Richey and Reimarus are said "to have prophesized, while he was still their student at the gymnasium, that this youth would become one of the most publicly useful and thoughtful men [*einer der gemeinnützigsten und denkendsten Männer*]" (M: I: 184 n.).[19] And in a 1771 publication Basedow refers specifically to both Richey and Reimarus as the two men "whose teaching profited him, whose confidence encouraged him, and whose patronage helped him."[20] Additionally, in one of his major early publications, the *Philalethie* of 1764, Basedow writes, regarding Reimarus: "I hope that this great friend of truth, to whom I am indebted since my youth for his instruction and favors, will not regard my deep respect for him and his service as suspicious, nor the impetus of my remarks as vain" (Basedow 1764a: II: 407). Armin Basedow also notes that Basedow sent Reimarus a copy of his 1753 book, *Versuch, wiefern die Philosophie zur Freigeisterei verführe,* "with the request that he judge it, just as he asked him in 1758 to review his *Praktische Philosophie für alle Stände* 'in a journal, so that the educated public could experience his intention to unite a really revealed [*wirklich geoffenbarte*] Christianity with reason.'"[21]

But the key questions—which unfortunately cannot be answered precisely—are the extent to which Reimarus and Basedow actually discussed theological matters with each other while Basedow was a gymnasium student, and the degree of Reimarus's influence on Basedow's later religious thought. Part of the problem is that there were two different Reimaruses:

> There was a public and a private Reimarus. Publicly, Reimarus ... took pleasure in showing that the demands of natural religion and those of Christianity agreed, or complemented one another ... Privately, Reimarus's views were those of rationalism, the total displacement of revelation by reason. The influences that shaped his private thought came primarily from two sources, Christian Wolff and English Deism.
>
> Talbert 1970: 6, 11

According to Armin Basedow, the 1743–6 register of lectures at the Hamburg Gymnasium indicates that during this time period Reimarus gave lectures and exercises (*Übungen*) on

> early Hebraic history, August Pfeiffer's[22] *Critica Sacra*, hermeneutics, the Protestant liturgies, early Jewish history, introduction to the Rabbinical writings; privately with students he pursued Hebrew, even Chaldean: but strangely enough one finds no mention of a lecture on Wolffian philosophy, of which Basedow speaks [in his vita].
>
> BA: 33

However, it is doubtful that Basedow would have spoken falsely in his 1752 vita, for this was an important public document submitted with his dissertation to the University of Kiel. Perhaps what he meant when he says in his vita that he heard "the expositions of Preacher and Professor Reimarus on the Wolffian philosophy" was that Reimarus spoke with him privately about Christian Wolff's philosophy. But if so, which aspects of Wolff's philosophy?

At any rate, regardless of the extent to which Basedow and Reimarus did or did not discuss Wolff's philosophy together at the Hamburg Gymnasium, their mature religious views are by no means identical. Basedow and Reimarus are often loosely labeled as "deists," but—at least in the case of Basedow—this is an inaccurate description. Max Müller, Basedow's great-grandson, in commenting on Basedow's personal interaction with Reimarus, observes that his ancestor "owed his first initiation in what were at that time very liberal ideas concerning the Christian religion, although in later years, after the appearance of the *Wolfenbüttel Fragments*, he regarded it as his duty to take decisive steps against the far-reaching consequences of his former teacher's [position]" (Müller 1967: 114). We will examine Basedow's voluminous religious writings in more detail later on. For now it suffices to say that although Reimarus—who held that "we need no miracle to make everything comprehensible"[23]—was indeed one of Basedow's favorite teachers at the Hamburg Gymnasium, Basedow's own religious perspective is quite a bit milder than his teacher's.[24]

But while Basedow clearly had several outstanding and influential teachers during his gymnasium years, he was hardly the most diligent student. In addition to his previously-commented-on poetry writing, other extracurricular activities (for which he also received remuneration) included tutoring well-to-do students and selling used books. Meier, as usual, offers the following negative assessment:

> 1) With great self-satisfaction Basedow took care to relate ... anecdotes and accounts of his youth, adding with an emphatic tone, "Yes! You can see who and what I was then, and how and why I have become what I am." 2) It is certain that Basedow took very little basic or systematic knowledge with him to the university from school, either in languages, the arts or the sciences; far less than one would assume of a youth who later became such a famous man. One remark more than a good many others deserves to be taken to heart in order to judge Basedow. His talents compensated for all his deficiencies. 3) Certainly at school and afterwards for his entire life, untimely praise and undeserved admiration became for Basedow very harmful and disadvantageous, for he imagined himself to be and to know what he was not and what he did not know; and he despised and did not learn what he should have prized and learned. In later years he himself recognized this very well, and he often had to strain his powers to a superhuman degree to compensate for these deficiencies. 4) Of his school years he took care to say that he was a merry companion [*lustiger Bruder*], a happy and cheerful associate, and a *bon vivant*: *vixi, dum vixi, bene* [while he lived, he lived well] ... 5) Just as

Basedow during these years acquired and became accustomed to his free, loose, and somewhat wild way of living, so he lived his entire life. He studied in a very disorderly and tumultuous manner; he despised and neglected the lessons of his instructors, he accustomed himself to immoderate delights that to him became indispensable needs; he cherished a too-great opinion of himself, and, finally, he did not wish to travel the customary paths and roads in order to seek knowledge and truth ... At school he already excused himself on account of his weak eyesight and his poor memory, and that is why he did not want to read or study the classics ... Thus Basedow lived, thought, and studied as long as he attended the Johanneum and the [Hamburg] Gymnasium.

M: I: 188–91

"His talents compensated for all his deficiencies:" Meier is certainly correct that this remark "more than a good many others deserves to be taken to heart" in evaluating Basedow, but for very different reasons than he suggests. What Meier means by the remark is well captured in the old saying (which he approvingly cites in a footnote) that "a smidgen of natural wit [*Mutterwitz*] is better and more fruitful, and often more useful, than a hundred pounds of school knowledge [*Schulwitz*]" (M: I: 189 n.). But a more sensible interpretation is that Basedow's professional accomplishments become even more remarkable when viewed in the context of his turbulent personal life. Basedow was no saint, he was not a regular guy, he was seldom a fun person to be around. "Until his death, he remained a restless, abnormal character" (Swrakoff 1898: 7). But he somehow found a way to leverage his numerous and notable personal deficiencies into an enviably productive and influential life as an author, educational reformer, *Popularphilosoph*, and liberal theologian. This is no easy task. At the same time, to focus exclusively either on his professional accomplishments while neglecting his personal life or vice versa is to only tell part of the story. The two belong together, and the latter may have even made the former possible. They are two sides of the same complicated person.

3

College Days

Basedow had ambitious but somewhat vague plans for his future after he graduated from the Hamburg Gymnasium in 1745. According to Meier,

> even in school his head was full of projects and plans for his future life, and with these squirming, still embryonic products of his mind he left his hometown. To become a great and famous man and make a mark in the world: this was what he constantly had as a goal before his eyes and in his heart.
>
> M: I: 192

Additionally, perhaps because the family legend of ancestors who had sailed the Eastern seas had been drummed into him since childhood,[1] the desire "to travel through the world and see foreign lands was already one of his favorite ideas in Hamburg, and the realization of many of his projects had a connection with this" (M: I: 193).

On the other hand, as noted earlier, Hinrich Bassedau hoped that his son would become a theologian, and Basedow must have also heard this message repeatedly during his youth. As Rathmann remarks: "His father, who wanted to make a pastor out of him by force, finally compelled him into it" (Ra: 8)—viz., Basedow's father steered Johann in various theological directions while he was still an adolescent in Hamburg. As Göring notes:

> His father's wish was that he should study theology. He appears to have already been amenable with this idea fairly early on, since he not only read dogmatic writings [*dogmatische Schriften*] before such studies could be useful for him, but he also preached at the churches in some of the neighboring villages near Hamburg while still a gymnasium student.
>
> Göring 1880: XXVIII; see also M: I: 205

After graduating from the gymnasium, Basedow left his parents' home in Hamburg to begin his university studies as a theology student. In early 1746 "he moved to the university at Leipzig, where he matriculated as 'Basedau' on May 12, 1746 under the Rectorship of Johann Erhard Kapp" (Swet 1898: 26). Founded in

1409, the University of Leipzig is Germany's second-oldest university, and includes among its famous alumni Leibniz, Goethe, and Nietzsche, as well as the composers Robert Schumann and Richard Wagner. Rector Johann Erhard Kapp (1696–1756) was also a historian and professor of rhetoric at the university. Gotthold Ephraim Lessing (1729–81), who would later become one of the leading figures in the German Enlightenment, also enrolled at Leipzig in 1746, and the poet Friedrich Gottlieb Klopstock (1724–1803), born in Quedlinburg, transferred there in 1746 from the University of Jena. In a letter written in the summer of 1760, Lessing comments very critically on one of Basedow's books[2] as follows: "You see, Herr *Basedow* exaggerates, he likes to be abusive, or he likes to praise. Hyperbole is his favorite figure in both cases. This unique man! ... I don't know at all what he wants" (as cited by Specht 1999: 82). Klopstock and Basedow, on the other hand, became good friends at the university, and Klopstock was later the godfather of Basedow's son Friedrich (b. 1771), who died six years after childbirth.

Two days after his matriculation date at the university, Basedow wrote to one of his patrons[3] back in Hamburg, focusing in particular on the new financial pressures he faced:

> Leipzig, May 14, 1746
> ... I have arrived safely, and the conditions at the university please me very much. Except for one thing, which I notice: I cannot get by on less than 200 thalers (a minor sum). I fear therefore that I shall not be able to hold out here for longer than a year, during which I must add to my scholarship the thalers I saved at Hamburg. But at the same time I also hope that before next Easter much can be arranged through the favorable attitude and kind intervention of some of the patrons in Hamburg. Your highness will not take it amiss, when my need again humbly urges you through your intervention and influence and the presentation of my precarious circumstances at your next meeting, to assure me of the continuance of the Penshorn scholarship for the following year, and to encourage others to imitate your magnanimity and consideration.
>
> I have already found the opportunity here to earn 80 thalers a year through my own work. This alone, however, is not a sufficient supplement to my present scholarship.[4]

At the end of a second letter dated October 10, 1746, after describing some of his professors and their seminars, Basedow repeats his request for additional financial support:

> Actually I am embarrassed, highly learned Doctor, to ask anything from a patron through whose unusual kindness I have already received so much. However, it

does not help to conceal one's poverty [*Mangel*] when one feels it. Your highness, then, will pardon the liberty with which I repeat my previous respectful petition of obtaining for me most graciously a continuance of the *Penshorn* scholarship for next year ...

In Pinloche 1896: 461

Other biographers confirm that Basedow faced considerable financial hardship at Leipzig. As his descendant Armin Basedow notes: "His living conditions at the university were not the rosiest" (AB: 48). Similarly, Meier observes:

Since Basedow received and could receive little or no support from his father, and from his patrons and friends he was provided with really only the barest necessities, and because he was also simply not a particularly thrifty housekeeper, I can readily believe that in Leipzig he often had to get by very poorly and barely.

M: I: 192

Indeed, Basedow himself states in one of his own books that "as a student in Leipzig for a course of time I ate *warm food* only three times a week" (Basedow 1783a: 172).

But what lectures did Basedow attend at Leipzig, and which professors influenced him while he was there? In the earlier-cited letter to his patron (presumably Wilckens) of October 10, 1746, he writes:

Leipzig still pleases me, and as I had the honor of informing you in my previous letter, Herr Professor and philosopher *Crusius*[5] causes more and more sensation here, and his sect [*seine Secte*] ... seems to grow daily ... I regret very much that my (frequent?) courses in theology and philosophy rob me of the time to work a little under the direction of this society of experienced writers.[6] I must allow myself to be content by serving to my advantage through contact with some of them, who will instruct me a little either by their lectures or criticism. In some of my leisure hours I have translated Cicero's book *De Amicitia*, and I think I will give it to a publisher with an appendix of the same material, and for my improvement submit it to the judgment of learned men.

In Pinloche 1896: 459, 460

Later in this same letter he offers further details concerning some of the professors at Leipzig and elsewhere:

The great physician Herr Dr. *Walther*[7] died here today, and we are already sure that Leipzig is expecting Herr Dr. and Councilor *Triller*[8] in his place. Herr Dr. *Baumgarten*[9] in Halle has recently published a short but thorough *Theologiam Dogmaticam* ... Herr Prof. *Crusius*, who, as is known, wants to construct a new philosophical system, has already published a Metaphysics and Ethics, his Logic is now in press, and the Physics will follow in a few years. Most of his opinions, in which he differs from the Wolffian philosophy, are to be found succinctly stated in the German translation of his *Disputation vom Determinirenden Grunde*, as well as in the *Disputatione de corruptelis intellectus ex gravis* [sic] *appetitibus*.

In Pinloche 1896: 460

In the 1752 vita that he submitted along with his dissertation at the University of Kiel, Basedow offers the following summary of his work at Leipzig:

Preacher and Professor Crusius presented to me in public lectures the central propositions of his philosophy and thetic theology, Doctor of Theology and Professor Jöcher[10] acquainted me with the history of constitutions (states). Deyling[11] guided me in the criticism of the Old and New Testaments. I listened to these famous men regularly and carefully, so far as I was able.

In AB: 9

However, according to his early biographers, Basedow did not in fact "listen to these famous men regularly and carefully." After his first semester, he rarely attended class at all. Meier writes:

The orderly and systematic pace of academic lectures was much too slow for his galloping way of studying. Therefore, after a short while he stopped being present at further lectures almost completely. He did not concern himself with the rest of the teachers, and gave no further effort in listening to or in examining their lectures ... He began now, again quite forcibly [*wieder recht gewaltsam*], to study alone under his own guidance, and more than usual, and perhaps more than he had ever done before in his entire life, to read, to meditate, to copy excerpts, and to put on paper his thoughts, doubts, and objections.

M: I: 198

Indeed, in later publications Basedow describes his student days in Leipzig in quite similar terms. For instance, in a 1771 book, *Vierteljährige Nachrichten von Basedows Elementarwerke und von andern Bemühungen*, he notes that during the two years that he lived in Leipzig, "I *studied almost entirely in my own room*" (Basedow 1771b: 5). And in the first volume of his 1764 *Philalethie*, he states that while he was in Leipzig "I divided up my effort into my own reading and reflection" (Basedow 1764a: I: 473). The reason for this intense period of self-study, he adds, is that after he had learned "the rudiments" of "the *Wolffian philosophy*" on his own he developed "strong doubts against some of its most important propositions," but also "doubts against some teachings of religion that

I had learned in my youth. So I stood *in the middle between Christianity and naturalism*, with a great desire to find conviction on one side or the other" (Basedow 1764a: I: 473). "In the middle between Christianity and naturalism"—this is an accurate description of Basedow's mature religious position, though he would also repeatedly maintain that the two outlooks, properly interpreted, were entirely consistent with each other. As he remarks in the *Philalethie*: "I now believed that I was at least convinced of natural religion, and I valued the Christian religion highly as one that agreed with it" (Basedow 1764a: I: 472). While his former teacher Reimarus and other deists could not possibly have agreed with Basedow's conviction that Christianity and naturalism are entirely consistent with each other, his own insistence that natural reason can and does support Christian doctrines, and that children should not be taught any religious ideas that they themselves cannot understand, does move him a bit in their direction. For instance, in the Preface to yet another work published in 1764 he writes that the "*first error*" in teaching religion to children is that "they become accustomed to thinking that without understanding and heart one can do merely with words and folding hands *that which deserves the name of prayer*" (Basedow 1764b: VII). And in the chapter entitled "Concerning the Religion of Young People" in the *Methodenbuch*, his "*first piece of advice*" is that "*we should teach children no words or sentences which mean anything relevant to religion as long as they either attach no concepts or false concepts to them*. For not even the smallest part of a religion consists in mere knowledge of words [*bloßer Wörterkenntnis*]" (MB VII.8; in G: 135). Other aspects of Basedow's mature religious outlook will be examined in a later chapter.

As a result of his decision to study "almost entirely" in his own room, Basedow attended Crusius's lectures on philosophy and theology for only a little over half a year. The famous professor "asserted that he drove the chimeras out of philosophy and also as a philosopher was completely in agreement with the Christian religion, which at that time I could only understand as Lutheran," but after a while, because Basedow could "no longer hear anything new enough in the lectures," he "chose the path of domestic diligence [*Weg des häuslichen Fleißes*]"[12]—i.e., he stopped attending Crusius's lectures.

However, "domestic diligence" appears to be an understatement. Basedow's new program of self-study was so intense that he almost ruined his eyesight (which was poor to begin with). Meier claims that Basedow later told him personally that "through excessive reading during his academic years and following [his eyes] had become so weak and wrecked that now he could barely read at all" (M: I: 200; cf. AB: 47). His extensive publication record is even more impressive when his poor eyesight is taken into account. Apparently, much of his writing was actually done with the help of an amanuensis who simply took dictation from him.

In his 1752 vita, Basedow notes tersely and rather cryptically that "after two years [in Leipzig] I matriculated at the University of Kiel" (as cited by AB: 9). But why did he leave the University of Leipzig? Was he bored? Homesick? Unhappy with the quality of instruction? Throughout his adult life, Basedow remained a stern critic of the German university system. For instance, in his 1768 *Vorstellung an Menschenfreunde*, he writes—in a remark that could just as easily be found in an op-ed column in today's newspapers: "Where are there now more obvious *useless formalities, more respectable lies and hypocrisies, than in . . . the academies [Akademien]*? I need to begin with what is most undeniable: who now for money and good words cannot *receive a degree [promovieren]*—PhD, licentiate,[13] MA, and BA . . ." (VM § 12; in R: 14)? Or did financial pressures force him to drop out? Basedow himself nowhere explains his decision to leave, but Meier speculates that "concerns for his future welfare" were the chief cause:

> It is true that he came to Leipzig full of restless anticipation, and with joyful restlessness, out of love of changes, to again leave the place; but he was also inundated with concerns for his future welfare, because he had expected no support from his family . . . In all of these pieces the central guiding hand of God prevailed over this man very strangely, which he soon knew, grasped, and kissed; but which due to stubbornness and sullenness he misjudged and even rejected . . . Basedow remained as he was, even after this change, a child of nature without a proper education, and during this time all youthful habits became rooted even deeper in him.
>
> M: I: 204–5

It is also not clear whether Basedow was still firmly committed to becoming a pastor at this point in his life. Diestelmann writes: "Whether Basedow preached during his time at Leipzig is not very likely [*wening wahrscheinlich*], but he probably did do this after he . . . returned to Hamburg, in order to continue his studies" (Diestelmann 1897: 15). Meier also notes: "Whether he preached in Leipzig, of that I know simply very little" (M: I: 203). At the same time, Quick's remark that "after an irregular life he left the university [of Leipzig] too unorthodox to think of being ordained" (Quick: 1896, 273) overstates the issue. We simply don't know with any certainty how committed Basedow was or was not to pursuing a career in the ministry at this particular point in this life.

At any rate, though the reasons for his departure remain cloudy, Basedow left the University of Leipzig in 1748—without obtaining a degree—and returned home to Hamburg. But he did not stay there for long. Armin Basedow writes: "According to information kindly provided by the Chancellor's office at the University of Kiel, in the matriculation list of May, 1748, under number 28, one finds the entry: 'Joannes Bernhardus Bassedau, Hamburg, free of charge'" (AB: 52). As Basedow himself remarks in his vita: "Two years after that [viz., 1748] I matriculated at the University of Kiel. Here I visited the lectures of the Reverend Herr Frisus on the Augsburg Confession. I also heard lectures on the rest of the sciences as often as circumstances permitted, through repetition and contact with learned men" (in AB: 9).

The University of Kiel, founded in 1665, is much closer to Hamburg than Leipzig is, and this suggests that economic pressures as well as a desire to study closer to home may have been the major causes behind Basedow's decision to leave Leipzig. But it is also possible that he simply wanted to hear other points of view and try something new. Martin Frisus (1688–1750; the last name is usually spelled "Friese"), born in Denmark and the only Kiel professor specifically mentioned by Basedow, was a theology professor who also served as Chancellor of the University after 1736. But no other solid information about his coursework at the University of Kiel is available. It is likely that here too—as had been the case earlier in Leipzig—Basedow was not the most avid attender of his professors' lectures, preferring instead "the path of domestic diligence." And here as well, he did not remain for long. As he notes in his vita: "In the following year [viz., 1749], I took on the scientific direction of an aristocratic boy, the son of Josias von Qualen, and lived on the kindness of his noble father" (in AB: 9).

So, after only a year at Kiel—and still without a university degree—Basedow again shifted direction. And by now it is apparent that he was beginning to have some doubts about becoming a pastor. Even in the earlier-cited letter of May 14, 1746 to one of his patrons—written while he was still in Leipzig—we see a revealing reference to his desire to acquire "the best knowledge of the sciences belonging to morals and theology" in order to apply it to "the education of young people" (although at this point he still states that he will use this knowledge "in the pulpit"):

> Thus would I live, as in Hamburg, more to quiet the pangs of my hunger than to improve my soul and to follow the chief goal of my life. This is to obtain the best possible knowledge of the sciences belonging to morals and theology. What efforts! Particularly since I must make myself prepared to use them as well in the pulpit as on the teacher's desk, and to apply them to the education of young people [*in Erziehungen junger Leute zu gebrauchen*].
>
> In Pinloche 1896: 458

And in a later letter of 1749 composed in Latin to his former gymnasium teacher Richey he offers the following explanation for his decision to work as a tutor for the von Qualen family: "I have accepted this position, not because it pleases me to live retired and to be inactive in the country, but rather that without any loss of income, I might have time for deliberation as to the course in life I particularly should adopt."[14] When we combine this remark about his wish to have time for deliberation over which course to pursue in life with the earlier comment concerning his interest in the education of young people and add to it his decision to accept employment as a private tutor, Basedow's future path begins to look clearer: he wants to become a teacher, but a teacher who also uses "the best possible knowledge of the sciences belonging to morals and theology" to inform his pedagogy.

4

A New Way of Teaching

In 1749 Basedow decided to take some time off from his studies at the University of Kiel and move to Borghorst, a small town just north of Kiel, in order to work as a private tutor. His employer, Josias von Qualen,[1] who had studied law at the University of Halle, is described by Meier as "a very smart, scholarly, and for his time, very enlightened [*sehr aufgeklärter*] man" (M: I: 209). Von Qualen had already hired a French governess to work with his five daughters (Emilie Dumas, whom Basedow would later marry), but for his seven-year-old son Josias, born on April 20, 1742, he wanted a male tutor "with the best recommendations. Basedow could have come by these recommendations only from the circle of his university teachers, or from one of the 'viri doctissimi' [learned men] with whom he associated, according to his Kiel vita" (AB: 53).

By all accounts, Basedow's experience as a private tutor at the von Qualen family home was extremely enjoyable as well as fruitful. According to Göring, "the boy loved his teacher as his closest and best friend and respected him like a father" (Göring 1880: XXI). And the boy's father also was quite pleased with his new employee's work: "Herr von Qualen was extremely satisfied with him for the entire time of his residence there and with all of his work with his child ... He often gave very flattering and favorable proofs of his satisfaction to his household tutor" (M: I: 209). Small wonder then, that "Basedow spent the happiest years of his life [*die glücklichsten Jahre seines Lebens*] here, as he himself often said" (Lauchkard 1848: 76).

Although von Qualen's son was not completely illiterate when Basedow first met him, he was a novice. Göring claims that "at the beginning of the instruction he could barely read" German (Göring 1880: XXXIII), while Basedow himself, in his *Methodenbuch*, states that "he could ... only read German" (MB VI.2; in G: 111) However, according to Swet, "when Basedow first came to Borghorst, the boy could read German well and some French. He possessed a lively nature and a quick grasp of things" (Swet 1898: 37). At any rate, Basedow had a relatively fresh canvas to work with. And at this point in his life, he felt free to try something new. He probably also sensed that he wanted to develop a different kind of pedagogical method than the formalistic, repressive, and authoritarian ones that he had been subjected to by most of his teachers when he was a student back in Hamburg.

Drawing attention to the ruinous effects of the dominant teaching methods in eighteenth-century Germany is a major motif in many of Basedow's later writings. For instance, in his 1768 *Vorstellung an Menschenfreunde*, which Reble regards as "without doubt the most important of all of Basedow's pedagogical writings" (Reble 1965: 258), he describes the Latin classes that he and his classmates were subjected to as follows:

> This method, as is known, is memorizing vocabulary, phrases, etymological and syntactic rules and exceptions together with entire passages of incomprehensible authors ... The Latin language is a torture [*eine Marter*] of these years, whose impression we never lose. In the entire period of youth when we have the excellent old men, they teach us to exchange construction with construction, sound with sound, word with word. The old men become disgusting [*ekelhaft*] to us.
>
> VM § 43; in R: 48–9, 51

Similarly, in the opening pages of his *Methodenbuch*, Basedow draws attention to the "useless knowledge of words" which brings "shame to the understanding and will" because it is only possible through "great pain and coercion [*große Unlust und Zwangsmittel*]" and "humiliates [*erniedrigt*] the souls of human beings for their entire lives" (MB I; in G: 17). And in his 1774 advertisement for the Philanthropin he again draws attention to the destructive effects of prevailing school methods: "I charge your schools with destroying nature [*die Natur zerpeitscht*], and of not strengthening, but rather paralyzing, the tendons of the soul, in which the life of man is determined" (DEP: XIII).

But now, in the von Qualen family home, Basedow had the opportunity to try out a new way of teaching, one based not on coercion but rather on the premise that learning should be enjoyable. As Meier remarks: "He lowered himself to the child and his capacities, and taught everything to him by playing [*spielend*]" (M: I: 212). Or, as Basedow himself puts it in the *Methodenbuch*, with a bit more qualification, "at first, our studying occurred unnoticed under the name of play [*unter dem Namen des Spielens*], and because of hard work dissatisfaction never or very seldom occurred and coercion was never or very seldom applied" (MB VI.2; in G: 111). Pinloche stresses Basedow's learning-through-play point even more strongly: "*Learning through playing* [*Spielend unterrichten*]: this is the main principle of his method" (Pinloche 1896: 31).[2]

One noteworthy application of Basedow's learning-through-play method involved the attempt to teach basic concepts of geometry by utilizing common, real-world objects with which the student was already familiar. And years later he would publish several different works on mathematical subjects, including one entitled *Arithmetic for Enjoyment and Reflection*.[3] Meier elaborates as follows:

> When, for example, he pushed his pupil in a stroller, or the pupil himself pushed it, Basedow drew attention to the wheels and their motion, and in the process showed the nature and use of the circle, in so far as the measure of the boy's years could understand. In the same manner he showed him the rhombuses in the windows, in the doors, in the tables, the chairs, and the benches, the walls and the floors, and in general in a hundred other small and large objects of art and nature; in the house and in the garden, in the stables and in the courtyard, the pupil was shown all the naturally occurring geometrical figures, together with their benefit and use—indeed, even the form and shape of books and their pages did not remain unused. Every reader who is at all well informed must approve of this system of teaching, if it does not degenerate into mere puppetry [*lauter Spielwerk*] and triflery.
>
> M: I: 212–13

Basedow also taught Josias aspects of simple arithmetic through play. Meier's example here is as follows:

> Just as playfully comfortable and easy was his way of teaching arithmetic, where, through the presentation of many small physical unities, for example, kernels of wheat or peas, the four principle alterations of the nine numbers [*die vier Haupt-Veränderungen der 9 Zahlen*], in which all of arithmetic consists, were taught with much patience. And in cutting up an apple or a pear into equal smaller parts of ½, ⅓, ¼, ⅙, ⅛, ⅑, and so forth he demonstrated clearly the doctrine of fractions.
>
> M: I: 213–14

Foreign-language instruction was of course also a major part of Basedow's tutorial work with Josias. "Because it was the advice of the father that his son should learn Latin through discussions [*durch Unterredungen*], he had to next devise ways and means for himself to acquire skills ... in this language" (Swet 1898: 37). And since Basedow's own knowledge of foreign languages was rather weak, this itself proved to be a formidable challenge. According to Göring: "As concerns language instruction, Basedow had to restrict himself to Latin, because he ... appears to have known only a little Greek, and at the time could not understand French or English at all" (Göring 1880: XXXI–II). Meier, as usual, is even more disparaging on this point:

> He restricted his language instruction merely to Latin, because he hardly understood other ... languages at all. To make matters worse, Basedow was so weak in Latin—a weakness which stuck to him for his entire life, and for which he was often rightfully reproached, that he ... could scarcely have been weaker and more unskilled. However, Basedow had courage and intelligence, and knew how to use his meager knowledge in order to dazzle and to grow, and he soon learned from experience how true it is: *docendo discimus* [by teaching, we learn].
>
> M: I: 215–16

Basedow himself, in his 1752 Kiel Master's thesis, which is based on his tutoring experience at the von Qualen home, describes as follows the arduous preparations he undertook in order to teach Josias Latin:

> At the very beginning I learned by heart a vocabulary book of words that are used in common company. Every day I translated in writing certain passages from books that dealt with similar matters, such as comedies, speeches, and so forth, from German into Latin, and also from Latin into German. With increasing skill I could soon do this orally. Almost never did I let Hedericus'[4] *Promtuarium* and *Fabri Thesaurum* out of my hands. Through much reading I almost memorized the speeches of Kromaier, Langen, Erasmus, and Corderi, and the comedies of Terence. Castalio was my Bible, and Thomas à Kempis ... my prayerbook. So that I might make myself more skilled at speaking good Latin about all household circumstances and the rudiments of the sciences, I read with the same purpose and attention the works of Cicero, Pliny, the biblical speeches of Castalio, Erasmus' ethics, Comenius' *Januam*, Suetonius' *Tranquillum*, Ernest's *Initia*, many parts of Wagenselius' *Pera*, and many other books. I read German fables and histories and recounted them to myself in Latin. Whenever I was not reading I translated all of my thoughts silently to myself. When I sat at the table or was with company, whenever anything was said in which I had no special interest, I also translated these conversations in my own thoughts, so that gradually all sorts of things came forth, and I could see for which sort I lacked the words or way of speaking. Afterward I made a note of this, wrote it down on the table and repeated it until I knew it. This was a labor which indeed improved my skill in Latin, but which also caused a noticeable injury to my powers. For the monotonous way of thinking, of translating everything, became so habitual to me that neither while eating nor in company could I free myself from it, even when I wanted to. Indeed, it often happened that I dreamed of groups of people whose conversations I translated, and thus I was not without work even in sleep, as a result of which my health was considerably weakened.[5]

After he had gained sufficient facility in Latin, Basedow began to teach the language to Josias. But the method he applied here was necessarily different than the one he had used on himself:

> After Basedow had been in Borghorst for not quite three weeks, he began to mix Latin words in his conversations with the boy, words which he could understand from the context. Soon after that he spoke short sentences to him entirely in Latin. If the boy did not understand this or that, then he would help with a German explanation. As far as possible, words and phrases that were not understood were replaced by other synonymous Latin words and phrases which the boy already knew, or Basedow tried to explain to him through his expressions and presentation of similar things the meaning of the Latin word or sentence. Actually, at the beginning, the conversations between Basedow and his pupil consisted of loud games, which amused him ... After another four weeks the boy could understand his tutor so well, that when Basedow said something to him in Latin "that concerned him," he began to mix "garbled and badly composed" Latin words into his conversation. From day to day there was less German, and to the same extent the Latin became more correct.[6]

At the beginning, nearly all of the instruction occurred during informal daily walks. (As Meier remarks, "for the most part or at least very often, he taught like a Peripatetic[7] out for a stroll" (M: I: 216 n.). But gradually, Basedow began to introduce more structure into the conversations and games:

> About six weeks later, Basedow began to schedule definite hours of the day for instruction for the boy. He was instructed in the rudiments of religion, geography, history, and grammar. Also, the necessity of human society, authority, and law were discussed, as well as the generation of plants, the earth and the sun, and the food and growth of human beings and animals. At first Basedow gave the instruction in German, then German mixed with Latin, and finally only in Latin.[8]

As noted earlier, in 1752—three years after he started his tutoring work at the von Qualen family home—Basedow publicly defended his *Magister* thesis at the University of Kiel. The thesis, written in Latin, entitled *An Unused, and also the Best Method of Instructing Distinguished Youth, Not Only in All Scholastic Pursuits, but Especially in the Latin Language* (see Basedow 1752a), is essentially a written report of his tutoring experience, and a German translation—the *Nachricht*, from which I have already cited a few times—was also published later in 1752 (Basedow 1752b). But in an even earlier publication consisting of a series of letters written in Latin to his former teacher Richey, we learn a bit more about some of the religious instruction that Josias received from Basedow. Although Basedow himself wrote the letters, some of them were dictated to him by his young student. As Swet explains it: "Three letters are added to the *Epistolae ad Richeium*[9] which Basedow wrote according to the dictation of his pupil Josias von Qualen, who at that time was a seven-and-a-half year old boy who did not know orthography sufficiently and whose hand was not firm enough for writing" (Swet 1898: 29). In the second of these letters, Josias states: "Concerning God, I know that He was not created, He is from eternity, He has no end and no beginning, He is all-wise and all-truthful. He can do all things at his own bidding. When He says: Let it rain, it rains."[10]

As Swet himself suggests (see Swet 1898: 29), there may be a Lockean influence here. In *Some Thoughts Concerning Education* (1693), Locke offers the following advice to tutors who wish to instill virtue in their student:

> As the foundation of this, there ought very early to be imprinted on his mind a true notion of *God*, as of the independent Supreme Being, Author and Maker of all things, from whom we receive all our good, who loves us and gives us all things. And consequent to this, instill into him a love and reverence of this Supreme Being. This is enough to begin with, without going to explain this matter any farther; for fear, lest by talking too early to him of spirits, and being unseasonably forward to make him understand the incomprehensible nature of that infinite Being, his head be either filled with false or perplexed with unintelligible notions of him. Let him only be told upon occasion that *God* made and governs all things, hears and sees everything, and does all manner of good to those that love and obey him.
>
> Locke 1996: §136

Locke and Basedow both held that, while it was important to teach a few fundamental points about God to young students, one shouldn't go too far too soon. Teachers should restrict themselves here to imparting to their young students only what they are capable of understanding by means of their own natural reason.

And in the first of the three letters appended to the *Epistolae ad Richeium*, we find a hint of yet another side of Basedow's new way of teaching. In this letter, young Josias writes the following to his aunt: "Dearest Aunt, My mother is about to have a baby boy or girl" (Basedow 1750: 13; as cited by Swet 1898: 29). As noted earlier in Chapter 1, sex education would later become yet another novel and controversial feature of the Philanthropin curriculum at Dessau. And it itself is a reflection of Basedow's broader commitment to pedagogical naturalism[11]—developing methods of teaching that work with rather than against children's natural development, but also viewing humans as part of nature, and placing a positive rather than negative value on nature. Both this latter point as well as his views about age-appropriate religious instruction would later become sources of tension and conflict between Basedow and a number of conservative religious authorities.

However, there were also several less controversial (but nevertheless progressive) aspects of Basedow's new teaching methods. In his *Nachricht* we read that "from the beginning he gave his student practice in writing letters" (Basedow 1752b: §10; as cited by Swet 1898: 44). And in yet another letter dictated to Basedow in the *Epistolae* collection, Josias—who had now been studying with his tutor for about ten months—states: "I am discussing the letters of Cicero" and, further, "we are writing stories" (Basedow 1750: 15; as cited by Swet 1898: 44). In the *Nachricht*, Basedow elaborates on this part of his teaching regimen as follows:

> I set up letter writing in such a way that in the beginning I started a fabricated exchange of letters with him in the name of another young man, which aroused him to greater industry. I talked over the contents of these letters with him beforehand, then I either read to him, or let him read a good example of, such a letter, and then let him write. Besides Latin, letters in German were also practiced.
> Basedow 1752b: §§10, 11; as cited by Swet 1898: 44

This particular aspect of Basedow's pedagogy involves an ingenious mix of writing and foreign-language skill development with practical life skills training. Traditionalists have often criticized Philanthropinist pedagogy on this latter point, labeling it "utilitarian," "flat [*platt*]", and "shallow [*seicht*]" (Krause 1994: 4). Neohumanist Immanuel Niethammer (1766–1848), in his influential 1808 work, *Der Streit des Philanthropinismus und des Humanismus in der Theorie des Erziehungs-Unterrichts unsrer Zeit*, offers a particularly strident but influential version of this criticism in the following remark:

> The promotion of real usefulness was now on the agenda; but real usefulness meant only profitability [*Einträglichkeit*], material production ... Thus began the spiritual revolution of the time ... under the name of the Enlightenment, a step backward from true culture, a hatred of all that is purely spiritual and ideal in art and science.
> Niethammer 1968: 15, 18

While it is true that Basedow and the Philanthropinists wanted education to have more practical efficacy and to help prepare students for life in the real world, Niethammer's claims that they were concerned only with "profitability" and that their pedagogical program amounted to a "hatred of all that is purely spiritual and ideal in art and science" are clearly over the top.[12] As young Josias states in one of his letters to Richey, "I am discussing the letters of Cicero." Rather, Basedow's goal was to put the classics to use: to find a way to integrate them into students' daily lives and use them to help prepare students for their future role as citizens, rather than treating them as esoteric luxuries reserved for the sons of the elite.[13]

Basedow was employed at the von Qualen home for a total of three years, from 1749 to 1752. Looking back on his experience in 1770, when the first edition of the *Methodenbuch* was published, he would later summarize the results that he had achieved with Josias through his new way of teaching as follows:

> 1) The Church could have received him among its adult members, in accordance with the religious knowledge customarily demanded, if his age had permitted it. 2) All of the textbook [*schülmaβig*] universal history and geography was known by him. 3) Because of my instruction, he was proficient in counting according to the rule of proportionality [*nach der Proportionalregel*]. 4) He had much background knowledge in miscellaneous philosophy and above all in physical science and geography [*Weltkunde*]. 5) His moral knowledge was the strongest of all. 6) He wrote letters in German and Latin. He held discussions, wrote compositions, and, after some meditation, gave short improvisational talks with equal facility in both languages on material that was appropriate to his knowledge. 7) He was so good in these languages that he could translate orally, and without difficulty, well but slowly, any book whose content he understood ... In short, this young gentleman was, at the end of his tenth year, as advanced as a well-trained student in the gymnasium.
>
> MB VI.2; in G: 112

Basedow's three-year residency in Borghorst is important above all because it is here that we witness the birth of his own progressive pedagogical methods. Although he articulates these methods in much greater detail in his later extensive publications, their real origin occurs in his tutoring experiences with Josias von Qualen. But there are at least two additional reasons for emphasizing this particular period of Basedow's life. First, an awareness of his 1749–52 tutoring work helps to dispel the still-popular opinion that "there is but little that is original in his pedagogical principles" (Seeley 1899: 255; cf. Graves 1914: 24–5), and that he is merely "a relatively mediocre thinker" (Parker 1912: 216) whose "root-ideas ... are those of Rousseau" (Quick 1896: 279). For it is important to remember that Rousseau's *Émile*—even if it is "the most important work on education after Plato's *Republic*" (Wokler 2001: 2)—was not published until 1762; i.e., thirteen years after Basedow arrived in Borghorst. And the "root-ideas" in Basedow's books that are allegedly taken from Rousseau—for instance, the conviction that one should "respect childhood and ... not hurry to judge it" and that one should "leave nature to act for a long time before you get involved with acting in its place, lest you impede its operations"[14]—were independently arrived at by Basedow at least a decade before the publication of *Émile*. As Landschoof rightly remarks in his 1933 PhD dissertation:

> While the name of Rousseau, to whom undeserved credit long has been given for any influence he is said to have had upon Basedow, was still unknown and unheralded; while the future great Pestalozzi, whose "natural, progressive, and harmonious development" of all the child's "powers and faculties" was to improve society through a new note in matters pedagogical, was, as yet, hardly out of his swaddling clothes; and while Herbart, the "psychologizer of education," was not to promulgate his theory of "many-sided interests" until more than a half century should elapse, or Froebel with his "play-way," was to revolutionize methods for young children ... [after] Basedow's own educational innovation at Dessau had long since been introduced, tested, adapted, and adopted in many like institutions, Basedow, as a young and inexperienced teacher, was laying the foundations of method, the practice, use, or origin of which, have been acclaimed for his successors.
>
> Landschoof 1933: 53–4[15]

At the same time, the Rousseau problem is exacerbated due to the fact that Chapter VIII of the *Methodenbuch*, in which Basedow presents his strongly gendered assumptions concerning "the different education of sons and daughters" (MB VIII.1; in G: 159),[16] contains a number of inordinately long quotations from *Émile*. Basedow is certainly correct when he prefaces these quotations by remarking that Rousseau "thinks with extraordinary acumen" and "writes with an imitable charm" (MB VIII.1; in G: 160). But he hurts his own case through his excessive quoting of Rousseau.

Finally, Basedow's residency in Borghorst is also important because it is here that he met his future wife. He and Emilie Dumas, the French governess whom von Qualen had hired to educate his five daughters, were married in Hamburg on October 1, 1752—four months after Basedow successfully defended his thesis at the University of Kiel on June 7. (It was at this point in his life that Basedow also officially changed the spelling of his last name from "Bassedau" to "Basedow." On the title page of the dissertation, which was written in Latin, his name is spelled "Joannes Bernardus Basedow.")[17] Unfortunately, their marriage lasted less than a year: "The marriage was already severed in 1753 through the death of his wife, who died in childbirth on August 1, 1753" (AB: 60 n. 1). In early 1753 the Basedow family moved to Sorø, Denmark, to the north of Kiel, where he began his first professorship at the *Ritterakademie*. Basedow's first son, Heinrich Josias (1753–95—he was presumably given his middle name in honor of Josias von Qualen) fortunately did survive, but Emilie's family seems to have blamed their daughter's premature death on her husband. According to Meier:

> Her nearest relatives wanted to prove that domestic displeasure and anger [*häusiger Verdruß und Aerger*] had been the cause of her death. It may be a misunderstanding. Basedow was now in a new situation in which he for the first time had to work very hard to fill his role well, and to act according to its big expectations. His temperament was impulsive; his way of studying was very strange, and in fact he had to apply extraordinary effort and special diligence if he wanted to replace the defects and fill the gaps, which were not permitted to be noticeable and conspicuous in him as a public teacher. Therefore it is easy to think that in his customary and tumultuous way of studying, he bothered himself little, or not at all, over domestic affairs, which were not his province at all. Indeed, the error stuck to this man throughout his entire life, and because of his moods he was often somewhat unbearable to his own family circle in their domestic life.
>
> M: I: 227

But here, as elsewhere, Meier is overreaching. Maternal mortality rates were extremely high in the mid-eighteenth century, and what the Basedow family experienced in Sorø was unfortunately an all-too-common tragedy. To claim that "domestic displeasure and anger" were the causes of Emilie's death—and neither Meier nor anyone else has ever provided any evidence to support this wild allegation—is to ignore the obvious. When Basedow and Emilie exchanged wedding vows in 1752, neither of them had the least inkling of the approaching catastrophe. Their marriage was short but sweet. And in 1769, when Basedow and his second wife Gertrude Elisabeth had a daughter together, they named her Emilie, in memory of Basedow's first wife.

5

The Professor

Basedow's three-year stint with the von Qualen family in Borghorst convinced him that his professional future lay in educational reform rather than the ministry, but it also provided him with the topic of his *Magister* thesis at the University of Kiel. Entitled *Inusitata et optima honestioris iuventutis erudiendae methodus* (An unused, but also the best method of instructing distinguished youth), the thesis was successfully defended on June 7, 1752 and was dedicated to Johann von Pechlin (1677-1757), who later helped Basedow obtain his first academic position at the *Ritterakademie* in Sorø, Denmark. The thesis is not examined in much detail by any of Basedow's German biographers, but Landschoof, in his 1933 doctoral dissertation, discusses it a great deal.

In the opening two paragraphs of his Introduction to the thesis, Basedow announces his theme as follows:

> I propose for public examination a new method for boys' studies, indeed not an unheard of one, but still an unused one... I have applied my thought to this idea, rather than to any other ... relying upon truth, and assured by experience... [I]t is evident to all who know me well, that more by chance and the plan of another, than my own discovery, that I happened upon this method... [T]hose points which are obvious, I shall touch on only lightly... To me now, science and scholastic pursuits are of great concern, among which, alas, the Latin language! Here, for boys, is the greatest ... anxiety, trouble, time, and toil. A plan for it is my chief concern.[1]

Four chapters follow the Introduction. Chapter One is entitled: "Concerning the Defective Attempts in the Common Method of Teaching Latin." In the opening paragraph, Basedow proclaims himself "a champion of boyhood" who has developed "a shorter and sweeter path [*dulce natura*]" for learning Latin.[2] We can see already that several of the central themes commonly associated with his later pedagogical writings—for instance, a more child-friendly approach to education, an emphasis on the importance of play in learning, and a commitment to working with rather than against nature (naturalism)—are already present in the 1752 dissertation. In the second and third paragraphs Basedow further emphasizes the importance of learning through play, in addition to stressing his commitment to a strongly empiricist theory of knowledge. From the second or third year, the student should be entrusted to the care of a

> well-trained teacher, who by his ingenious games, his pointed jesting, his artfully designed stories, by revealing objective things to the sense-perception, and by wisely explaining their relationship, by his friendly and serious counsel, may instruct the mind of his pupil by these aids for the more serious pursuits and duties of life, and may teach him to read and count in such a way that ... the pupil does not sense that he is being taught.
> All our knowledge begins with the senses, and experience is the teacher.[3]

Although Basedow's conversational method of teaching Latin is the major theme in the dissertation, other important aspects of his mature pedagogical outlook also make brief appearances. For instance, in the fourth and fifth paragraphs, he criticizes the authoritarian manner in which religion is taught to children in schools—its overemphasis on rote memorization, and its underemphasis on reasoned discussion:

> not by inclination of the soul, but commanded and forced, they worship God, with the mouth, and not in their hearts ... How are these matters for those who do not even grasp a noun, to say nothing of the thought of the Trinity, the kingdom of God, the Blood of Christ? ... It is enough, is it not, to learn and recite those things which they understand now?[4]

What Basedow proposes in place of this is a more age-appropriate introduction to religion. In religion as well as elsewhere, young children should be taught only what they are capable of understanding.

In paragraph eight Basedow begins to settle in on his main theme of an "unused, and also the best method" of teaching Latin. As was also the case with religious instruction, one of his major criticisms of the prevailing methods of foreign language education is their heavy stress on memorization, which often leaves students with a strong aversion against the study of literature generally, in addition to harming their health: "Who would wonder then, that boys are driven reluctantly to learning a book by heart; a too-heavy burden is laid, one that is but poorly endured; thus arises that distaste for all literature; abilities are deadened, health is shattered."[5] And in the twelfth paragraph he presents his own motto for teaching Latin: "Let use come first; let the rule follow [*Usus praeeat, regula sequatur*]."[6] Foreign language students should of course eventually learn the relevant rules of grammar and syntax for their language(s), but this should come later rather than earlier. If teachers emphasize it at the beginning, students are much less likely to develop a genuine interest in the language.

Chapter Two of the thesis is entitled "The Unused and Natural Method of all Scholastic Studies, chiefly, Latin." Here Basedow reflects back on his own tutoring experience in Borghorst and offers more specific advice concerning his "natural method." Ideally, students should have teachers who speak directly to them in the desired foreign language(s) at as young an age as possible:

> If a boy should have several teachers, I should advise that one of them speak the vernacular, and the others, from the very cradle, Latin and French with him. Or, if there is such an ability in only one instructor, let him converse with the pupil, either on certain days or at definite hours, in Latin, and at other times in German.[7]

And, at least at the beginning stage of education, sitting at a desk in a school building for a fixed length of time each day is not recommended:

> There is no need—indeed it is harmful—that he hold school during fixed hours of the day. Here conversation, during play and while walking, is most significant, spontaneously developing the boy. We seek here fluency in Latin and in the vernacular. By explaining the names and reasons for domestic articles of cooking, farming, clothing, trading, and merchandise, the impressionable mind is not only informed with food for reflection, but is also trained in using keenness of judgment in matters that come to its attention.[8]

In this passage one sees not only Basedow's famous emphasis on learning through play and his concern for educating the body as well as the mind, but also the practical bent of his approach. The proper way to study Latin, at least at the beginning stages, is to learn the Latin terms for everyday objects in one's immediate environment. In this way, a "dead" language can be resurrected and once again brought into useful contact with the daily world.

After the student has successfully navigated what Basedow calls "the first mile" of education, he is ready for a more structured and intellectually challenging regimen, albeit one that still strives to make relevant connections to the student's daily world:

> Let him enter upon the second mile of scholastic pursuits. On different days I give him an hour of drill on previous work, so arranged that the pupil seeks to express what has been said or read to him, either orally or written, in his own words... We shall devote a second hour to theology, certainly the reading of the

Bible [and] the *Confessions* of St. Augustine ... The business of the third hour will be this. Alternately explain to pupils grammar in the following fashion: Latin in Latin, and the vernacular in the vernacular... Train the pupil in all things illustrated by examples taken from daily conversation. Analysis will occupy the fourth hour. I would have you use the next three hours in such a way that you may assign two of them for a student of history... But never apply yourself to this work until there are geographical charts, tables, and genealogies at hand ... Whatever remains of the day, we shall devote to calligraphy and arithmetic.[9]

Physical education, another pedagogical innovation later associated with Basedow's Philanthropin, also has a designated place in this second mile of education, though here, too, more structure is added to it: "Thus, with a part of each day sufficiently occupied, during the remainder, let him spend it with me, in writing, arithmetic, French, physical exercise, and finally leisure."[10]

The third chapter of the thesis is entitled "An Elementary Outline of Syntax Adopted to the Understanding of a Pupil Who has Learned Facility of Speech from Practice, and How to Recognize Authors." Landschoof passes over this part ("with the third section of the thesis, we need have but little concern"—Landschoof 1933: 87), but according to both Pinloche and Diestelmann it contains not only a discussion of Latin grammar and syntax minutiae but also further advice concerning how to teach both Latin and German authors, as well as the recommendations that "very little philosophy and metaphysics" be offered and that "morals and theology should be taught more through practice than through instruction [*mehr durch Übung als durch Unterricht*]" (Pinloche 1896: 163; cf. Diestelmann 1897: 20–21). At this third level "the pupil should also be instructed in physical exercises; and also undertake travels, either alone or with the teacher" (Diestelmann 1897: 21).

Finally, in the concluding fourth chapter—"Refutation of Certain Objections and Doubts; Proof of the Method, by a Few, but the Most Distinguished, Testimonies"—Basedow responds to criticisms, arguing that his own approach is "quicker, better, easier, and more convenient"[11] and names earlier authors such as Morhof,[12] Erasmus,[13] Gesner,[14] and Locke as forerunners of his own conversational method. But he adds that his largest debt is owed to his former high school teacher, Michael Richey:

> that most brilliant star of Hamburg, a man whom I am never to recall without the greatest respect and the unbelievable affection of a grateful heart, that most learned Professor Richey, who in a group of Latinists at Jena, introduced a method of teaching Latin more at variance with the customary one than my own.[15]

Although Landschoof overstates matters a bit in claiming that Basedow's later extensive writings are "in large measure ... but an elaboration of the thesis that he had already defended at Kiel" (Landschoof 1933: 88), it is certainly the case that several key aspects of the innovative pedagogical methods that would later make Basedow famous are already present in a rudimentary form in his impressive *Magister* thesis of 1752.

After the successful oral defense of his thesis in Kiel on June 7, 1752, Basedow returned to his previous residence at the von Qualen home in Borghorst. But he did not remain there for long. He and Emilie Dumas, the French governess whom von Qualen had earlier hired to instruct his five daughters, were married in Hamburg on October 1, and in late 1752 he also published a German revision of his thesis under the title *Nachricht, inwiefern besagte Methode wirklich ausgeübt sei und was sie gewirket* (Basedow 1752b). And soon he began preparations for yet another move. But this time, it was for a solid academic appointment. On the collective recommendation of von Qualen, Johann Freiherr von Pechlin, Count Adam Gottlob von Moltke (both of whom were occasional guests in von Qualen's home), and his college friend Friedrich Gottlieb Klopstock, who had by now become a prominent poet, Basedow was appointed Professor of Rhetoric and Moral Philosophy at the *Ritterakademie* in Sorø, Denmark, to the north of Kiel.

The *Ritterakademien* (literally, "knights' schools") were originally designed as educational institutions for sons of noble families. They originated in German-speaking areas of Europe in the late sixteenth century, during a time when education was becoming more important to the nobility, and they were still fairly popular in the mid-eighteenth century when Basedow received his academic appointment. However, by the end of the eighteenth century most of them had either closed or been converted to other uses. (In many cases, they were downgraded into gymnasia or high schools.) For instance, the *Ritterakademie* that employed Basedow in Sorø closed in 1793, due in part to competition from the University of Copenhagen. But various successor institutions have occupied the property since then, and at present there is still a boarding school on the grounds. The elite single-sex American liberal arts colleges of a century or so ago (particularly in their role as finishing schools for children of the upper class) are a (very) rough analogy to European *Ritterakademien*.

Armin Basedow, in his biography, provides (in a German translation of the original Latin) the following excerpt of his ancestor's first teaching contract:

> We herewith announce that we have engaged and contracted, and herewith do engage and contract our beloved Johan [sic] Bernhard Basedow as Professor of Rhetoric and Moral Philosophy at our *Ritterakademie* in Sorø; at the same time we appoint him to teach the German language. In this office he is to follow and behave according to the charter [*Gründungsurkunde*] which we have most graciously arranged for our *Ritterakademie*, in so far as it can bear any connection to him.
>
> AB: 61

The contract is dated December 22, 1752, and was signed by Basedow on January 26, 1753, soon after he and his wife had arrived in Sorø. But Armin Basedow notes further that in the original contract the sentence "'and shall enjoy a yearly salary in this office of the Academy of 500 *Reischsthaler*' was crossed out" (his actual salary was only 400 *Reichsthaler*) and that "the teaching assignment was changed at Count Moltke's request, who … wished that 'philosophy and history' would be taught by the new professor, and by philosophy was understood 'a useful, practical philosophy, as is proper for young people of the great world'" (AB: 61).

Basedow's first official lecture, delivered in Latin (*De philosophiae studio a procerum filiis prudenter moderando*), was also subsequently published under a slightly different title (see Basedow 1753a). Here he takes up Count Moltke's suggestion of stressing "above all the usefulness of philosophy in the future professions of the students, for the cultivation of judgment, [and] development of eloquence and good style [*Redegewandheit und gutem Stile*]," adding that while "noble youth need the study of philosophy for their future leadership of the state, the instruction must be organized so that it not take away from the remaining equally necessary subjects of instruction" (AB: 63). As regards the specific areas of philosophy that are most relevant, he then writes:

> Although all parts of philosophy are important, nevertheless noble youth need less of metaphysics and physics and much more of logic, the rudiments of mathematics, and practical philosophy, they must be able to distinguish the true from the false, the probable from the less probable,[16] the narrowness and uncertainty of natural theology, the magnificence and strength [*die Herrlichkeit und Festigkeit*] of revealed theology, and so forth. If conducted in this manner, the study of philosophy is not wasted time. A general education demands that one have the capacity to speak and write well, and "that the seeds of virtue and prudence be sown."
>
> AB: 63[17]

Despite a heavy teaching load and the challenge of adapting to a new job in a foreign country, Basedow's first year at Sorø also marks the real beginning of his extremely prolific writing career. A second work published in 1753 is *Versuch, wiefern die Philosophie zur Freigeisterei verführe* (An Investigation into how far Philosophy leads to Freethinking).[18] As Overhoff notes, in this short, early work Basedow "shows that, despite their different premises, the academic disciplines of philosophy and theology without doubt can and should mutually complement each other" (Overhoff 2004: 108). Armin Basedow summarizes the work as follows:

> After an overview of the history of philosophy, he formulates his theme: Can freethinkers (that is, those who find contradictions in the Bible and do not want to recognize it as the source of truth) appeal with justice to philosophy, and how is such an evil best avoided in case this actually contributes to their temptation? His explanations come together in sentences at the conclusion of § 63: "different philosophies really contain only a few sentences which tempt one to freethinking. True philosophy is poorly explained by most deists. The doctrines of Christian sects, regardless of the universal truth of the Christian religion, can contain something which conflicts with true philosophy and sound reason. Most freethinkers who appeal to philosophy do not understand the nature of religion. A careful [*vorsichtige*] philosophy is the best means to convince those fools, who call themselves strong spirits, of their weakness."
>
> AB: 64

In this passage one can see that, while Basedow in fact tries to distance himself from deism (a label that many commentators over the years have incorrectly used to describe his religious orientation), he also—like many deists—sees no conflict between reason and religion. Properly understood, philosophy and religion are not at war with one another but rather support one another. As Overhoff notes, in his summary of Basedow's *Versuch*, "correctly taught, he [Basedow] believed, philosophy was never harmful to religion and it could very well be used in the attempt to solve the most pressing theological problems of the age" (Overhoff 2010: 61). Nevertheless, the dogmatic manner in which Basedow presents his middle position seems not to have pleased many of his contemporaries. Armin Basedow cites an anonymous reviewer of the work who predicts that "without doubt neither theologians nor philosophers will be satisfied with this [book]; for although it contains much truth, one also finds much that is ungrounded in it and, it appears to us, careless [*Unvorsichtiges*]" (AB: 64).

Still, in spite of this negative review, it is clear that Basedow was off to a very productive start in his new position in Sorø. But then tragedy struck. As noted earlier, his wife Emilie died in childbirth on August 1, 1753, leaving Basedow a widower with their newborn son, Heinrich Josias. His meager salary of 400 *Reichsthaler* now proved insufficient to manage the household, and he soon fell into debt. Looking back on the situation thirty years later, he wrote:

> As a professor in Sorø through my marriage, the move, preparations for the birth of our child, and the death of my wife, I fell into debt of 150 *Reichsthaler* and was left with a son. I wanted to pay the debt, and have a year to live *independently*. But as a widower I must have been deceived. Thus I made a contract with my housekeeper that she would receive no greater wages for the week than had been arranged, but that I would say nothing if she occasionally had to give me boiled hay to eat. Matters came to such a point that the Saturday evening meal of the rather distinguished *professor* was beer soup without sugar or herring.
>
> Basedow 1783a: 172

In 1754 Basedow published only one book (he usually averaged three per year)—*Von der Glückseligkeit des Königsreiches Dänemark und der Regierung Friedrichs V* (On the Felicity of the Kingdom of Denmark and the Government of Frederick V) (see Basedow 1754). This short book falls outside of his usual pedagogical–theological–philosophical concerns and was indeed perhaps written, as Landschoof notes, "with an eye ... to future favors" (1933: 92). But the relative paucity of publications during this time period can most likely be traced to changes in his personal life. On June 28, 1754 Basedow married for the second time. His new wife was Gertrude Elisabeth Hammer (1733–88), the only daughter of a minister in the village of Flaville, not far from Copenhagen. Nine years younger than her husband, Gertrude would go on to raise four children with him, only two of whom survived childhood. Shortly after his second wedding, Basedow also received a substantial increase of 200 *Reichsthlaer* in his annual salary, due in part to the retirement of a senior colleague. But the raise had substantial strings attached to it. He was now required "to give eight different lectures each day, a colossal workload" (Specht 1999: 18).

Basedow's next book appeared in 1756—*Lehrbuch prosaischer und poetischer Wohlredenheit in verschiedenen Schreibarten und Werken, zu akademischen Vorlesungen eingerichtet von M. J. B. Basedow* (A Textbook of Prosaic and Poetical Eloquence in Different Writing Styles and Works, Arranged for Academic Lectures; see Basedow 1756). In the Introduction he describes this 600-page collection of his lectures as a textbook whose thorough exposition [*gründliche Erklärung*] at gymnasia and high schools would be able to give every listener as much knowledge as is demanded for eloquence in every field, so that without further guidance he is enabled to help himself with the sections of greater texts of various subjects, for example grammar, letter writing, sermons, homilies, and poetry.

As cited by AB: 67

In 1758 Basedow published a eulogy for a deceased colleague entitled *Akademische Trauerrede über den Herrn Friedrich von Rosenkranz, Freiherrn, Hofjunker des Königs und Akademisten auf der königlichen Ritterakademie zu Soroe* (An Academic Eulogy for Herr Friederich von Rosenkranz, Baron, Nobleman, and Academic at the Royal *Ritterakademie* in Sorø; see Basedow 1758a). But by far his most notable publication during his early years at Sorø was the two-volume *Praktische Philosophie für alle Stände* (Copenhagen and Leipzig, 1758; see Basedow 1758b). Building on the reconciliationist position between philosophy and religion that he first presented in his 1753 *Versuch*, in his Preface Basedow announces that one of his main goals is "to also make the friends of philosophy friends of the Christian religion, or to protect them from doubts about this."[19] For, as he argues near the end of the book, "practical philosophy is useful in general because the grounds of motivation to recognize duties as duties and to perform them despite strong stimulations [*starken Reizungen*] to do the opposite" can only be expected "from a Christian who combines revelation with reason, which is much more powerful than a mere philosopher" (Basedow 1758b: 1003).

As Overhoff notes, for Basedow "the real difference" (Overhoff 2010: 61; 2004: 114) between a "merely philosophical" and a religiously grounded ethics consists in their contrasting conceptions of self-love. Natural law theorists such as Grotius[20] and Pufendorf[21] made self-love the starting point of their doctrines, and viewed egoism in a positive light. But Basedow warns readers in his Preface that he "would not want to be taken as a student of these great men" (Basedow 1758b: Preface). Instead, he defends a Christian conception of self-love, which tells us "to love our neighbors as ourselves" (Basedow 1758b: 31). Egoism must be rejected, because "it is a duty to love others or to take care of the other's well-being ... Love of fellow man is the greatest part of one's duty to the city of God [*Stadt Gottes*] or to the human race" (Basedow 1758b: 31). Every other human being "is exactly as important a member of the divine republic as I am" (Basedow 1758b: 31–2). Self-love properly construed means that "*one should act toward others as he would wish them to act toward him in the same situation*" (Basedow 1758b: 32). "Mankind is more important to me than the Fatherland and my religious sect; these are more important to me than my neighborhood and my family; and these are more important than I am to myself" (Basedow 1758b: 33). In the latter citation, one can already see the double emphases on cosmopolitanism and human friendship (*Menschenfreundschaft*) for which the Dessau Philanthropin would later become famous, and which would also endear Kant and many other liberal Enlightenment intellectuals to his project.

Basedow's biographers are far from united in their assessments of *Praktische Philosophie*. Göring, for instance, is extremely critical:

> What does it contain? Nothing more than a compilation of sentences which had taken hold as the coarser sediment of contemporary enlightenment in the author's conviction ... There is nothing in it of a purely scientific interest and a rigorous method of research. He refutes the idealists as well as the materialists with the simple turn [*Wendung*] that either they are crazy or they dissemble; he grounds the acknowledgment of the origin of the world on a clumsy circular argument with the sentence that the world exists because of a sequence of events, one of which was the first; out of that the unity of God is proved, [and he argues] that the belief in it assures us the greatest peace in our hearts, facilitates the hopes of immortality, and recommends love of humanity.
>
> Göring 1880: XXXIV

On the other hand, Meier (for once!) is extremely positive: "This book is, in my view, the very best and most splendid of all of Basedow's publications" (M: II: 268).

But even if the support Basedow offers for his positions in *Praktische Philosophie* is sometimes weak, the sheer scope of this work is impressive. As he states in Chapter I: "Not a particular part, but the complete philosophical science of human conduct, is my subject" (Basedow 1758b: 5). A glance at the Table of Contents shows that this is no idle boast:

(First Part) I. A Statement of Practical Philosophy
II. Of the Advancement of General Happiness
III. Of Life and Security
IV. Of the Hostile and Charitable Inclinations
V. Of Duties in View of Pleasure and Displeasure
VI. Of Sincerity
VII. Of Honor
VIII. Of Property and Contracts

>   IX. Of the Means of Making Oneself Usefully Pleasant
>   [*brauchbar angenehm*] and Happy
>   X. Of the Family
> (Part Two) I. Of our Duties toward God and Religion
>   II. Of the Highest Form of Philosophical Statescraft
>   [*philosophischen Staatslehre*]
>   III. Of Reason and Truth
>   IV. Of the Human Will and its Desires
>   V. Of the Common Ground of Duty and Right (Basedow 1758b: end of Preface)

As is the case with most of his works, Basedow is writing here for the larger reading public, not merely for academics. As he sees it, "a good practical philosophy must be pleasant, thorough, and of benefit to the public. It will be pleasant on its own, if only it avoids certain common mistakes" (Basedow 1758b: 18).

One of the most admirable aspects of the *Praktische Philosophie* is Basedow's argument in defense of civil rights for Jews. Jews would be "better citizens ... if one allowed them to have equal rights with Christians" (Basedow 1758b: 740), for at present "they are not allowed to occupy public positions, they cannot buy property, they cannot pursue the crafts [*Handwerke*], they are not allowed to persevere as day laborers and soldiers. Where should the poor descendants of Abraham begin?" (Basedow 1758b: 798). As Overhoff remarks, "Basedow's vehemently-presented demand here for extensive civil equality of Jews is a noteworthy early example of the humanitarian idea of tolerance in German-language literature of the eighteenth century" (Overhoff 2004: 117 n. 148). And it also provides strong support for Max Müller's claim that Basedow was "one of the boldest pioneers in the fight for human rights and human dignity" (Müller 1967: 114).

Some of Göring's strong criticisms of *Praktische Philosophie* have already been noted. But he is not entirely negative: "The best that the thick book contains are two chapters, 'Of the Education and Instruction of Youth'" (Göring 1880: XXXV). What does Basedow say about these topics in *Praktische Philosophie*? "*The main goal of education is that children become happy and useful human beings*" (Basedow 1758b: 540). However, here as elsewhere, the end does not justify the means—one "is not justified in seeking to demand the happiness of children through depraved means" (Basedow 1758b: 540). And this leads to his first rule of education: "Do not overwhelm your children with a lot of commands" (Basedow 1758b: 542). Instead, one should try to "connect, with increasing knowledge, the grounds of your commands with them; then obedience will come more willingly and more reasonably" (Basedow 1758b: 543). "*If one wants children to love and trust their fellow human beings*, then do not limit their innocent desires" (Basedow 1758b: 545). And "above all one should be a friend of one's children as often and as soon as one can, and a master [*Herr*] only as often and as long as one must" (Basedow 1758b: 545). "The *deep respect* of children toward parents and guardians will be promoted" when they become accustomed to their duties toward their fellow human beings "without force [*ohne Zwang*]" (Basedow 1758b: 545). Here as well, one can see the beginnings of some of the curricular innovations that would later make the Philanthropin famous: a deemphasis on corporeal punishment, an attempt to work with rather than against nature, and a high regard for children's own reasoning abilities.

Basedow also discusses a number of issues in applied ethics in his *Practical Philosophy*. For instance, he is strongly opposed to dueling, a practice which was still deeply rooted in European culture at the time:

> *Dueling by monarchs* and princes, through its shameful example, is highly dangerous ... A peasant may duel with his pitchfork, and a nobleman and officer with pistols and daggers, and a mischievous boy with sticks and stones ... Through duels, life, body, health, fortune, and family are destroyed, or shamed, or at least endangered.
>
> Basedow 1758b: 68–9

But as regards food and animal ethics, he adopts a traditional Christian "dominion over creation" position:[22]

> It is the entirely trustworthy will of God that the milk, skins, work, flesh, and other parts of animals, as well as all inanimate things, may be utilized for the needs and pleasures of human beings ... Whatever man needs for his sustenance, for clothing, for dwelling, for pleasure, or for security, are partly gifts of nature, partly the results of work to promote, multiply, improve, preserve, and bring into the necessary form and condition, these natural gifts.
>
> Basedow 1758b: 246–7

The sexual ethics advocated in Basedow's *Praktische Philosophie* is also rather conventional, though on this point there will be some significant shifts in his position later on:

> Our clothes must conceal all those different parts, the sight of which is wont to arouse the mutual fleshly passions of both of the sexes ... Indeed, perhaps some young women have become wives, because by deviating from this rule, they

have aroused a passionate male ... Therefore it is contrary to modesty if persons of different sex gaze upon the other either sleeping or in bed, or in nightclothes, or in the sleeping chamber, or when a married couple in the presence of the young recall in jest matters of conjugal intimacy.

Basedow 1758b: 141–2

On the topic of lotteries, however, Basedow is much more liberal:

Lotteries are a good means of imposing voluntary taxes upon a people; they are a not unpleasant anticipation of loss, provided that the participants in them are those who without noticeable frustration can lose their stake. But whoever regards them as a regular or probable method of making money does not understand reckoning.

Basedow 1758b: 328

In 1759, Basedow published a text for teaching German—*Neue Lehrart und Übung in der Regelmäßigkeit der deutschen Sprache* (The New Art of Teaching and Practice in the Regularity of the German Language; see Basedow 1759). His prolific publishing record, which continued unabated from the mid-1750s until just a few years before his death in 1790, and often resulted in three or four different books being published in a single year, is all the more impressive when one factors in his congenital eye weakness, which grew worse with age. By the late 1750s Basedow "can only see with the help of a large convex glass, and he must ask to be released from all written work at the Academy" (AB: 68; cf. Specht 1999: 18). Basedow himself, in a 1767 publication entitled *Hauptprobe der Zeiten in Ansehung der Religion, Wahrheitsliebe und Toleranz* (Final rehearsal of the times with regard to religion, love of truth, and tolerance), writes: "Because of the weakness of my eyes, I could not read my own manuscripts without effort, which hindered me ... in making an orderly whole" (Basedow 1767a: 120). And apparently his health issues during this period of his life were not just limited to eye problems. Basedow seems to have often been on the edge of a nervous breakdown from overexertion. Armin Basedow, for instance, cites a note of Count Johann Hartwig Ernst von Bernstorff's (1712–72—Bernstoff was one of Basedow's key supporters in Sorø), in which he recalls that during this time Basedow "'fell into such a great weakness of body and mind' that he always, even in the following decade, must have feared 'a derangement [*Verrückung*] of his intellectual faculties'" (as cited by AB: 68). A second note from Count Friedrich Danneskiold-Samsøe (1703–70), who served as *Oberhofmeister* of the *Ritterakademie* from 1760 to 1766, tells a similar story: "One could have compassion for him; for he had become partly confused [*halb verwirrt*] in the head ... I lament his already-mentioned weakness of mind and spirit, which perhaps has partly to do with this confusion in his writings" (as cited by AB: 68–9).

Nevertheless, at least at the beginning of his tenure in Sorø, Basedow was a huge success: "the innovation in his instruction, the originality of his lectures, the warmth of his spoken word inspired his audience from his first lecture" (Pinloche 1896: 34). As Meier remarks: "But this is the truth and the fact of the matter ... Basedow did not teach like the scribes and the Pharisees ... When he began his lessons, people pricked up their ears, as if to say: 'This is an entirely new man, it is a new teacher, a prophet has come among us'" (M: I: 233).

And Basedow's popularity increased even more (at least for a short while) when he began lecturing on theological topics. As he would recall later in his 1767 *Hauptprobe*:

> A little while ago, religion in the Academy had become so overgrown [*verwildert*] that theology found no audience among the members of the young nobility and their tutors. But God reprieved me with bliss that my lectures, which concerned themselves first with the truth of the Christian religion, later with the important parts of church history, and in the third year with the most important interpretation of the New Testament, almost always attracted all of the numbers of masters and tutors at the Academy.
>
> Basedow 1767a: 115–16

However, Basedow's initial success in this area would later lead to his undoing, for the more he lectured on theological topics, the more he began to acquire enemies. Some of this was undoubtedly due to jealousy on the part of his colleagues at the *Ritterakademie*, who soon noticed that his lectures were much better attended than theirs. But his religious liberalism and the frequent challenges he posed to orthodox positions eventually proved to be too much for others. As Pinloche notes:

> The entire orthodox tribe rose up with outrage, in order to hand over the bold one to the severity of the government. Despite the always-growing patronage of citizens and students, despite the attempt at mediation by the brave pastor *Hammer* ... despite the protection of Bishop *Harboe* of Zealand [Denmark], and despite the friendship of the liberal minister *Bernstorff*, Dean *Friedrich Danneskiold[-Samsøe]* brought it about that Basedow would be released from his position and would finally have to stop causing offense to the well-thinking theologians through his subversive theories.
>
> Pinloche 1896: 35–6

And so, on January 19, 1761, Basedow was dismissed from the Sorø *Ritterakademie*. Soon afterward, he was demoted ("transferred") to a professorship at a gymnasium in Altona. But while his disagreements with religious conservatives would continue and deepen for at least another decade, the move to Altona, as we shall see in the next chapter, eventually turned out to be a blessing in disguise. For Basedow's new position (in large part because of the growing controversies surrounding his lectures) came with an extremely light teaching load, and this gave him more time to write.

6

That Old-Time Religion

Basedow's transfer (in fact, a demotion) from the *Ritterakademie* in Sorø landed him at the *Gymansium Christianeum* in Altona, only a few miles from his birthplace in Hamburg. Altona, presently a western borough of Hamburg with a population of about 250,000, was an independent city until 1937, and during Basedow's life it was under the administration of the Danish monarchy. Pinloche describes part of the context of Basedow's move as follows:

> Although the Danish government endeavored to ameliorate the unfavorable impression which his dismissal from office [*Amtsentsetzung*] must have caused, nevertheless it was impossible to prevent the conditions connected with his transfer from being known in his new sphere of activity. Rightly or wrongly, the clergy had accused him of heresy [*Irrglaubens*]: from now on nothing could protect him against the consequences of such an accusation. Although Altona was large enough to enable him to live unnoticed when he gave up his eccentric ways and dissipation [*Ausschweifung*], which unfortunately had become more and more frequent with him, nevertheless the society which he relied on through his position was not free enough from the spirit of intolerance of that time to receive without mistrust a man who was pursued by accusations of the orthodox.
> Pinloche 1896: 37

Toward the end of this passage Pinloche hints that both Basedow's drinking problem and his mood swings were exacerbated by the move to Altona, and the following remark of Diestelmann's offers some additional support for this hypothesis:

> How different was the beginning in Altona, in comparison with the first entrance at Sorø! Basedow came there with burning enthusiasm for his new calling and was welcomed and celebrated by students who, according to the reputation that preceded him, expected great things from him. In Altona indifference and ridicule [*Gleichgültigkeit und Spott*] welcomed him.
> Diestelmann 1897: 30

On the other hand, while his "eccentric ways and dissipation" probably did become more frequent as a result of his forced move to Altona, in looking back on the situation years later Basedow himself was able to put a much more positive spin on the situation: "Because I wanted to get out of the way of a powerful enemy [einem mächtigen Hasser], I became professor at the (at that time) academic gymnasium in Altona; or rather, due to special favor I became a paid writer, and once again had extraordinary luck" (DEP: 24–5). Nevertheless, his initial situation in Altona was quite a bit more precarious than he admits in this passage. Göring offers the following details:

> Everything aroused powerful protest from the side of the orthodox [altgläubigen] theologians, under whom in particular the Hamburg clergymen, Senior Goeze[1] as well as pastors Winkler[2] and Zimmermann, excelled in fanatical attacks from the pulpit. In addition to these, schoolmaster Ziegra in Hamburg, Pastor Paulsen in Wedel, and Professor Profe[3] in Altona inveighed against him in journals and special leaflets. Basedow's teachings were declared unChristian, even immoral, his person was disparaged and his character defamed, he was described as a fanatic [Phantasten], a dangerous lunatic [gefärhlichen Irrgeist], a contemptible seducer and detestable heretic who was unworthy of a public office, indeed, all governmental pay. With the usual tactics of crude persecutors of heresy, his opponents stirred up the rabble, always incapable of judgment, against the harmless innovator who as a result could no longer allow himself to be seen without endangering his life, since he had been threatened with stoning.
>
> Göring 1880: XXXVIII

To be sure, Basedow still had supporters, but there were limits to what they could do to help him without endangering their own positions:

> At the time of these struggles powerful patrons still stood by his side to protect him from his enraged opponents. There was the worthy Bishop Harboe of Seeland,[4] Court Chaplain Cramer,[5] Klopstock,[6] Funk,[7] Schlegel[8] and above all the noble, wise Minister Bernstorff.[9] Due to the intercession of this man alone, Basedow was indebted for his whole existence, above all for protection from removal from office and imprisonment.
>
> Göring 1880: XLI

Although neither the threat of removal from office nor that of imprisonment was carried out,[10] life for Basedow and his family in Altona was often extremely unpleasant:

> Indeed, clerical zeal went so far that the municipal authorities of Hamburg were induced to forbid, first through a public ordinance, the preservation of all

polemical and paradoxical writings [*aller polemischen und paradoxen Schriften*], and then through a publicly posted mandate, dated April 23, 1764, to warn the citizens against reading such writings, to demand that children and young people keep away from them, and finally to prohibit all schoolteachers from using such books in the instruction of the young, under penalty of banishment [*unter Androhung der Landesverweisung*]... The city of Lübeck was also seized by the zeal of intolerance: booksellers were ordered to remove all copies of [Basedow's] *Philalethie* and *Unterrichtes in der natürlichen und biblischen Religion*[11] from the city, and were forbidden under a penalty of 50 Thaler from bringing them back in. In other places as well honorable people could be brought into discredit through buying, selling, reading, or praising Basedow's writings; indeed, their official positions were endangered... Personal or written contact with him was regarded as improper [*als ein Unrecht*]... In Hamburg there were no longer any clergymen who would allow him to attend confession. Finally, he and his family were excluded from Communion and thereby from the entire religious community in Altona and the whole surrounding area.

Göring 1880: XXXIX

But—to return to Basedow's rosier description of his new situation of having become "a paid writer"—his new salary in Altona of 800 Thaler was nearly double his earlier Sorø salary (400 Thaler plus housing benefits), and—because of the controversy surrounding him—his teaching duties were greatly curtailed. He was now allowed to lecture publicly only three hours per week, whereas in Sorø he had a twenty-one-hour teaching load.[12]

Basedow and his family moved to Altona in the summer of 1761, and on October 7 he gave his inaugural address (*Antrittsrede*) in Latin[13] under the title: "Concerning Various Important Questions Relative to Moral Axioms." It was dedicated to Michael Richey, his favorite teacher at the Hamburg Gymnasium, who had died five months earlier. ("I cannot find words which worthily praise enough your good deeds. I can only express in all simplicity what my grateful heart urges"—as cited by AB: 38; see also 81). But Basedow's most impressive achievement during the Altona period is his intense literary productivity (carried out, as we saw earlier, while he was under continual threat of public stoning and imprisonment). Göring lists 38 publications during this ten-year period (G: 514–16); Reble, 42 (R: 267–70). And even more impressive than the sheer quantity of publications is the wide scope of topics covered. They range from works on applied mathematics education (*Überzeugende Methode der auf das bürgerliche Leben angewandten Arithmetik, zum Vergnügen der Nachdenkenden und zur Beförderung des guten Unterrichts in den Schulen* (see

Basedow 1763)—A Convincing Method of Applied Arithmetic Employed in Civil Life, for the Pleasure of Reflective Men and for the Advancement of Good Instruction in Schools) to books on religious epistemology (*Philalethie. Neue Aussichten in die Wahrheiten und Religion der Vernunft bis in die Grenzen der glaubwürdigen Offenbarung, dem denkenden Publiko eröffnet* (2 vols.; see Basedow 1764a)—Love of Truth. New Points of View on Truth and the Religion of Reason up to the Limits of Credible Revelation, Presented to the Thinking Public); from multiple polemical religious tracts (e.g., *Schutzschrift für seine neuesten Bücher gegen den Herrn Göze* (see Basedow 1764c)—A Defense of his Latest Books Against Herr Goeze) to works on political philosophy (*Agathokrator oder: Von der Erziehung künftiger Regenten, nebst Anhang und Beilagen* (see Basedow 1771c)—Good Power: Or, On the Education of Future Rulers, with an Appendix and Addenda); from defenses of religious toleration (*Betrachtungen über die wahre Rechtgläubigkeit und die im Staate und in der Kirche notwendige Toleranz* (see Basedow 1766a)—Observations on True Orthodoxy and Necessary Tolerance in State and Church) to one of his most famous and influential books, *Das Methodenbuch für Väter und Mütter der Familien und Völker* (see Basedow 1979/1770)—The Methodbook for Fathers and Mothers of Families and Nations.

Because Basedow is known primarily as an educational reformer, biographers tend to ignore his religious writings. The following remark of Landschoof's is typical: "with the purely religious material this paper has no concern" (Landschoof 1933: 113). But this is a mistake, for religion played a central role throughout Basedow's life, and his pedagogical theory is strongly influenced by his religious orientation. As we have seen, his father hoped he would become a minister, he studied theology at the Universities of Leipzig and Kiel, the theme of religious toleration is perhaps the single most important legacy of his Philanthropin, and many of his writings, including those that are often tagged as pedagogical works, contain extensive discussions of religious issues. Additionally, for at least the first seven of the ten years he spent in Altona, the focus of his writing was religion. But what was Basedow's basic religious outlook? Why was it controversial? What were the main points of disagreement between Basedow and the "orthodox theologians" mentioned earlier—Goeze and co.?

Basedow's religious perspective is best described as a middle position between radical Enlightenment deism and conservative Protestantism. Like the deists, he is a fan of natural religion—that is, he believes that religious beliefs should be supported by empirical evidence and reason. As he notes near the beginning of his 1764 book, *Methodischer Unterricht der Jugend in der Religion und Sittenlehre der Vernunft*, "the theology and ethics of this book is simply the natural [*bloß die natürliche*]" (Basedow 1764b: I: XLVI). But like traditional Protestants, Basedow also takes the Bible very seriously—that is to say, he regards the statements in the Bible as true. In the second volume of this same book he proclaims: "The Holy Scriptures are the only guiding principle [*die einzige Richtschnur*] of our faith and life" (Basedow 1764b: II: 44). As David Stern remarks, in his analysis of Basedow's theology:

> Basedow is a supporter of natural religion and at the same time Christianity ... He insists that an irreconcilable opposition [*ein unüberbruckbarer Gegensatz*] between the two does not exist ... Basedow's efforts basically come down to the attempt to prove that true natural religion does not lead to any results that conflict with revealed truths in the Holy Scriptures.[14]

More radical deists reject those parts of the Bible that contradict reason and empirical evidence. Perhaps the most famous American example is Thomas Jefferson's version of the New Testament, *The Life and Morals of Jesus of Nazareth* (1820). In this severely condensed text, all references to miracles have been deleted, there is no mention of the Resurrection or any other supernatural events, and all passages that portray Jesus as divine have also been excluded. As Jefferson explains in a letter to John Adams of October 12, 1813:

> We must reduce our volume to the simple evangelists, select, even from them, the very words only of Jesus, paring off the Amphibologisms into which they have been led by forgetting often, or not understanding, what had fallen from him, by giving their own misconceptions as his dicta, and expressing unintelligibly for others what they had not understood themselves. There will be found remaining the most sublime and benevolent code of morals which has ever been offered to man. I have performed this operation for my own use, by cutting verse by verse out of the printed book, and arranging the matter which is evidently his, and which is as easily distinguishable as diamonds in a dunghill. The result is an 8 vo. [octavo volume] of 46 pages of pure and unsophisticated doctrines, such as were professed and acted on by the *unlettered* apostles, the Apostolic fathers, and the Christians of the first century.
>
> Jefferson 1984: 1301–2

Or, as Forrest Church notes in his Introduction to *The Jefferson Bible*: "As with many Unitarians of like spirit who have followed him, Jefferson's was a search not so much for the historical as for the intelligible Jesus" (Church 1989: 31).

One might think that any effort to find common ground between natural religion and strict adherence to the Bible (according to Basedow, "*die einzige Richtschnur* of our faith and life") is doomed to failure. Either one sides with empirical evidence and reason, or one subscribes to Holy Scripture. The possibility of an irresolvable conflict between these two commitments would seem to always be present, and when it occurs, one must choose one side or the other. And in fact Kant—despite his later enthusiastic support for Basedow's educational reforms at the Philanthropin in Dessau—seems to have reached a similar conclusion regarding Basedow's theological outlook. In Johann Gottfried Herder's notes from Kant's practical philosophy lecture from 1763–4, Kant points to Basedow as an example of a regrettable tendency he calls "syncretism": "here one tries to develop contradictory doctrines as if they were in agreement. It seldom catches on; is usually futile and often damaging—Basedow is syncretic" (V-PP/Herder 27: 78).[15]

However, during the Enlightenment very, very few authors argued that the Bible could be dismissed entirely. Basedow's theological project of finding common ground between reason and revelation, however fanciful it may strike some of us today, struck a deeply sympathetic chord when it was first presented. Many liberal readers hoped he would succeed in his reconciliationist project.

At the same time, when Basedow turned his attention to the religious education of the young—and in his adult life he was always a pedagogue first, and a theologian second—his conservative opponents felt strongly that his natural religion sentiments had gained the upper hand. For just as he would later promise parents of students who enrolled at the Philanthropin that "there will be very little memorizing with us" (ES: 39) when it came to secular texts dealing with, say, foreign languages or geography, he also argued repeatedly that young children should not be forced to memorize extensive passages from the Bible. For instance, in his "Treatise on the Instruction of Children in Religion," which was included in place of a preface in one of his 1764 publications, he writes: "Barely can the weaned infant stammer than one teaches him to recite prayers with a broken voice, whose meaning is not understood and cannot be understood without being instructed beforehand in the deepest mysteries of Christianity" (Basedow 1764b: I: IV).[16] This longstanding habit of pastors to immediately force young children to memorize prayers and passages from Scripture that they cannot possibly understand leads to what Basedow calls "the first error" of religious instruction: "Children are accustomed through this to think that, without understanding and heart [*ohne Verstand und Herz*], merely through words and folded hands, they can accomplish *what serves the words of the prayer*" (Basedow 1764b: I: VII). Additionally, the motto Basedow chose to place on the title page of the book: "*Denket selbst* [think for yourself]" (Basedow 1764b: title page)—while eerily similar to Kant's later (1784) famous definition of the

Enlightenment ("Have courage to use your own understanding! This is ... the motto of enlightenment"—WA 8: 35?),[17] also slants the discussion toward natural religion and away from blanket acceptance of the words of the Bible.

All of which was extremely upsetting to traditional German Lutheran pastors, the most well known of whom was Johann Melchior Goeze (1717–86), son of a pastor and later an influential minister in Hamburg. Goeze is primarily remembered today as one of the last champions of Lutheran orthodoxy against the rising tide of liberal Enlightenment religious writers. He vehemently attacked not only Basedow but many other major figures in German Enlightenment religious thought, including Lessing—primarily because of his association with the controversial *Wolfenbüttel Fragments*, whose author was eventually revealed to be Reimarus, Basedow's former teacher at the Hamburg Gymnasium. Other targets of Goeze's attacks include Johann Salomo Semler (1725–91) and Carl Friedrich Bahrdt (1714–92).

Goeze interpreted Basedow's plea for more reason and less memorization in the religious instruction of children as a direct assault on the profession of the ministry itself. What meaningful work would there be left for ministers to do in the area of religious education if they were no longer encouraged to teach young children to recite prayers and passages from the Bible? As he writes in one of his tracts against Basedow:

> If Herr Professor Basedow gains approval and credence in our community, who will then send their children to catechism in the future? For if the Basedowian fantasies of religious education have a foundation and spread further without hindrance, then we must at the same time request that the church doors be garrisoned by sentries, so that no children [who cannot yet follow a minister] would be allowed in and to their greatest injury hear the name of the Redeemer called.[18]

Additionally, Goeze interpreted Basedow's recommendations as a direct assault on both the Bible and Protestant customs. For instance, in a letter of March 1764, he accused Basedow not only of having made "the symbolic books of our church contemptuous and hated by human beings," but also of "favoring a way of instructing children" that contradicts all of our customs (Goeze, as cited by Overhoff 2004: 164). He also accused Basedow of trying to prevent young children from learning Christian doctrine. In the same letter, Goeze claimed that, according to Basedow's guidelines, each and every child should remain "with the greatest diligence in a state of uncertainty regarding the foundations [*Unwißenheit der Grundlagen*] of the Christian religion until the twelfth year."[19]

And of course Basedow's ardent ecumenicalism ("a state, viewed as a state, acts intelligently and justly when it tolerates all politically good religions [*alle politisch guten Religionen*] next to one another")[20] could also not have sat well with Goeze and other traditional Lutherans.

Given Basedow's basic reconciliationist stance—his conviction that "biblical religion stands in great agreement with true natural religion" (Basedow 1764b: I: XLVII)[21]—it should come as no surprise (the attacks of Goeze and company notwithstanding) that his views on a number of core religious doctrines are not terribly radical but fairly mainstream.[22] For instance, unlike most deists, Basedow believes in miracles, defining them in the *Philalethie* as events "in which we discern divine intention, through which human beings become attentive to a divine instruction and command, and which we should regard as proof of the truth of this instruction" (Basedow 1764a: I: 239). Similarly, he "denies neither the immortality of the soul" nor the Resurrection,[23] he rejects materialism, and he endorses the doctrine of Communion (despite his own family's exclusion from this practice while they lived in Altona—see Basedow 1764c: 55).

At the same time, however, Basedow did advocate heterodox views on several other theological issues. For instance, he did not subscribe to the doctrine of eternal damnation, and he did not regard child baptism as an urgent necessity. Also, unlike many of his more conservative theological contemporaries, he believed that sound religion should not be viewed as static and unchangeable. "The enlightenment [*Erleuchtung*] of our time will also soon extend over religion" (Basedow 1764b: I: XI). Or, as he remarks in the 1764 *Defense of his Latest Books Against Herr Goeze*: "What 300 years ago was very orthodox here is now called false, wrong, papist ... Is it then now so determined that our current orthodoxy is free from all error?" (Basedow 1764c: 36) Finally, and most importantly, Basedow was a strong advocate of religious tolerance. No single religion has a monopoly on truth, and this is why he would later insist that all instructional texts used at the Philanthropin would be "*free from theological verdicts* against Jews, Muslims [*Mahomedaner*], and Deists; or for this or that church against so-called Dissidents, who in some places are called *heretics* ... For *cosmopolitical education* must be universal, and cannot advise against clergy of any denomination" (ES: 65).

Turning now to general issues in the philosophy of religion rather than specific theological doctrines, Basedow is probably best known for his position regarding the duty to believe (*Glaubenspflicht*). First presented in his 1765 work, *Theoretisches System der gesunden Vernunft, ein akademisches Lehrbuch* (Theoretical System of Healthy Reason, an Academic Textbook), in this book and several others Basedow defends the claim that *"there are practical propositions that are only probable [nur wahrscheinlich] to us in theory*, and remain only probable, but which must [*müssen*] be regarded as true in practice if we do not wish to act against important ends [*wichtigen Zwecken*] and put ourselves in danger" (Basedow 1765: III: § 27). In other words, we have a duty to believe those propositions that have an essential bearing on our life and conduct ("practical propositions"), even if their truth is only probable rather than certain, where the consequences of doubting them, should they in fact turn out to be true, will cause us to violate our core convictions and goals ("important ends") as well as put ourselves in danger. Commenting on the latter point in the second edition of his *Practische Philosophie für alle Stände* (1777), he notes that "the universal rule" of "*the duty of belief and doubt*" is the following: "you must want to believe, when you know that the doubt will harm you or put you in danger, and you must then also endeavor to believe" (Basedow 1777a: II: xiii. § 8).

American readers will no doubt sense a connection between Basedow's *Glaubenspflicht* and William James's later "will to believe" doctrine,[24] and both authors did of course use their respective positions to defend belief in God. But within German philosophy, it is also evident that "Basedow's views are important antecedents to Kant's arguments for the postulates"[25] of God and the immortality of the soul, as presented in the second *Critique* and elsewhere. Both Basedow and Kant argue that it is morally necessary to believe in God and immortality even though we do not have sufficient evidence to prove that either proposition is true.

Philalethie (see Basedow 1764a), which has been referred to several times already, is without doubt another of Basedow's key works from his Altona decade. But in addition to lengthy discussions of religious issues, it also contains a substantial chapter called "On Teaching [*Von der Unterrichte*]," which offers early hints of many ideas that would later be put into practice at the Philanthropin. For instance, in this chapter Basedow advocates a school library; viz., "a collection of school books which should serve pupils from their elementary grades up through entrance into a university" (Basedow 1764a: I: 325). Such a library would contain works on moral education (*Kindermoral*) (Basedow 1764a: I: 326), elementary physics (*Kinderphysik*) (Basedow 1764a: I: 326), geography and history (Basedow 1764a: I: 328), as well as a collection of all types of realia (Basedow 1764a: I: 329). Basedow is here essentially sketching an idea that he elaborates on later in his four-volume *Elementarwerk* (1774), one of his most influential works. Early in the *Methodenbuch*, Basedow describes the forthcoming *Elementarwerk* in part by predicting that children themselves "should love no game and no delight as much as this book, arranged for their nature and illustrated continuously with educational copperplates" (MB II; in G: 20).

In the following passage, Basedow summarizes his basic position regarding what is needed in a school library:

> The textbooks used in schools must not only present something from history, but also from physics, religion, and grammar; but each science also requires its [own] book. However, it would be very useful if all of them were done by only one man, who in his preparation begins with the earliest knowledge of children, and then progresses as the natural order requires. In this order he must therefore place physical truths in physics [and] historical knowledge in history; each time he must reflect whether it would be advisable that instruction in school should go out from one science to another and then return to the former, so that the parts of his work follow one another. Then it should be noted in which volume of the school library this instruction will be continued, if one does not wish to wander from this path. Such a school library would not require as many different volumes ... as the books which are now needed. For one would not need to have the same things printed many times, as is now frequently necessary, since often the same knowledge in history, religion, geography, chronology, and genealogy will be presented at the same time. In short, the wished-for school library should be a book which is sufficient for students studying and at the same time gives a plan of instruction.
>
> Basedow 1764a: I: 330–1

The school library project was also a major component in Basedow's overall school reform strategy. As he describes it in a later publication, such a library would be

> an orderly sequence of useful school books, which would progress uniformly to the most important goals; which would begin from the alphabet of human understanding; which would set forth all necessary knowledge to all classes [*zu allen Ständen*]; and after that would give average citizens the opportunity for instruction and end with the principles of the sciences ... in which each earlier part would be made easier than the one following it, in which verbal knowledge [*Verbalerkenntnis*] would not be the main thing; which would not ignite the conflicts of the churches in common schools ... which would unite that knowledge that is scattered with shame; which would be equipped according to the needs of our times with all diligence ... *Necessary, of highest necessity is such a work.*[26]

And in fact Basedow was working on the idea of a school library even before the 1764 publication of the *Philalethie*. He alludes to it in a letter to Bernstorff of

July 10, 1761 when he says that he has finished working out "theorems [*Lehrsätze*] of the most useful sciences for children and youth" (as cited by AB: 93–4),[27] and he discusses it explicitly in a later letter to Bernstorff of November 9, 1763:

> I will gradually start the following writings ... a school library, in which all sciences that pertain to youths studying in school follow one another according to the gradual development of human mental faculties in the necessary order and mixture. This book will enable others, either in public or special schools, to practice the same plan of instruction on which I myself had decided in the beginning. For without such a well-ordered school library, in which vocabulary words, phrases, and classical authors must no longer be the main element, the true improvement of school conditions is not possible.
>
> As cited by AB: 94

Göring also notes that several other key aspects of Basedow's pedagogical vision are already present in the *Philalethie*:

> Already the basic idea that the child ought to view the entire world only optimistically [*nur optimistisch*], that in every relationship he must experience the full truth, that a lively, general education is more useful than extensive erudition—all this was in ... the *Philalethie*.
>
> Göring 1880: XLIV

And Basedow's employer, the Danish court, relieved to see both that he was once again writing about issues of educational reform and that the theological quarrels with Goeze and others were beginning to quiet down, "gave him free rein for this work, relieved him of what little teaching he had in the gymnasium, but continued the salary stipulated for his professorship" (Landschoof 1933: 118). By this point, as Basedow notes later in a 1774 booklet about the Philanthropinum, he had indeed become "a paid writer" (DEP: 24)—one who also made extremely good use of his newly acquired leisure time.

One of Basedow's most popular and influential works[28] published during his ten-year residency in Altona was his 1768 *Vorstellung an Menschenfreunde und vermögende Männer über Schulen, Studien und ihren Einfluß in die öffentliche Wohlfahrt. Mit einem Plane eines Elementarbuchs der menschlichen Erkenntnis* (Presentation to Friends of Humanity and Men of Means regarding Schools, Studies, and their Influence on Public Welfare. With a Plan of an Elementary Book of Human Knowledge). Reble, who reprints the entire text in his edited collection of Basedow's *Ausgewählte pädagogische Schriften* (1965), calls it "the actual groundwork of German Enlightenment pedagogy," and judges it to be "without a doubt ... the most important of all of Basedow's pedagogical writings.

Basedow here became the interpreter and spokesman for the fundamental pedagogical tendencies of the entire epoch" (Reble 1965: 258). In the *Vorstellung an Menschenfreunde* Basedow's readers learn more about some of his by now familiar themes of religious toleration, his critique of existing pedagogical methodologies, and the need for new teaching methods. But there is now a rhetorical directness and tightness to his presentation that was missing in earlier publications. Regarding religious toleration, for instance, he asks readers: "Because he was a pagan, can Euclid's *Elements* not be useful?" (VM § 5; in R: 8). And in § 22 he defends *"the right of everyone, even dissenting citizens [dissidentischen Bürger], to attend public schools"* (R: 23) in part by asking: "cannot languages, rhetoric, all of philosophy, mathematics, and morals be presented in writing and orally, so that *no decision against Catholics, Greeks, Lutherans, Arminians, and Socinians* will be given" (R: 24)? Section 43 is entitled *"Judgments concerning the Foolish Methods [törichten Methoden]* [of teaching] *the Latin Language"* (R: 48) and ends by noting that "the Latin language is a torment of those years, whose impressions we never forget ... The old teachers become disgusting [*ekelhaft*] to us" (R: 51). Section 47 is entitled "Of a very new school method" (R: 57), and emphasizes that, "as much as possible, all frustration and revulsion in learning must be avoided" (R: 57).

But the most impressive aspect of this short book is its call for the total transformation of the existing school system. Basedow is no patient reformer content to work within the existing system. Section 24 is entitled: *"Of the Necessity and Nature of the Total Transformation [gänzlichen Umschaffung] of Schools and Programs of Study"* (R, 28), and earlier in the treatise he informs readers that the needed improvement of schools cannot be brought about "through a small change" because "wounds which have a bottomless depth because of burning pus will not be healed through ointments and bandages" (R, 12). As noted earlier, Kant was particularly impressed with Basedow's call for radical and immediate change in educational institutions, and in the second of his two short essays praising the Philanthropin he employs the same language of total transformation. Existing schools, he notes, "must be transformed [*müssen umgeschaffen werden*] if something good is to come out of them because they are defective in their original organization ... Not a slow *reform* but a swift *revolution* can bring this about" (AP 2: 449).[29]

Basedow followed the success of the *Vorstellung an Menschenfreunde* with four more related publications in 1768 alone: 1) *Das Nötigste von der Vorstellung an Menschenfreunde und vermögende Männer wegen einer versprochenen Folge von untheologischen Schulbüchern nach dem Bedürfnisse und Geschmacke unsrer*

Zeiten (The Most Necessary Part of the Presentation to Friends of Humanity and Men of Means, due to a Promised Series of Nontheological Textbooks according to the Needs and Tastes of our Times—essentially, an abridged version of the earlier *Vorstellung*); 2) *Ehrerbietiges Schreiben an diejenigen Menschenfreunde und vermögende Männer, welche um Beförderung der Schulbibliothek und des Elementarbuchs ersucht zu werden verlangen* (Respectful Writings to those Friends of Humanity and Men of Means Who Requested that the Promotion of the School Library and Elementary Book be Demanded); 3) *Die ganze natürliche Weisheit im Privatstande gesitteter Bürger*[30] (The Complete Natural Wisdom in the Social Class of Well-Mannered Citizens); 4) *Vierteljährige Unterhandlungen mit Menschenfreunden über moralische und dennoch unkirkliche*[31] *Verbesserungen der Erziehung und Studien* (Quarterly Correspondence with Friends of Humanity concerning Moral and nevertheless Secular Improvements of Education and Studies)— this last text, which appeared in several different issues, contains a collection of letters Basedow had received testifying to the value of his work, as well as a summary of the results of his efforts thus far (see Basedow 1768a, b, c, and d).

Basedow's star was clearly on the rise at this point: money began to finally pour in from a variety of sources, due in no small part to his own indefatigable letter-writing campaigns and fundraising trips. Rathmann reports that in 1768 alone Basedow wrote to

> the Empress of Russia, King Friedrich the Second of Prussia, the Queens of England, Denmark, and Poland, the Elector of Saxony, the General Secretary [*Generalstaaten*] of Holland, different academies of science, six respected Free Masons' lodges, famous ministers of state in multiple European kingdoms ... and noble-minded and famous scholars inside and outside of Germany.
>
> Ra: 42

And in 1768 Basedow also traveled to

> Copenhagen, where he sought out Klopstock, Cramer, Schlegel, Resewitz, Preisler and others. December found him in Berlin, where Spalding,[32] Lampert, Sulzer,[33] Gillet, Mendelssohn, and others encouraged, advised, and supported his plans. He also discussed his plans with famous artists ... On his return trip to Altona he also visited Dresden, Leipzig, Halle, Braunschweig, Hannover, and Bremen.
>
> Ra: 47–8

Biographers often speak of a pedagogical *Wendung* or *Rückkehr* that occurs in Basedow's life in 1768—a (re)turn to his earlier critique of the school system that would continue to occupy him for the remainder of his life. Göring, for instance, writes: "A new period, indeed, the decisive turn [*die entscheidende Wendung*] in Basedow's life, begins in the year 1768, when the all-round busy man definitively turned to the educational system" (Göring 1880: XLII). Similarly, Pinloche also stresses Basedow's "return [*Rückkehr*] to pedagogy" in his study (Pinloche 1896: 25). But these are brusque overstatements. It would be more accurate to say that the adult Basedow was always concerned with education, from his first tutoring work in Borghorst in 1749 onward, and that *religious* education was also always a strong topic of interest. Reble describes the situation more accurately in the following remark:

> It should not be overlooked that this return to pedagogy in 1767–68 was not an actual '*Wendung*' but rather merely a shift of emphasis … Basedow's bigger works before this period, especially *Practical Philosophy for all Classes* (1758) and *Philalethie* (1764) already contain … extensive chapters on education and school questions.
>
> Reble 1965: 257

But to return to the *Vorstellung*: its earnest call for fundamental change in education found an extremely receptive audience, and soon after the book's publication Basedow's professional career definitely took a turn for the better. As Fritzsch notes:

> The success of the *Vorstellung* was enormous [*ungeheurer*]. "From friends and strangers, from scholars and the unlearned, from clergy and members of different churches, from pedagogues and school principals, from subjects and great monarchs, over 7000 *Reichsthaler* in aid and payments was given," as Basedow himself reported. In a short time the sum he was supplied with was over 15,000 Thaler.[34]

During this same time Basedow's turbulent private life also finally began to take a turn for the better. In 1767 his second wife Gertrude Elisabeth (1733–88) gave birth to their first son, Franz, who unfortunately died at age 10. And on March 18, 1769 their only daughter was born. Named in memory of Basedow's first wife, Emilie not only survived into adulthood but also became one of the star pupils (and, as a result, an invaluable promotional tool) at the Philanthropin. Tutored primarily by Basedow's first assistant Christian Heinrich Wolke (1741–1825), Emilie learned to read before she was three, spoke French at four, read Latin at four and a half, and could also perform a number of impressive arithmetical feats at an extremely young age. And "all of this knowledge" was, of course, acquired in the recommended Philanthropinist manner—through "playing [*Spielend*], that is, without exertion or harmful sitting still" (DEP: 47).

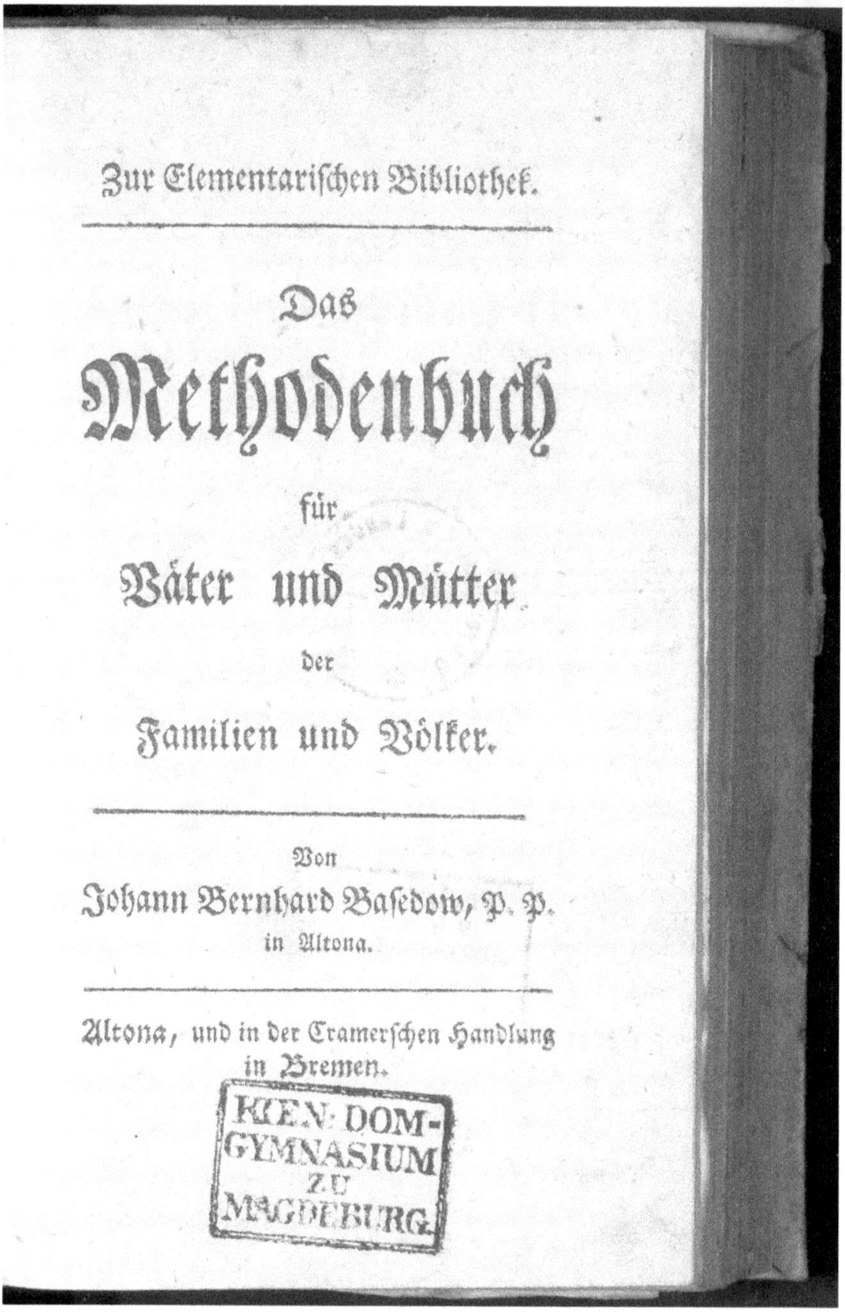

Zur Elementarischen Bibliothek.

Das
Methodenbuch
für
Väter und Mütter
der
Familien und Völker.

Von
Johann Bernhard Basedow, P. P.
in Altona.

Altona, und in der Cramerschen Handlung
in Bremen.

Figure 2 The original title page of Basedow's *Methodenbuch*, 1770. By permission of the Universitäts- und Landesbibliothek Sachsen-Anhalt, Halle (Saale).

7

"For Fathers and Mothers of Families and Nations:" The *Methodenbuch*

One considerable challenge facing anyone who seeks to understand Basedow's work is his extremely lengthy list of publications. He was the author of well over a hundred different books, and many of them are very difficult to obtain at present.[1] Part of the explanation for Basedow's extensive publication record can be attributed to his productive use of insomnia. According to Goethe,

> He never went to bed, but dictated constantly. Sometimes he laid down on a couch and slumbered, while his amanuensis, pen in hand, calmly remained sitting in order to be ready at once when Basedow, only half awake, would again give free rein to his thoughts.
>
> *Dichtung und Wahrheit*: XIV; in R: 242

But there are two points that lessen the shock of dealing with such a huge quantity of writings. First (as is often the case with authors who publish a great deal), his works are extremely repetitive. Reble, for instance, in summarizing the "radical formation and diverse grounding" of Basedow's pedagogical principles, tells readers that we learn about them "in Basedow's innumerable [*zahlosen*] writings (with correspondingly frequent repetitions and amplifications)" (Reble 1965: 253). Second, there are two books in particular that stand out above the rest, both in terms of their public impact and in their overall significance: namely, *Das Methodenbuch für Väter und Mütter der Familien und Völker* (1770, 2nd ed. 1771, 3rd ed. 1773) and *Das Elementarwerk. Ein geordneter Vorrat aller nötigen Erkenntnis zum Unterrichte der Jugend von Anfang bis ins akademische Alter, zur Belehrung der Eltern, Schullehrer und Hofmeister, zum Nutzen eines jedes Lehrers, die Erkenntnis zu vervollkommen*, 4 vols. (1774, 2nd ed. 1785). Regarding both books, Göring writes:

> In the *Methodenbuch* and in the *Elementarwerk* Basedow offers the sum of his pedagogical intentions and abilities. As the earlier publications of the author

have only fragmentarily prepared what these works have delivered in complete form, so his later writings almost without exception turn back to these main works. And Basedow could rightly demand that every teacher who wanted to teach in his Philanthropinum first needed to include a thorough study of both of these works in his principles of education.

G: 3

Accordingly, in this chapter and the next I shall present an overview of and brief commentary on each of these two central books, with the aim of giving readers a better sense of Basedow's basic pedagogical theory.

The Table of Contents for the *Methodenbuch* reads as follows:[2]

> *First Part*
> I. Regarding the Complete Plan of the Book
> II. Continuation, Especially Regarding the *Elementarwerk*
> III. Of the Relationship of Secular Schools to Churches
> IIIa. Attempt at a Contribution to a Plan for the Education and Instruction of Princes
> IV. Of Education in Civilized Classes [*gesitteten Ständen*]
> V. Continuation: Of Instruction
> VI. Particularly Concerning Instruction in Languages
> VII. Of the Religion of Youth
> VIII. Of the Different Education of Sons and Daughters
> *Second Part*
> IX. Of State Supervision [*Staatsaufsicht*] over Morality, Education, Schools, and the Sciences
> X. Of the Encyclopedia for Instruction and for Readers

Chapter I is only three pages long, and is not subdivided into any sections. Basedow begins by informing readers that the basic plan for the book was first presented in his 1768 work, *Vorstellung an Menschenfreunde*. But then he gets down to business:

> The morality and happiness of the human race are now ... in great danger and decline ... The sources of this evil are for the most part the universities. Nevertheless, it is a futile wish to improve this incessant river of the scholarly class ... as long as the high schools and elementary schools are not improved. For the river receives its essence from the brooks that flow into it, from whose confluence it comes into being.

MB I; in G: 16–17

Although Basedow is known primarily as a reformer of elementary and secondary school education, he is also not shy about criticizing German universities—a reflection, in part, of his own personal experience at Leipzig and Kiel universities. But as this passage makes clear, he believed that fundamental educational reform must start at the beginning. What is needed is fundamental bottom-up transformation, not top-down reform.

Chapter II, which is also quite short, is essentially yet another pitch for Basedow's forthcoming *Elementarwerk*. "Children themselves, when one acts according to my provision, should love no game and no delight as much as this book [viz., the *Elementarwerk*], which is organized according to their nature and elucidated throughout with instructive copper engravings" (MB II; in G: 20).

Chapter III, "Of the Relationship of Secular Schools to Churches," another very short chapter, opens by stressing the underlying unity of the world religions: "Jews, Muslims [*Mahomedaner*], and Christians (in their different churches and sects) stand both in complete agreement with each other as well as with true naturalists concerning the content of some very important religious propositions" (MB III; in G: 21). These propositions, he continues, "I will prove through all possible proofs from nature and experience ... But instruction in a revealed religion ... I gladly leave to the individual churches and their teachers" (MB III; in G: 21). Schools should emphasize the connecting points between different religions, not their doctrinal differences. Similarly, the forthcoming "*Elementarwerk* will be absolutely useful [*vollkommen brauchbar*] without any offense to conscience not only for children of all Christians but also to Israelites and Muslims" (MB III; in G: 22). Toward the end of his discussion Basedow stresses the importance of intellectual content over origin, what over where:

> In such important matters as those that concern the human race and the improvement of instruction and study for countries, it should never be asked "from whom?" but rather "what is proposed?" ... Can Euclid's *Elements* not be useful, because he was a pagan? ... Is it forbidden for Protestants to hear the political truths of a Montesquieu ... because he was a Catholic?
>
> MB III; in G: 24–5

Basedow recast much of the material in Chapter IIIa ("Attempt at a Contribution to a Plan for the Education and Instruction of Princes") in his 1771 work, *Agathokrater oder: Von der Erziehung künftiger Regenten, nebst Anhang und Beilage* (The Good Ruler, or: On the Education of Future Sovereigns, together with an Appendix and Supplement—see Basedow 1771c). He sent a copy of the latter book to Kaiser Joseph II,[3] for which he received a royal medallion. Meier finds it "strange, that a man would want to write on the education of princes who had never associated with children of this kind, much less instructed them" (M: II: 309). But in fact this particular chapter played a decisive role in Prince Leopold Friedrich Franz of Anhalt-Dessau's generous invitation to Basedow to move to Dessau in late 1771 to establish what would later become the Philanthropin. For the prince was "intrigued particularly" (Landschoof 1933: 173) with the chapter in the *Methodenbuch* concerning the education of princes.

Basedow opens Chapter IIIa by asking:

> How should princes be brought up and educated? This is one of the most important questions for the fatherland, for the ruling house [*das regierende Haus*], for the court, and for moralists ... If only the hundredth part of what I will say should somehow work out for the good of the education of princes, then all the trouble over the remaining ninety-nine parts by a friend of humanity will be amply repaid. In this hope I shall express my thoughts briefly.
>
> MB IIIa; in G: 27

He then offers a detailed list of thirty-three recommendations concerning the education of princes:

1. No matter how young the prince may be, particularly if he is destined to rule, all care must be taken to prevent him from boredom, irksome work, fear, and anger ... (MB IIIa; in G: 28).
2. Everything which one seems to need through a violation of these rules for one's knowledge, physical exercise, and obedience is a real harm [*wahrer Schaden*] (MB IIIa; in G: 28).
3. No *costs* are too great for the state, if through their use the education and instruction of the future ruler can be made even the least degree better ... (MB IIIa; in G: 28).
4. A prince must never be brought up and instructed alone, without the company [*Gesellschaft*] of other youths ... (MB IIIa; in G: 28).
5. Next to his rooms, the prince must also have a special garden, which may be arranged or changed according to the purpose of his instruction ... (MB IIIa; in G: 28).
8. A young prince must not read any more than is required to acquire and retain this skill [of governing]. Also, he must not write more when he does not enjoy it ... (MB IIIa; in G: 29).
9. A prince must have at least three full-time teachers ... one with the name of "teacher," two perhaps with the name of "companion" ... (MB IIIa; in G: 29).

11. Because it is not necessary that princes ... know how to write in an orthographically correct manner or avoid seldom-occurring errors in speech, paradigms [*Paradigmata*] and grammar are simply no occupation for them (MB IIIa; in G: 29).
12. It is not necessary that a sovereign be a superb master in any other art than the art of ruling ... [But] since he is seen by the people when he rides or dances, in these arts a prince should be at the highest degree of decency [*Anständigkeit*] ... (MB IIIa; in G: 29).
13. The future ruler and the sons of the aristocrats who may someday be of service to him are the only ones of whom it is expected that they have a full knowledge of all agricultural products and manufacturing in the realm ... From the age of eleven until fifteen, the prince should devote two hours each day to studying these products and the necessary layout of the workshops (MB IIIa; in G: 29–30).
14. The prince should know his own country—the notable regions, shorelines, mountains, mountain passes, fortresses, buildings, public amusements, and, when there are several religions, their worship service customs ... (MB IIIa; in G: 30).
15. From the eleventh or twelfth year onward a prince must spend about two months each year traveling in his own country ... (MB IIIa; in G: 30).
16. ... The prince must learn to respect highly the farmer, the gardener, the shepherd, the fisherman, the hunter, the cobbler, the tailor, the sailor, the freight-carrier, the blacksmith, the mason, the carpenter, the cabinet maker, the wood cutter, the water carrier ... (MB IIIa; in G: 30).
17. Those customs and verities which if misjudged put princes and rulers in great danger must be learned through constant repetition in verses and written maxims ... (MB IIIa; in G: 30).
18. Skill in difficult algebraic calculations is absolutely superfluous in a prince ... His knowledge of mathematical truths must concern first and foremost the practical parts of geometry, mechanics, and architecture (MB IIIa; in G: 31).
19. The history of art and artists, which would actually be useful for a prince, must be set up in an elementary fashion ... (MB IIIa; in G: 32).
20. ... A prince must know the history of his own country very well, but not actually as it is written about in public books [*öffentlichen Büchern*]. It seems to me that a prince should have a special historical manuscript to compose the best governance of his land ... only for the use of the rulers and the privy council (MB IIIa; in G: 32).

21. Skill in speaking is necessary for a prince... The teachers and companions must possess the gift of skill in speaking. If, as I have advised, the greatest part of instruction consists in instructive conversation... then all rules and artificial words of rhetoric, which he does not yet know, can and must remain unknown to him (MB IIIa; in G: 33).
22. I hurry on to the actual virtues of princes. These are tender love of humanity without dreadful soft-heartedness, proper confidence in princely interaction with all classes, the habit of not carrying out anything for someone without advice and insight... and finally, the capacity to rule in the future (MB IIIa; in G: 33).
24. ... It is very useful if the prince, from youth onward, is accustomed in every way to see and speak with human beings from all classes as well as from the common herd. The castle guards, parades, marketplaces, and harbors... all provide opportunities for this (MB IIIa; in G: 34).
26. ... A full-grown prince in his manly years should know how to rule in a wise manner... This art consists in the capacity to know human beings, in the wise use of legislation and the judiciary, the use of the public treasury, and the establishment of a military system (MB IIIa; in G: 35).
27. Skill in the knowledge of human beings [*Menschenkenntniß*] is required... The prince should be taught how difficult it is to know human beings and to surmise their intentions (MB IIIa; in G: 35).
28. The wisdom of legislation follows for the most part from love of humanity and a very exact knowledge of one's country... Nevertheless, some exercises are still necessary for it... (MB IIIa; in G: 35).
29. A prince should pass judgment in the highest court exactly as seldom as he himself invents laws [*Gesetze erfinden*], but he must nevertheless be able, as often as he wishes, to examine whether the proposed laws are good and whether the pronouncements [*Ansprüche*] of his judges are in accordance with them. He must have exercises in the administration of justice or jurisdiction... (MB IIIa; in G: 36).
31. As to what a prince should be prepared to do as ruler in the observation of international law [*Völkerrechts*] and military affairs, a writer who understands nothing of either of them should give no advice (MB IIIa; in G: 37).
32. I have mentioned neither some arts of instruction nor some very necessary exercises in certain virtues (for example, love of honor), not because I have forgotten them but because in regard to the prince there is nothing to say that I haven't already stated concerning the education of children of all civilized classes (MB IIIa; in G: 37).

33. Which religion the ruler must educate his prince in can be decided neither from the truth nor the value of the religion, because each person regards his own religion as the true and correct one, and the conscience of the ruling prince and father alone must decide which religious principles ... should have influence ... (MB IIIa; in G: 38).

Granted, there is a strategic intent behind all of this advice. Basedow knew that in his era effective pedagogical reform was only possible with the support of princes.[4] Pragmatically speaking, the chief value of Chapter IIIa lies not in the specific content of his advice regarding the education of princes, but rather in the amount of attention and financial support he was soon to receive from royalty and heads of state. It was huge.

Chapter IV of the *Methodenbuch* ("Of Education in Civilized Classes") opens with the following claim:

> The primary goal of education should be to prepare children for a publically useful [*gemeinnützigen*], patriotic, and happy life. A respectful station in life, an ample income, learning, artistic skill, and a pleasant outward appearance are advantages which one may provide for one's children only in such a way that they do not endanger the primary goal.
>
> MB IV.1; in G: 42

In Section 2 (Chapter IV is subdivided into fourteen sections), Basedow offers some enlightened, naturalistic advice on early childcare:

> The cradle is superfluous [*überflüssig*]. With benefit and without danger I have used a gradually cooler bath with very young children. I have accustomed very young children to raw air, damp weather [*rauhe Luft, an nasses Wetter*] and light clothing. I find it true, that they need much sleep, but as soon as possible with increasing maturity they should be accustomed to early rising. Some exercise in swimming I regard as beneficial ... A hard bed, whose linen is often changed, is more healthful to children than a soft, too warm and comfortable feather bed ... The simplest foods are best. However, a lot of salt, spice, wine, and warm drink are very harmful. No meat before the third year; bread, vegetables, and fruits should be their usual food; thin beer their usual drink ... As early as possible they must be accustomed to move all of their limbs in every way that will later be necessary ... If they lie on the ground after a fall, there is no new danger: pick them up slowly and quietly, provided that they cannot help themselves, so that they are not needlessly frightened. Fresh air in the child's room is an important and nevertheless often neglected means for health.
>
> MB IV.2; in G: 42–3[5]

In Section 3 Basedow turns to the topic of obedience (*Gehorsam*). Surprisingly, despite his famous emphasis on "learning as play" and his opposition to corporal punishment in school, he is a strong defender of discipline and conformity:

> The first strong medicine is *obedience* or the inclination to follow the will of another in an orderly manner as a predominant motive. This inclination can come into being simply from love and trust; it can also gradually develop at the beginning from fear of the special consequences of displeasure [*des Unwillens*] ... No one may doubt the importance of this simple virtue [*dieser kindlichen Tugend*].
>
> MB IV.3; in G: 44

He also admits to a rare change of mind on the topic:

> Actually, I had been of the opinion that one must reason with children as soon as possible concerning the causes for the command. But through reflection and experience I have found that the certainty of obedience is thereby delayed ... A command is an explanation of the will [*eine Erklärung des Willens*] and nothing more. To cite reasons for it is only necessary in advice and instruction. Not infrequently children will become so confused [*so zerstreut*] by the presentation of multiple reasons that they do not correctly understand or remember the content of the command. Furthermore, there are those parents and teachers who are accustomed to rationalize [*zum Vernünftelen*] by their commands, often in dangerous situations, to express completely invalid or very insufficient reasons: as a result they hinder the growth of children's insight, even if, in some cases, obedience is not thereby hindered.
>
> MB IV.3; in G: 46

In Section 4 Basedow turns to the topic of reward and punishment:

> Reward the good, even if it has not been previously demanded, so that future stimulations to the opposite [*Reizungen zum Gegentheile*] do not gain the upper hand ... Do not be extravagant in praise, for the understanding of children is so tractable that through praise one can make them do everything one wants, even if it is not pleasant by nature ... A bouquet of flowers, a ribbon, a picture, a small mirror, a well-bound book, a polished writing box, a pencil, a special place at the table, the company of this or that person, a visit to this or that place, permission to imitate the parents in this or that manner, in short, countless objects and liberties [*Freiheiten*] can be made into rewards.
>
> MB IV.4; in G: 47

In his discussion of punishment, he begins with an apology:

Oh, if only I were permitted not to speak of *punishments*! And indeed, if children had no bad examples and corrupters [*Vorführer*] among their housemates and playmates, if the parents and teachers devoted enough time and care to it, if they observed the above rules regarding advice and rewards, then the disobedience of children would not only be rare, but it could also be successfully dealt with through very mild means [*sehr gelinde Mittel*].

MB IV.4; in G: 47

Unfortunately, children (not to mention adults) do sometimes need to be punished, but here enlightened teachers and parents need to learn about the proper limits of punishment. For instance, neither solitary confinement nor punishments arrived at in a state of anger are justifiable:

> Through darkness, solitude, and confinement [*Gefängnis*] children are either not improved, or at the same time they are filled with harmful prejudices [*schädliche Vorurtheilen*] ... [And] we may not carry out any punishments in anger, rather we should wait until we are rational again.
>
> MB IV.4; in G: 48

Section 5 deals with the social dimension of education: "The best education has some difficulties, unless more children are educated *together*, or if the only child of the parents does not associate with other playmates of his own age. This is more necessary in the tenderest days of youth than in the following years" (MB IV.5; in G: 50). Basedow also emphasizes here that parents and teachers must be in agreement with each other concerning children's education: "If one wants to make the education of the heart of young children easier, every person in the home must be brought into agreement regarding this goal ... The agreement of both parents and teachers is the most important point" (MB IV.5; in G: 50). And he recognizes that some of the most important goals of education—particularly as regards character development—are best achieved outside of the classroom:

> Education is the most important thing in all of life. Morality makes the strongest demands on the best education. Therefore I consider it indispensable that every family have in its neighborhood a group of sensible friends who try to win the trust of children, to make moral education easier through the presentation of such matter as redounds to the advantage of the parents and teachers ... Thus three or four sensible families should meet often, agree upon some good proposals as well as carry them out, with the goal of making the education of their children easier through such means ... But, oh God! How far are we still from moral perfection?
>
> MB IV.5; in G: 50–1

In Section 6 Basedow offers some practical advice on self-control:

> Some *moderation* of sensual desires, some *power* over a necessary revulsion [*nöthigen Ekel*], some *patience* with adversity and pains, and some *steadfastness* in danger are useful for young children, and can be promoted through certain conduct of the parents and guardians. Do not be too hasty to satisfy their innocent sensual desires; accustom them to negative answers, refuse them something now and then merely with the intention that definite desires for certain things whose enjoyment is often impossible will not be strengthened, and with that it remains easier for children to endure quietly the denial of many requests.
>
> MB IV.6; in G: 53–4

And (despite Basedow's strong association with learning-as-play pedagogy) he also emphasizes that children need to be taught early on that life is not all fun and games: "In describing human life and world conditions you must never forget to make young people aware of the normal mixture of good and evil and at the same time the greater sum total of good: *Now you have health and joy; but, my child, it will change; you will also feel pains, hardship, and frustration* [*Verdruß*]" (MB IV.6; in G: 56).

At the end of Section 6 he also offers some advice on physical education:

> When their limbs have the proper strength and flexibility, accustom them in a safe fashion to those *movements* which at times are necessary and which, when one has not practiced, are dangerous; accustom boys, for example, to swimming, to going over a narrow footbridge,[6] to letting themselves down a rope, to sitting firmly on a horse, or guiding it and stopping it in riding; to go down hills and then to climb them, to jump over small graves and fences [*kleine Gräben und Zäune*], to use the pogo stick [*Springstock*], to get out of the way of a thrown ball, to flee from a dog that is pursuing them, to go over smooth ice, and so forth.
>
> MB IV.6; in G: 56–7

The introduction of physical education into the school curriculum would soon become yet another innovation for which Basedow's Philanthropin became famous. As Kant remarks in his discussion of physical education in the *Lectures on Pedagogy*: "Since the Dessau Philanthropin has led the way here with its example, many experiments of this sort have been made with children in other institutes" (Päd 9: 467).

In Section 7 Basedow offers some advice concerning vindictiveness and envy:

> Seek in every way to remove *vindictiveness* and *envy*, those furies of human beings, from your children. Earnestly forbid your servants to ascribe the

accidental frustration of children to innocent bodies, animals, and persons, and to strike these so-called mean things [*diese sogenannten häßlichen Dinge*] for their false slander.

MB IV.7; in G: 57

And he repeats his earlier warnings against anger-fuelled corporal punishment and the need for a more rational approach to punishment: "All blows, pushing, and throwing from disgust [*aus Widerwillen*] are an unpardonable misdeed toward your children ... One of the first moral truths that children can understand is that *evil must never be returned by evil by a reasonable man, except with the intention of preventing a repetition of wrong*" (MB IV.7; in G: 57).

Section 8 contains advice on sincerity and dissimulation in both children and adults:

Accustom children very early to *sincerity* [*Aufrichtigkeit*] in word and in deed; be yourself as sincere and honest as virtue demands under the present world circumstances. If you permit yourself some dissimulation [*Verstellung*], make sure that children seldom or never notice it, and as soon as they come to a degree of understanding, make them aware of the reasons why a wise and virtuous man is justified and obligated at times to use some *dissimulation* in the case of the foolish, the deceitful, and the evil-minded, who would either misunderstand or misuse the truth.

MB IV.8; in G: 59

Although Basedow is clearly not an absolutist with regard to the duty to tell the truth when it comes to adults, he does urge that children should be taught to always tell the truth:

But even in earliest youth let it be a law [*Gesetz*] for your children, one whose violation must not be pardoned, to utter no untruth either to their superiors or to the disadvantage of others. Let such lies bring about their own harm, and for a while regard the small liars as children whom one would dare not believe ... Children often utter *a few falsehoods* without evil intent, merely in order to be able to give an account of something.

MB IV.8; in G: 59

Section 9 deals officially with modesty and chastity, "the dangerous parts of some good books," as Basedow remarks in his section title (see G: viii). But, as we saw earlier in Chapter 1, parts of it can also be viewed as an enlightened primer on sex education, a topic that would later play a prominent role in the Philanthropin curriculum:

> *Modesty* is the strongest fortification of chastity, and is necessary among civilized people [*gesitteten Völkern*]. If circumstances permit, give each child not only a special bed, but also a separate room for sleeping and dressing, which is at the same time a special room. Children of different sexes must neither sleep together nor undress in each other's presence. I would like to advise light nightclothes, through which nakedness would be covered with certainty. Accustom your children, when possible, to be alone in secret places during the evacuation of bodily waste.
>
> MB IV.9; in G: 60

He continues with similar advice concerning modesty for another ten lines or so, but then there is a definite shift of emphasis:

> Of the procreation of animals and human beings, one should speak with even young children, at least from the tenth or twelfth year, with truthfulness,[7] though not entirely in detail, seriously and frequently with the proper expressions, as with other natural phenomena, in relation to God's providence, so that they may be acquainted with these ideas in the right way. If one seeks to conceal these natural things entirely, or satisfies their curiosity through fables,[8] then without the knowledge of parents or guardians, in such years as the abuse of them may be quite possible, experiences of the truth will strongly tempt their new desires, and in a harmful manner. They will discuss the newly discovered secrets with one another, whose dangerous consequences I dare not explain.
>
> MB IV.9; in G: 60

The most striking example of Basedow's emphasis on sex education in the Philanthropin curriculum is the first in the group of four copper engravings in plate XXIX of the 1774 *Elementarwerk*. It is described tersely in the "Content of the Copper Plates to the *Elementarwerk*" (which was probably written by Basedow's assistant, Christian Heinrich Wolke) as follows: "Plate XXIX... a) Preparation during pregnancy of the mother" (E, III: 27). The inclusion of this engraving was extremely controversial at the time. Including a picture of childbirth in a school textbook was—and in many regions today still is—a radical move. And a student discussion of its meaning (led by Wolke) was apparently featured in the public examination of the school held on May 13–14, 1776 in Dessau, as recorded in Letter IX of *Fritzens Reise nach Dessau*:

> Mr. Wolke brought out a painting, hung it up [on the wall] and then said: "Dear children, I am bringing you here a picture, which you have not yet seen, but I am telling you beforehand that it is concerned with the most serious thing in the world, therefore you be serious too!" And the children were. And now I must tell you, dear mother, what was in the picture. First, a very pregnant woman was

sitting in a big grandfather's chair, and beside her stood her husband, holding her by the hand. On the other side stood a table, on it lay two small caps, one for a girl, the other for a boy, and under it stood a basin with water and a sponge in it. Then Mr. Wolke began to ask questions concerning what kind of woman this was, and why she looked so sad, and why her husband was holding her hand: and then the small pupils said that it was a pregnant woman, and that the one standing next to her was her husband, who wanted to comfort her, for soon she would be in great danger and could perhaps even die ... "Listen, dear children," he said, "consider once what your mother has undergone for you! She has been in danger of death, and for your sake she has suffered unspeakable pain, your parents already cared for you before you came into the world: do you think then, that you could ever be thankful enough to them?"

In R: 231

Section 10 of Chapter IV sounds stereotypically German: "Of the Promotion of Diligence [*Fleiß*], Order, and Cleanliness" (G, viii), and begins as follows:

Diligence, love of order, and *cleanliness* are virtues in which children also need some preliminary exercise. Speak in their presence of the need for diligence, but never with frustration. Don't say to them: "*I'm pleased to have survived the arduousness of this work;*" rather, "*I'm glad to have ended this good performance and after some recuperation I can begin another task*." Show children often that the greatest number of happy [*vergnügter*] human beings is not to be found among those that give the most time to their own pleasures, but among those who, through choice or necessity, work diligently ... Young children from four or five years on should gradually and when possible become accustomed to work, without force, and indeed only to such tasks as exercise the limbs and strengthen health.

MB IV.10; in G: 62

Basedow's emphasis on *Fleiß* here helps to dispel the common complaint that students at his school did not learn the value of hard work, but at the end of this passage we also see a hint of two additional themes of Philanthropinist pedagogy: preparing students for the work world and the importance of physical education. Both of these emphases mark a clear departure from traditional curricula. Later in Section 10 he returns to the theme of an education that will help prepare students for the real world, linking it now with one of his dominant concerns—learning as play:

The cabinet maker, the carriage maker, the blacksmith, the weaver, the book binder, the pharmacist, the grocer, and others must from time to time be persuaded to teach such boys ... In youth one has therefore to see a double type of diligence; in the above-mentioned manual work and in study. The latter must be less sour [*weniger sauer*] to them than the former, and at the beginning its goal must be unnoticed and promoted through instructive play [*lehrreiches Spiel*].

MB IV.10; in G: 63

In Section 11 Basedow turns to the topics of charity (*Wohltätigkeit*) and service (*Dienstfertigkeit*):

> I continue on to *charity* and *service*. Show philanthropic compassion before your children whenever you see misery, not merely in words, but where it is possible and advisable, in deed. "*The man is miserable; I must help him as much as I can. What would we wish, if we were in his position* [?]" ... Practice many acts of charity and service in the presence of your children ... Among civilized families there will be only a few who after mature reflection will not regard it as a duty (especially when the state demands no contribution for poverty) to use at least five percent of their yearly income, and of their savings at least ten percent, for good deeds ... Notify your children, as soon as they can count, and accustom them, from the weekly or annual money that is entrusted to them for their pleasure, to voluntarily use such a deduction for good deeds ... Praise your children, when they are compliant, but do not punish them, for charity cannot be forced. You should say, "*people love charitable children more than the others;*" and with these words a pleasant result should now and then be associated, and then shaming of selfishness is unnecessary.

MB IV.11; in G: 65–6

In Section 12 Basedow turns to love of honor, and how to instill it in children:

> In education a great deal must aim at awakening the souls of children to noble love of honor and to guarding against ambitious vanity. They must learn to protect the honor of others as their own ... Reprimand them only in their presence, if you must; never scold them, and praise them as often as you can.

MB IV.12; in G: 66–7

His recommendations on how to instill love of honor in children are also worth citing:

> Place before your children true *patterns* or ones fabricated with probability, which they can already imitate in accordance with their years; speak of these patterns always with great pleasure, and wish often that they become similar to them; and compare without further reprimand or rebuke their imperfect actions with the perfection of their patterns. If they become worthy of reprimand,

never take from them the hope that they will soon again attain honor ... For the children who are increasing in age, prepare a white book and a black book; in the one, write down the particularly good deeds, and in the other, the particularly bad deeds. From time to time, read parts of the books to them, and at certain times let there be a family ceremony, at which, for each good deed which appears in the book, a mark of praiseworthy conduct be noted, and for every bad deed, a mark of blameworthiness, according to the agreement of the friends taking part, and let them be balanced against one another in order to judge, according to the nature of the remaining sum, the quantity of certain good deeds.

MB IV.12; in G: 67[9]

In Section 13 he offers readers advice on how to inculcate "civil and economic prudence [*bürgerlichen und ökonomischen Klugheit*]" (G: viii) in their children:

We need to exercise our children in *prudence*; that is, in the skill of discovering and applying infallible or probable means to permissible ends. Instruction will fulfill the greatest part of this goal ... Much *social intercourse* with adults as well as with children, and selected *stories* of specific types of prudence, and of the effects of ignorance and imprudence will also contribute much to it. However, among the sciences natural history is first and foremost, and practice in measuring probabilities is an excellent aid to prudence. The supervisor, or whoever represents his position, must at times accustom children to be attentive to many circumstances of a matter, without passing over any of them. Another exercise is to accustom them to give attention only to the more important matters in many circumstances, and to progress with attention from one point to another, being attentive at once with both eyes and ears ... As soon as the understanding permits, one should make them take an interest in those goals they could achieve in a week, in a month, or in a year, and for the sake of which something must happen almost every day. ... In order that they gradually become accustomed to the careful *use of money*, give your children, from about their ninth year on, if they can already count and write, some money in hand that is adequate not only for minor needs of clothing, writing materials, and the like, but also from which a portion remains that they may use as they please, but with the exception that certain types of expenditure remain forbidden to them. For example, no *gambling* must be allowed before the age of sixteen or eighteen.

MB IV.13; in G: 67–8

Section 14—the final (and by far the longest) section of Chapter IV—is subdivided into seven parts, and deals primarily with relations between children and adults:

> Something very important still remains regarding the advantageous *relationships of youth toward their parents, guardians,* and other *adults*... Your birthday parties and even your wedding anniversaries should be family celebrations in which the children take an especially pleasant interest. Such arrangements are very helpful in properly grounding love and respect for you in their hearts. Your presence is a great good for them: but the usual enjoyment will remain more pleasant for them if you do not seem overwhelmed with it.
>
> MB IV.14; in G: 69

In the third edition of the *Methodenbuch* (1773—this is the edition that Göring has reprinted in his anthology, and from which I have been citing), Basedow concludes Book IV with nearly twenty pages of citations from the work of "a Swiss philosopher" (MB IV. *Zusätze*; in G: 72), a.k.a. "the wise Rousseau" (MB IV.14; in G: 70). All of the citations are from Rousseau's *Émile* (1762), and while Basedow promises readers that he "has only borrowed what is useful from him, when he thinks or says it better than I can" (MB IV. *Zusätze*; in G: 72), his excessive quoting from Rousseau in this part of the *Methodenbuch*, has, as noted earlier, contributed to the widespread tendency to view him as only a "mediocre thinker" (Parker 1912: 216) whose "root-ideas," as put forth "in his 'Book of Method,' and other writings, are those of Rousseau" (Quick 1896: 279). But, as demonstrated earlier, Basedow in fact developed all of his central pedagogical concepts and theories on his own, at least thirteen years before the publication of Rousseau's *Émile*, when he working as a private tutor for the von Qualen family in Borghorst. His abundant and imprudent quoting from *Émile* can be partly explained simply as a desire to ride on the coattails of someone who was fast becoming one of Europe's most influential authors.

Book V is entitled "Continuation: Of Instruction," and is divided into eight sections. It begins on the following moralistic note:

> *Instruction* [*Unterricht*], in the civilized classes, is indeed an important part of *education* [*Erziehung*] but (in comparison with the culture [*Bildung*] of the heart toward virtue, which can also occur without formal instruction), merely the *smallest part*. For it is possible to educate a child to a considerable degree of virtue, prudence, modesty, and happiness even if he never learns to read, write, or memorize, and instead of all formal instruction only enjoys an instructive social intercourse [*lehrreichen Umgangs*]... For the years of early youth belong, for the most part, to growth, liveliness, the exercise of the body, and to interest in outer activities [*äußerlichen Handlungen*], but not to exercises of understanding and memory.
>
> MB V.1; in G: 93

Educating the heart toward virtue is the primary goal of Philanthropinist education—not memorizing facts and figures. Toward the end of Section 1, Basedow also touches on two other core themes of Philanthropinist education: the joy of learning (which teachers are to inculcate in young students by devising games to help them learn) and a well-structured curriculum that is age-appropriate and in line with children's cognitive development:

> The *knowledge*, therefore, which a wise man may expect in the first years of youth, must stand in a well-thought-out relationship to the goal of the whole education. Not a great deal, but with joy! [*Nicht viel, aber mit Lust!*] Not a great deal, but in an elementary arrangement which progresses from the easier to the more difficult, and allows no gaps and weakness to remain in the foundation that with time can harm the entire structure!
>
> MB V.1; in G: 94

In Section 2 Basedow again emphasizes the importance of the joy of learning, but now he uses this theme to argue against the use of corporeal punishment and compulsion in school:

> I must advise against all *compulsion* [*Zwang*], in order to promote industriousness in school, as a highly dangerous matter... Most of the actions that one wants to enforce in school, are by nature not enforceable. One punishes a child today, for example, so that tomorrow he will be industrious in this or that way. It is true that the method does not always miss the goal, but it is always unnecessary, and, it seems to me, harmful, on account of the side effects ... If one makes instruction as pleasant as one can according to the child's nature, if one does not want to lead the child to a height where he must feel dizzy, if one lightens the difficulties of schoolwork as much as possible through imperceptible instruction from social intercourse ... then I assert firmly that none of the students who are able to serve the public good through industriousness at school [*durch Schulfleiß*] could make themselves guilty of laziness at school [*Schulfaulheit*] for a long time.
>
> MB V.2; in G: 95–6

In Section 3 he extends the argument against compulsion to include forced memorization work—a standard means of instruction in schools of his day, and another traditional curricular tool that the Philanthropin would later fight against: "Never plague your children with the command that they busy themselves with memorization ... Never let them memorize a *list of words* which will one day be forgotten without loss" (MB V.3; in G: 98).

Section 4—"Of Pedantry in both Knowledge of Words and Facts" (G: ix) presents yet another argument against boring curricula that stifle students' natural capacity to learn:

> Teaching facts must actually give the understanding new ideas [*neue Vorstellungen*], not merely fill the memory with words. Schools and teachers, however, can just as well be guilty of a very harmful pedantry if they push word-knowledge instead of fact-knowledge, as when they burden youth with so much and such fact-knowledge, which is either useless to them, or in case there is some need for it, could be known better through inquiry and experience, or through books later on. A small measure of useful and complete knowledge is better than a mixture of numerous kinds of knowledge that appear to have been thrown together by chance, and to none of which can the necessary attention be given due to lack of time.
>
> MB V.4; in G: 99

In place of this hodgepodge of disparate kinds of knowledge that appear to have been thrown together by chance, Basedow instead advocates a more unified curriculum centered around "a cabinet of natural objects and models"—a theme which he will elaborate on at greater length later in the *Elementarwerk*:

> I turned to the resolution of urging instruction in fact-knowledge only so far as it is necessary in order to make an understanding of it practical through some applications, to help oneself under ordinary circumstances, and to understand useful languages and writings about trades [*Schriften von Gewerben*] ... At various times I have mentioned a cabinet of natural objects and models which would be far more useful than copperplates[10] in teaching languages as well as facts [*Sachen*].
>
> MB V.4; in G: 100

In this passage we also see Basedow's repeated emphasis on the need for a more practical and worldly education, one that will better prepare students for life outside the academy.

Section 5 is entitled "Of Instruction in Morals" (G: ix), and begins as follows:

> Next to the publicly useful truths [*gemeinnützigen Wahrheiten*] of mathematics and natural history, *ethics* is the most excellent fact-knowledge [*die vozüglichste*[11] *Sacherkenntnis*]. But whether it will be of much or little use, depends on the choice of method. *Fear of the Lord is the beginning of wisdom*:[12] this sentence is true, but one must understand it such that its content does not contradict experience.
>
> MB V.5; in G: 100–1

He then offers readers twelve maxims that he believes comprise "the true genealogy [*die wahre Abstammung*] of moral knowledge" (MB V.5; in G: 101). These maxims include the following:

> 1) Seek happiness. 2) Pay attention to experience and advice, so that you find it [moral knowledge] all the easier and more surely... 11) Promote God's will for the common good of human beings, as much as it is in your power to do so. 12) But think primarily about what is best for your *neighbors* [*Nächsten*], that is, those human beings whose concerns you know, and whom you have the most certain opportunity to serve, and so forth.
>
> MB V.5; in G: 101–2

Section 6—"Of Instruction in History" (G: ix)—offers readers a limited defense of the value of history:

> Ethics and the rules of prudence are grounded on *experience*:[13] our own, however, is limited, and often comes too late; therefore we need information from strangers [*Nachricht von Fremden*]. Only in this aspect does *history* have a true worth, although the love for it at the beginning is perhaps based merely on natural thirst for knowledge of human beings.
>
> MB V.6; in G: 102

And in Section 7—"Of Instruction through Fables" (G: ix)—we find a qualified defense of the use of fables in moral instruction. The section begins as follows:

> Moral rules, when they are not confirmed through *narrative* [*nicht durch Erzählung bestätigt*], occupy only the understanding but not at the same time the imagination. However, such representations have neither a strong nor a lasting effect in the soul; they are easily forgotten and seldom repeated, because the repetition of them cannot be arranged differently other than through words, not through sight or through the recollection of sensory objects. On the other hand, when the rules can be confirmed through narratives, they find an easier entrance into the depths of the soul and the heart of the human being. For the *moral rule* is a universal truth which is thought by the understanding with abstraction or with omission [*mit Auslassung*].
>
> MB V.7; in G: 104

Basedow prefers true stories or narratives (*Erzählungen*) over fables (*Fabeln*), and he thinks that many unenlightened educators have allowed the latter to play too big a role in children's moral education: "Most fables aim at moral doctrines that children and early youth do not need. In each collection [of fables] known to me I find only a little that schools cannot do without" (MB V.7; in G: 105–6). The proper role of fables in moral education is thus quite limited: "I say only that we do not need fables, when we protect the best of each part of moral instruction, and have collected and brought into order invented narratives [erdichteten Erzählungen], which are not fables" (MB V.7; in G: 105).

Section 8—the last section in Chapter V—is entitled "Of Instruction through Pictures. Remark concerning the Copperplates of the *Elementarwerk*" (G: ix). Basedow's main points regarding instruction through pictures are as follows:

> I must still say something about the use of *paintings* and *copperplates* in the instruction of children. 1) Experience shows how much everything that looks similar to a picture pleases children, even if only everyday matters are represented, or things to which they have become accustomed to be indifferent. 2) The considerations and moral doctrines that are displayed by such figures are livelier than others, last longer, and are shared and repeated from one child to another. 3) During lessons one can give no conception of many sensory things without pictures [ohne Abbildung], because they are in foreign lands [ausländisch], or at least absent. 4) Through the help of pictures, the teacher is more easily understood when he repeats known facts in a foreign or a dead language ... [and] through this natural method of teaching children learn most easily and most quickly achieve skill.
>
> MB V.8; in G: 107

The note regarding the copperplates in the forthcoming *Elementarwerk* is rather long, and consists primarily of advice concerning the ordering and presentation of the plates. For instance, "the first panels must present objects which are already familiar to children before the picture [is seen]; for the transition from the presentation of the picture to the presentation of the object requires some exercise of the power of imagination" (MB V.8; in G: 107–8).

Chapter VI—"Particularly Concerning Instruction in Languages"—draws both on Basedow's earlier experience as a private tutor in the von Qualen family home in 1749–52 as well as on his 1752 Kiel dissertation, and is divided into seven sections. In Section 1 ("Proposals regarding the Best and Unrecognized Language Methods," G: ix), he condenses some of his proposals into numbered rules such as the following:

> 3) I regard it as useful that a child not be occupied with a foreign or dead language before the end of the sixth year ... 4) From the beginning of the seventh to the end of the eighth year ... the time of fact-instruction must be divided so that the child hears, reads, and speaks twice as much in the *French*

language as in the German. Then until the end of the twelfth year fact-instruction in the *Latin language* must occupy one half of the time.

MB VI.1; in G: 109

Other proposals, particularly regarding his more radical views on the limited place of grammar in language instruction, are listed after the numbered rules: "Yes, I am of the opinion that one could become a masterly author in a language without ever knowing anything of its grammar... [However,] I do not want to banish grammar from the range of studies [*Zahl der Studien*], but only to allocate it to the correct place at the end of the exercises in skill" (MB VI.1; in G: 109–10).

In Section 2 he addresses the objection that it is very difficult for families to secure qualified teachers (particularly in Latin) for their children with the following reply: "I answer that a decent number of such teachers must be cultivated in a seminar" (MB VI.2; in G: 110). Here Basedow is alluding to a key component of his future Philanthropin. From the start, the school was intended to be not just a progressive school for students but also a teacher-training institute. As he indicates in the title of a 1774 publication, the "Philanthropinum established at Dessau" was a school both "for Pupils and Young Teachers [*junge Lehrer*]" (DEP: title page). It was designed to be a "*mother school*" and "planting center [*Pflanzort*] of teachers for everyone" (DEP: XVI). In Section 2 he also refers to his earlier tutoring work with Josias von Qualen, noting that "at the beginning our studies took place unnoticed under the name of 'play', and due to his diligence frustration never or very seldom occurred, nor was compulsion used" (MB VI.2; in G: 111).

In Section 3 Basedow replies to another objection to his proposed method as follows:

> *Second objection*: The touted method of making a beginning in the Latin language through exercises of speech *is at any rate not possible in public schools*— Why not? Are the French teachers who, without vocabulary- and grammar-books, begin to teach thirty or forty students very happily and very early through conversation and later through reading, more capable of instruction than most of the Latin teachers? Or is the Latin language alone of such a special nature that one cannot speak it?
>
> MB VI.3; in G: 114

In principle, Latin is not radically different from other natural languages, and thus it should be teachable in the same manner. Similarly, in Section 4 he replies to the objection "that through my method boys would attain an incorrect and coarse skill in Latin, but not correct and genuine Latin" (MB VI. 4; in G: 115–16) by responding that this depends primarily on the skill and training of the specific teachers employed. "The teachers must not only be qualified to speak Latin, they must also speak it correctly"—and once "a seminar is established" at the future Philanthropin to achieve this goal, qualified candidates will no longer be lacking (MB VI.4; in G: 116). In Section 5 he attempts to rebut another objection:

> For (and precisely in this way is the *fourth objection* refuted), I merely want to shift the *classical authors* from the children's school to the gymnasium for students, and in this way I believe I will be acting not only in accordance with the dignity of these great men but also for the benefit of youth. Languages are only a means of study, not the highest end; everything must aim at fact-knowledge.
>
> MB VI.5; in G: 116–17

Section 6, "Of Grammar," addresses questions concerning when and how to focus on issues of grammar in teaching foreign languages. Basedow's conversation-based approach to foreign-language instruction does not ignore grammar, but he does advocate postponing instruction in grammar until later in the course of study, and he does have definite ideas about how to teach it:

> If one waits until the right time, and then chooses a reasonable method, one then finds less difficulty in *grammatical instruction* than one might think ... Without practice in the concepts of substance and quality, of relation, cause, action, object and effect, etc., all the work of grammatical instruction is futile or a disadvantageous overloading of the memory with things which through mere exercise in the language would be voluntarily presented by the imagination ... The grammar of the *vernacular language* must be the first thing for each student.
>
> MB VI.6; in G: 119–20

But the key point of Basedow's method of foreign-language instruction is the emphasis on learning through conversation. In the last section of Book VI he writes:

> According to my plan, the teacher must for the most part teach students by means of conversation; however, they must translate a great deal of well-known materials and be encouraged to have a real exchange of letters with their parents, teachers, friends, and playmates. That is, they must carefully set down in writing a great deal that they were otherwise accustomed to say only in a hurry.
>
> MB VI.7; in G: 121

And although he does recommend that students be exposed to "some notion and foretaste [*einigen Begriff und Vorgeschmack*] of the best-known sciences and of the different prose and poetry styles of eloquence" before the end of their studies, he also recommends that "more practice in the art of writing and taste and an orderly recitation of rhetoric and poetry is unnecessary before the fifteenth year" (MB VI.7; in G: 121).

Chapter VII—"Of the Religion of Youth"—is divided into fifteen sections. In Section 1 Basedow clarifies what he means by "religion":

> No matter how ambiguous the word "religion" may be, my readers may nevertheless easily remember that in the *Elementarwerk* I understand not more and not less by it than the real, complete, and active *belief in God*, the universal father of human beings, the sustainer of their souls after the death of the body, and the just rewarder [*gerechten Vergelter*] of good and evil.
>
> MB VII.1; in G: 122

Although this is an intentionally broad-based, nondenominational conception of religion, it is important to note that Basedow *does* believe that religion—in his nondenominational sense—should be taught in schools.

Sections 2 to 5 focus on the "Duties of Parents (also of Skeptics)" (G: ix) regarding the religious education of their children. First, they are obligated to see to it that *"their children, before they reach maturity, at least have this religion"* (MB VII.2; in G: 123)—viz., "religion" as defined in Section 1. Believers as well as "irreligionists" are both obligated to educate their children into this religion (MB VII.2; in G: 124), in part because of what Basedow sees as a strong connection between religion and moral virtue, as well as between virtue and happiness. "Hence I may also establish the truth, that virtue is a true means of earthly welfare. *Therefore an irreligionist who can still obey reason on this point and who truly loves his children must educate them toward virtue*" (MB VII.3; in G: 129). A "strong" but not quite a *necessary* connection, for as he says at the beginning of Section 4:

> However, I do not say that the care and prudence through which youth can be brought to an active belief in God as a future rewarder of good and evil are *the first and only means* to bring them to the path to virtue and afterward to maintain them there; much more do I regard this seemingly pious error [*fromm scheinenden Irrthum*] as one of the most dangerous. Nevertheless, it is ... the most certain and easiest means.
>
> MB VII.4; in G: 129

But (as if conceding to the limitations of this argument) he also warns readers in Section 5 that

I have nothing to accomplish with completely senseless or wild irreligionists who are no longer capable of any reasonable reflection whatsoever and do not love their children: rather I speak only with the others, and primarily with skeptics [*Zweifelern*] in whom reason and love of human beings have not entirely died out.

MB VII.5; in G: 131

In Sections 6 and 7 Basedow continues this imaginary discussion with skeptics and irreligionists by responding to two possible objections, but in Section 8 he presents to all readers one of his core religious doctrines: "*My first piece of advice is this: that we teach children no words or sentences whose meaning belongs somewhat to religion so long as they either associate no concepts whatsoever with them or extremely false ones*" (MB VII.8; in G: 135). Adults should not try to teach children religious doctrines until the children are mature enough to understand and evaluate what they are hearing. As we saw in the previous chapter, many conservative religious educators in Basedow's time took this as a direct assault on their professional obligations.

Basedow's core position that religious education should be age-appropriate then leads him to offer additional bits of advice in subsequent sections of Book VII. Each of them is in effect a subsidiary proposition derivable from the core claim. Thus his "*second piece of advice*" is that "we must *proceed very methodically or elementarily* in the endeavor for our religion," incorporating well-designed exercises in our teaching so that it "has been made understandable and can be effective" (MB VII.9; in G: 136). And ("*third piece of advice*") "if children are already well off [*vermögend*] with certain true religious propositions" but still lack a clear understanding of the concepts involved, "one should not allow this initially unavoidable incompleteness of their concepts" to remain (MB VII.10; in G: 137). Instead, examples need to be offered to students that will increase their grasp of core religious concepts.

> *Fourth piece of advice*: One must encourage children to no action that one calls *praying* and which for that reason is no prayer, because they do not understand the wording, or are incapable of the feelings which should be expressed or aroused through it. For such an exercise would directly contradict the first important piece of advice.
>
> MB VII.11; in G: 137

Teaching prayers to children before they are in a position to understand what they are saying is contrary to the true spirit of religion. However, at the same time ("*fifth piece of advice*") "*as soon as children are capable ... of thinking of an immortality after the death of the body . . . we must . . . not only hurry to get these concepts across to them, but also . . . present them as true*" (MB VII.12; in G: 138). But he immediately qualifies this advice in the next section when he writes: "*Sixth piece of advice: However, one must not extend the practice of the previous rule further than the proof of its use reaches*" (MB VII.13; in G: 140). The result is a kind of pragmatic tempering of the earlier advice to make religious education more age-appropriate. Religion is vitally important in human life, so one shouldn't wait too long to teach children about it. At the same time, children must first be in a cognitive position to understand religion's importance before they receive instruction in it.[14]

Section 14, in which Basedow presents his "*seventh piece of advice: the elementary order of bringing children to faith and to the conviction of religion*" (MB VII.14; in G: 141), also contains a list of seven main steps (several of which are subdivided into additional steps), and ends with another brief discussion of his famous "duty to believe [*Glaubenspflicht*]" doctrine (MB VII.14; in G: 143), according to which we have a duty to believe propositions that are necessary for human happiness, even if no rational proofs for the propositions exist. According to Basedow, belief in God and immortality are both necessary for human happiness, and so humans have a duty to believe in both. First introduced in his 1765 work, *Theoretisches System der gesunden Vernunft* (see Basedow 1765: esp. 5, 76, 144), Mendelssohn would later criticize Basedow's *Glaubenspflicht* in his *Morgenstunden* (1785; see Mendelssohn 2011). But as noted in the previous chapter, Basedow's *Glaubenspflicht* doctrine is also quite similar to Kant's later arguments for the postulates of God and immortality in the second *Critique* and elsewhere, and some have speculated that Mendelssohn's real target was in fact Kant.[15]

Section 15, "The Order in which the Propositions of Belief in Natural Religion Should Be Promoted," is the final section in Chapter VII, and concludes with an eleven-page list of notes in which he criticizes a number of philosophers, including his former teacher Reimarus, Mendelssohn, Wolff, and Baumgarten. Each of these notes constitutes a "warning of the harmful trust in bogus demonstrations [*Scheindemonstrationen*] of natural religion, which are not capable of strict demonstration" (G: x).

Chapter VIII—"Of the Different Education of Sons and Daughters"[16]—is, as noted earlier, a disappointment for contemporary readers. Here one finds no Enlightenment challenge to traditional norms. Boys and girls are different by nature; therefore they require different educations. As Basedow proclaims in the opening section ("Natural or Very Customary Differences [*Natürliche oder sehr gewöhnliche Unterschiede*] of the Sexes, on which the Art of Education is Based"—G: x):

> The *male sex* is by nature and through our customs [*von Natur und durch unsre Sitten*] more skilled to work a great deal, to take in experiences from a distance, to learn skills, arts, commercial arts or sciences; as a result to acquire needs [*Bedürfnisse zu erwerben*]; to hold offices, and to be able to use his superior strength to care for the family. All of this, and in many religions it is a divine command, gives man decisive dominion [*die entscheidene Herrschaft*] in the family... On the other hand, a *person of the other sex* is most skilled [*am geschicktesten*] in pleasing man through her charm ... She is under dominion [*unter der Herrschaft*], consequently she must know how to bear this; however, she has part of the dominion rule over children, tenants, and servants; she must therefore also possess the gifts and virtues of a domestic sovereign [*häuslichen Regentin*]. From this it follows that in the education of a daughter the performance of all of these duties which are in store for her must be made easier.
>
> MB VIII.1; in G: 159

A second, related weakness in Chapter VIII is Basedow's excessive quoting from Rousseau's *Émile*. He defers once again to "the already often-cited Swiss philosopher" because Rousseau "thinks with extraordinary acumen, he writes with an inimitable charm" (MB VIII.1; in G: 160). Sections 2 to 8—nearly fourteen pages in Göring's text—consist almost entirely of lengthy citations from *Émile*. Here Basedow essentially endorses without comment Rousseau's well-known views concerning the "duty *of chastity* in the female sex" (MB VIII.2; in G: 161), his claim that "the whole education of women ought to relate to men" (MB VIII.3; in G: 161),[17] his beliefs regarding "*the occupation, dependence, and gentleness* of the female sex" (MB VIII.4; in G: 162), with special reference to "*finery* [*Putz*] *and the graceful arts*" (MB VIII.5; in G: 164), "*talkativeness* [*Gesprächigkeit*] *and the necessary sciences of the more agreeable sex*" (MB VIII.6; in G: 165), and "*domesticity*" (MB VIII.7; in G: 167). In Section 8 he offers readers seven more pages of quotes from *Émile*, because "the philosopher makes many of these teachings perceptible to the senses through the example of his fictional *Sophie*" (MB VIII.8; in G: 168).

But in Section 9, when he turns to the topic of "Love and Marriage of Adult Daughters" (G: x), the excessively long quotes from *Émile* finally stop. And at this point Basedow does diverge slightly from Rousseau's strongly gendered views concerning education. For while the "Swiss philosopher" treats "Sophie or the Woman" exclusively as being destined to become a spouse, mother, and housewife, Basedow acknowledges that some daughters will not marry. How should they be educated? In Section 10 he writes:

> Because the fate of the family is variable, all parents must educate their daughters as much as they can to contentment and wise behavior, in case they are not sought in marriage. But for this I know no better means than that one make them skilled and adaptable in an agreeable *association* of happy and upright women, helpers in the education of their children or in the oversight of their domestic matters... One must therefore educate a daughter so that she becomes capable of educating the children of others.
>
> MB VIII.10; in G: 177

Contemporary readers will still find much to object to in this passage, but it is nevertheless one of Basedow's most progressive comments on the issue of *Mädchenerziehung*. For he acknowledges here that it is not every woman's destiny to become a spouse, mother, and housewife, and that a daughter's education should therefore not be constrained by this assumption. Some girls will lead independent lives as adults.

What sort of education does Basedow therefore recommend for girls, keeping in mind that some will "not be sought in marriage?" In Section 11 he writes:

> Girls must learn to speak intelligently and *with propriety what they resolve to say*; they must read clearly and according to the sense, but for them to be able to declaim eloquently or dramatically is superfluous. One must teach them to *write* legibly and with such lines that the appearance causes no displeasure.—In our regions I regard no *language* as necessary other than the vernacular and French... She must know the rules of meter and verse, but I won't give a penny to him who wants to make my daughter a *poet*. One must arrange some practice in *accounting and in bookkeeping*... Girls need *history, geography, mythology, knowledge of antiquity, natural history,* and *some philosophical knowledge* only when the mothers and attendants are accustomed to teaching them in an informative manner... *Concerning music, singing, dancing, and drawing* ... I wish that my daughter acquire as much of these skills as is necessary for her now and then with practice to amuse herself and arouse no disgust in casual critics. But I could not myself rejoice if she were to become an expert in this or that art.
>
> MB VIII.11; in G: 182

In sum, on Basedow's view girls do require a modest education, for those who don't marry will need to become "capable of educating the children of others." But in his final sentences in Book VIII he once again endorses the conventional norms that governed girls' education in eighteenth-century Europe:

> One must educate daughters for the possibility of a happy *marriage. And when they come to the proper age, I wish that* ... [they will be given] formal instruction in the duties and rules of maidenhood, of betrothals, of the married state, and of the wise conduct of a mother, a housewife, and female companion.
>
> MB VIII.11; in G: 184

However, Basedow's position on girls' education becomes more complicated when one looks at the education of his own daughter, Emilie. A star pupil at the Philanthropin, she received extensive personal tutoring from Basedow's assistant Christian Heinrich Wolke at an extremely young age—not just in the "female art" of pleasant conversation but also in mathematics and Latin. According to Wolke, by the age of four Emilie could already

> read printed and written German and Latin, knew a considerable number of natural objects and tools, together with their origin and use, distinguished mathematical lines, surfaces, and bodies with application to particular cases, counted forward or added to 100, counted backward or subtracted by ones or pairs from 20 or 21 to 0 or 1, practiced drawing and writing by following the copies in pencil which were set before her, [and] sometimes dictated a letter to her father.
>
> DEP: 47

And all of this knowledge was of course learned "through playing [*spielend*], that is, without exertion and without harmful sitting still" (DEP: 47). Fortunately, when it came to his own daughter's education, Basedow did not practice what he preached.

Chapter IX, which is divided into twenty-seven sections, is entitled "Of State Supervision over Morality, Education, Schools, and the Sciences" (G: x).[18] In Section 1, he proposes the establishment of a *"moral education council"* which would

> *concern itself with the morality of the nation* and in this department recommend necessary changes in the law. The jurisdiction over *all charitable institutions*, over *all correctional houses*, over *orphanages*, over *education of the young*, over [elementary] *schools, high schools*, and *universities*, over the *status of scholars* honored [*betitelten*] by the state, over *literature* [*Bücherwesen*], over *plays*, and over *artistic productions that serve for enjoyment*, in short, over everything that has a very clear influence on the morals of the nation ... [T]he entire oversight, whose parts naturally belong together, could well be entrusted to this moral education council and facilitated through subordinate colleagues and civil employees.
>
> MB IX.1; in G: 187–8

Some of this is clearly too authoritarian for contemporary liberal tastes. And it is unfortunate that Basedow, whose family personally experienced some of the devastating effects of political and religious authoritarianism and censorship, does not speak out more strongly in favor of freedom of expression:

> *Political and moral censorship*, which either hinders books not yet published or punishes those already published, cannot be abolished [*nicht aufgehoben*] to the advantage of human beings, rather it must with wise strictness or gentleness [*Gelindigkeit*] be retained or be replaced by something else. But what should I say of an authoritarian [*obrigkeitlich*], effectively mere theological censorship? This much is clear: once errors are protected with the rifles of theological censorship, truth cannot be victorious, indeed, it cannot even fight [*nicht einmal streiten*]. I will say no more, so that this work will not be rejected by such a censor.
>
> MB IX.9; in G: 190

And while he grants that university students, unlike younger elementary and high school students, "live in civil freedom in accordance with their maturity" (MB IX.17; in G: 198), he also wants to regulate their conduct, recommending that universities be placed not in "*heavily populated cities*" but in smaller communities where "supervision over morality would be more strictly practiced" (MB IX.19; in G: 198).[19]

However, Chapter IX is not wholly devoted to centralized political control over "everything that has a very clear influence on the morals of the nation." In Section 5 Basedow puts forward a proposal that is remarkably similar to recent efforts to outsource government services to private entities:

> Are *orphanages* beneficial [*nützlich*]? Or would it be better if one estimated their previous upkeep and then removed the children, placing them in groups of about half a dozen among poor families, particularly out in the country, where supervision could still be exercised? From youth up, let them continue with farming and horticulture, and with the stipulation that foster parents care for their life and health, promise them some reward at the end of their education.
>
> MB IX.5; in G: 189

But the main point to emphasize here is that Basedow sought to raise educational standards, and that he offered concrete proposals for achieving this goal. Some of his specific proposals are certainly open to criticism, but here as well—in an era when very few educational standards even existed and state oversight of education was virtually nil—Basedow was a very progressive voice. Most fundamentally, he was making an early case for public education. As he writes later in Chapter IX:

> At present, only the *churches* look after moral instruction, primarily in schools ... that are for the most part dependent on clergymen. Does it not matter to the state, in order to be secure, that those who in adulthood will achieve this or that degree of citizenship be instructed sufficiently in the duties of their class?
>
> MB IX.7; in G: 189–90

Chapter X, the final chapter of the *Methodenbuch*, is entitled "Of the Encyclopedia for Instruction and for Readers" (G: xi), and is partly a sketch of the forthcoming *Elementarwerk* as well as an outline of the school library that Basedow hoped to establish for high schools. Both projects were motivated in part by what Basedow perceived as "the great disorder in the usual style of teaching in schools" (G: xi), described in Section 1 as follows:

> Hardly does a child learn to stammer than he stammers something about commandments against adultery and about duties toward the government; he learns to talk about duties without knowing them ... The eight- or ten-year-old pupil chatters about phalanxes and legions, consuls and proconsuls, ovations and triumphs; and the thirteen-year-old barely begins to recognize and know the properties of a triangle, [or] that air is not nothing. What a pitiful order! And much greater are the errors in the more important method of leading the heart to virtue.
>
> MB X.1; in G: 209–10

The remedy for this pedagogical chaos, Basedow believed, involved a two-step process:

> I shall stay with my already-determined decision, to provide in the *Elementarwerk* for an orderly, progressive instruction until about the end of the fifteenth year—that is, to the time youths destined for the sciences taught at the Gymnasium will be admitted ... My plan for desired texts therefore has two parts: *first*, the *Elementarwerk*, which I intend for private instruction and schools, and for which I myself almost alone must guide the pen, *second*, an *elementary library in the gymnasia*.
>
> MB X.1; in G: 210

What Basedow envisioned with his *Gymnasienbibliothek* was not merely a well-organized library for high school students, but one that would also serve general readers and adult learners. As he writes in Section 2:

> This same small library that I wish for schools and gymnasia can and must be so constituted that even outside of the places of instruction the needs of every reader would be remedied through the proper use of it—those who regret either the brevity or bad quality or their own failing of former school instruction—by

filling the gaps, by instructing themselves in their own necessary areas of knowledge, and for this purpose, helping themselves by reading an elementary, well-ordered, and complete *encyclopedia*.

MB X.2; in G: 211

What were the proposed contents of the library? Basedow addresses this question in Section 3:

> *But what then belongs ... to such a cabinet-library or encyclopedia, whose general nature I have described above? ... First*, the elements or rudiments of much general knowledge must be in the work, which is to be in the first book and therefore can be called the *Elementarbuch*, in a useful admixture and alternation for the instruction of children, in order to make a beginning in *factual knowledge* ... Due to the many aims, which have been frequently indicated, this work must be accompanied by a collection of copper engravings. I maintain that the *Elementarbuch* must contain a mixture of elements of many types of knowledge ...

MB X.3; in G: 215–16

Ten more points follow this first one. His second point concerns the need to include an "easy reader:" "It is particularly necessary that a small *elementary book of the art of reading* be written (indeed, one in every national language). I have already delivered this in the small books, *For Parents and Teachers of all Classes* and *For Children of all Classes*"[20] (MB X.3; in G: 216). Basedow's third point outlines the natural science contents of the library:

> One of the *reference books* [*Hilfsbücher*] can introduce terms in *natural history* and *mathematics* [*Größenlehre*] ... namely, from arithmetic and geometry and through natural history, experiments, mathematical truths and through inductive reasoning over causes and effects ... This part will also require a number of copper plates and will end with the rudiments for a general understanding of the mechanical and fine arts.

MB X.3; in G: 216–17

His next point focuses on arithmetic:

> *Fourth*. The arithmetic of this book will be more theoretical than practical in the commercial trade ... There will follow a *reference book of domestic and commercial transactions* ... and finally such instruction in bookkeeping as is sufficient for all who are not destined for elaborate commercial activity, but which is sufficient and prepares them for understanding future tradesmen.

MB X.3; in G: 217

Basedow then turns to the coverage of history:

> *Fifth.* Just as necessary is a *reference book of history, and with many copperplates explaining world knowledge* [*Welterkenntniß*] ... The design will apply to everything historical that is of general use, to folk history, geography, genealogy, mythology, and ancient history.
>
> MB X.3; in G: 217

His sixth point focuses on the coverage of grammar:

> With the help of a necessary collaborator I will write *a grammatical reference book*, in the following four parts: a) A general preparation for instruction in grammar ... b) Application of this material to the German language ... c) For the unskilled, noteworthy differences between the French and German languages. d) An equally limited presentation of the differences of Latin from both.
>
> MB X.3; in G: 221

The seventh point touches on the need for a book on persuasive speaking and style: "In another reference book provision will be made for the benefit of the unskilled in the German language for exercises in persuasive speaking and for taste in various styles of good German works" (MB X.3; in G: 221).

In his eighth point Basedow turns to "*knowledge of the soul, ethics,* and *natural religion,*" emphasizing that "in this secular library I am not concerned with instruction in *church-religion*; rather, I leave it for parents or for church-teachers and church-schools" (MB X.3; in G: 221). The ninth point hints at closure, but Basedow is not done yet:

> *Ninth* ... In my opinion there is nothing further lacking in the encyclopedia and school library than *the general reference book for the elementary school library.* This will make all preceding parts fully useful as a single set. It will contain: a) an *alphabetical index* of the scattered materials in the complete work, with an indication of the books and places where they are to be found ... b) a *tabular arrangement of all the types of knowledge,* and ... the best *reference books* that one can use in case there is need for an expansion of knowledge. *Tenth.* One more point! This *Methodenbuch* is a necessary part of the entire work. It is continued in instructions to parents and teachers, how and when the individual books and plates are to be used ... *Eleventh.* Still one more point! The books of advice for the instruction of the young must also have another reference book, which can be called ... *The Book of youthful Delights.* In it will be collected a host of pleasing and instructive stories, songs, puzzles, theatrical presentations, and other games, which are really appropriate to the inclinations and abilities of children.
>
> MB X.3; in G: 221–2

In Section 4 of Chapter X Basedow offers several more suggestions concerning additional books to add the cabinet-library, viz.: "a) a somewhat *complete political history of the fatherland*...b) a brief and comprehensible *summary of the laws of the land* ... c) a *collection of summaries* of domestic and foreign *books*" (X.4; in G: 222–3). Finally, in X.5, the last section of the *Methodenbuch*, he makes the following recommendations for books for older students "after the fifteenth year" (MB X.5; in G: 223): "a) A *Latin anthology* of the ancient, classical authors, both in prose and verse"[21] (MB X.5; in G: 224) ... "b) A short *Latin dictionary* ... c) An *anthology* of the *classical Greek authors* ... d) Finally a *dialectic* or *art of differentiation* [*Unterscheidungskunst*] for students and authors" (MB X.5; in G: 225).

In a well-known quip on Basedow's *Methodenbuch* included in the Foreword to his 1771 German translation of La Chalotais's *Essai sur l'éducation nationale*, August Ludwig von Schlözer (1735–1809) complained that "nothing is more unmethodical than this so-called method-book" (as cited by Pinloche 1896: 165). The above tour of the *Methodenbuch* unfortunately provides ample evidence in support of Schlözer's criticism, but it nevertheless remains the case that Basedow's work "for fathers and mothers of families of all nations" is without doubt one of the most outstanding testimonials and influential examples of Enlightenment educational policy (cf. Krause 1979: IX).

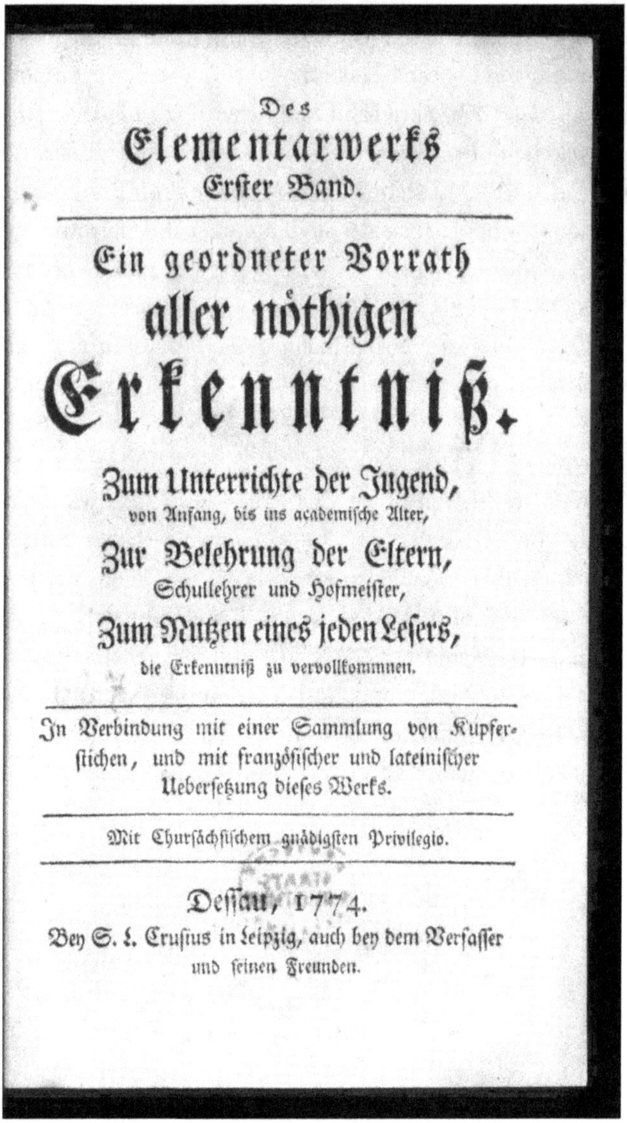

Des

Elementarwerks

Erster Band.

Ein geordneter Vorrath

aller nöthigen

Erkenntniß.

Zum Unterrichte der Jugend,

von Anfang, bis ins academische Alter,

Zur Belehrung der Eltern,

Schullehrer und Hofmeister,

Zum Nutzen eines jeden Lesers,

die Erkenntniß zu vervollkommnen.

In Verbindung mit einer Sammlung von Kupferstichen, und mit französischer und lateinischer Uebersetzung dieses Werks.

Mit Chursächsischem gnädigsten Privilegio.

Dessau, 1774.

Bey S. L. Crusius in Leipzig, auch bey dem Verfasser und seinen Freunden.

Figure 3 The original title page of Basedow's *Elementarwerk*, 1774. By permission of the Staatsbibliothek Berlin: PK: https://digital.staatsbibliothek-berlin.de/werkansicht/?PPN=PPN1016516983.

8

"A Well-Ordered Stock of All Necessary Knowledge:" The *Elementarwerk*

In the final sections of the *Vorstellung an Menschenfreunde* (1768), Basedow plugs yet another forthcoming work: his *Elementarbuch*. Described earlier in the *Vorstellung* as the "first work in every improvement of the school system" (VM: § 41; in R: 46), later he effuses over its fundamental necessity as follows:

> You noble friends of humanity, . . . you wish for more public happiness in many regions. O, that more insight, more virtue, more patriotism would spread! O, that scholars could have primarily inner worth and external reputation! O, that the universities would actually be improved! This is not yet possible! Further back with our desires! O, that secondary and primary schools in many regions would be what they should be! This is not yet possible! We must once again go further back with our desires! O, that we only had some seminaries for future schoolmen and professors, as friends of humanity must have wished! This is also not yet possible! First we must have a well-ordered school library for rational instruction, after that we ourselves or our descendants can slowly climb the steps that are now much too high for us. An elementary book [*Elementarbuch*], an ABC-book of real and nominal human knowledge, a work, whose presentation until now is missing, is the first thing that united friends of humanity together . . . can make for the fulfillment of such marvelous goals with plausible hope of good success.
> VM: § 55; in R: 75

In sum, the *Elementarbuch* was declared to be the key that would unlock the entire Philanthropinist program of educational reform. Without it, no improvements in education were possible; with it everything hoped for could become a reality. Furthermore,

> the *Elementarbuch* should begin with the very first knowledge of a child . . . The book should be written so practically that even in the absence of schooling and tutors every mother who has understanding or can obtain it will find the way completely to an agreeable and useful instruction for the early years of childhood.
> VM: § 56; in R: 75–6

Surprisingly, the manifold fundraising efforts for this ambitious project proved extremely successful—indeed, "Basedow had a much more favorable success than he himself or his friends expected" (Fritzsch 1972: I: XV). And with the help of his two recently hired research assistants, Christian Heinrich Wolke and Christian Wilhelm von Dohm,[1] in spring 1770 the *Elementarbuch* was finally published—a three-volume primer "for Youth and their Teachers and Friends in Civilized Classes" containing over 900 pages of text and 53 copperplates prepared by Daniel Chodowiecki. Six months later, the *Methodenbuch* (discussed in the previous chapter) was also published.

Both books met with strong public approval and received glowing reviews, and, at first, Basedow referred to both of them together—along with their French and Latin translations and an expanded list of 100 copperplates—as his *Elementarwerk*. Christian Garve, for instance, in a well-known review of both books published in the *Neuen Bibliothek der schönen Wissenschaften und der freien Künste* in 1771, wrote: "If it is possible to get to know a man through his writings, then Basedow is one of the most insightful and honest men who lives among us; if it is possible to make conclusions about the worth of a work from its outline and a part of its execution, then Basedow's undertaking is a good deed [*Wohltat*] for his era and his nation" (Garve 1771; reprinted in E: II: 547). And an anonymous reviewer in the *Allgemeine Deutsche Bibliothek* proclaimed: "We know of no book on education in which so many clear and precisely determined rules have been concentrated together as in this [*Methodenbuch*], and we are convinced that future experts will place Basedow as the third man next to Locke and Rousseau" (as cited by Fritzsch 1972: I: XXI).

But there were also some criticisms, particularly of the *Elementarbuch*. The most severe critic was the earlier-referred-to August Ludwig von Schlözer, a history professor at Göttingen. In his 1771 translation of a work of Chalotais's (*Versuch über den Kinderunterricht des Herrn von Chalotais*), Schlözer argued that "a universal *Elementarbuch* was at present not possible," that "with assistants under Basedow's direction" the project was not feasible, that Basedow's *Elementarbuch* "did not have the very first quality which belongs to such a book and which is presupposed by educated scholars," and (last but not least) that "the whole thing looks like a money grab" (as cited by Fritzsch 1972: I: XXII–III; see also G: 237 and Ra: 59).

Although Basedow on the whole seemed satisfied with the *Methodenbuch* (the second and third editions of this work differ only slightly from the first), in his Preface to the *Elementarbuch* he himself acknowledges that the work was far from perfect ("*occasionally real flaws in the order and completeness occur*"— Basedow 1770: VII). And while he defended himself against Schlözer's charges in his usual manner—viz., by publishing yet another book (*Documented Description of Schölzer's Actions Against the Elementarwerk, the Author and some of its Supporters, with Remarks on La Chalotais's Essay on Childhood Education*— see Basedow 1771d), in the end he decided to rework the entire text, giving it the new title of *Elementarwerk* (the Elementary Work). But by now Basedow, along with his family and two recently hired assistants, Wolke and Dohm, had relocated to Dessau, having left Altona on December 1, 1771. And his new patron Prince Leopold Friedrich Franz's first demand was that the work be brought to completion as soon as possible, so that Basedow could concentrate on setting up the Philanthropin. Basedow immediately promised to complete the *Elementarwerk* by Easter 1772, but multiple factors caused a delay in publication. In addition to the challenges of acclimating himself to a new living situation, his health, always precarious, took a turn for the worse, and his congenital eyesight problems flared up again. His spells of melancholy and depression also returned, which led to yet more drinking, and soon he developed gout. In a letter to his friend Isaac Iselin dated July 24, 1773, he writes: "Since Easter I have been plagued by gout, which occasionally is very painful. The baths at Lauchstädt,[2] where I have continued my work, have not helped me" (reprinted in G: 497).

But while Wolke was helping to get the copperplates part of the *Elementarwerk* project into better shape (particularly those dealing with the natural sciences— see, for instance, Plate XXI, Numbers 2–4, and Plates XC–XCIII), Basedow somehow found time to publish three more books, each one dealing with issues in mathematics: *Arithmetic for Enjoyment and Reflection* (see Basedow 1774b), *Demonstrated Principles of Pure Mathematics*, vol. I: *Theory of Numbers and Algebra*, vol. II: *Geometry and Infinity* (see Basedow 1774c), and *Theoretical Mathematics* (see Basedow 1774d). According to Reble, at this point in his career he had already managed to publish sixty-three separate works on an astonishingly wide range of topics (R: 270).

Yet another delay in the publication of the *Elementarwerk* was weather. During 1771 and 1772, Dessau and the surrounding region suffered massive flooding, which left many citizens homeless and without food. The resources of Prince Leopold were severely tested by this catastrophe, and Basedow was forced once again to appeal to the general public for funds. In a footnote in the Preface of the first edition of the *Elementarwerk*, he describes the "continuous flooding" and resulting "famine of many poor people," "1,500 of whom the Prince fed daily" (E: I: XLV n.).

But in summer 1774 the massive four-volume *Elementarwerk* was finally published—"*A Well-Ordered Stock of all Necessary Knowledge for the Instruction* of Youth from the Beginning up to the Academic Age, for the Guidance of Parents, Schoolteachers, and Tutors, for the Needs of Every Reader, to Perfect his Knowledge" (see Basedow 1774e).

By all accounts, the *Elementarwerk* is definitely one of Basedow's best-known and most influential books. Göring and Reble both include ample selections from it in their respective anthologies of Basedow's writings, and it is one of his only books that is currently still in print (in an edition published by Georg Olms Verlag in 1972—a facsimile edition of the 1909 version of the text edited by Theodor Fritzsch, first published by Ernst Wiegandt). The first edition (1774) was out of print by 1780, and a second edition was published in 1785. The initial plan called for Ernst Christian Trapp (who taught briefly at the Philanthropin before being appointed to the first university professorship in pedagogy at Halle in 1779) to edit the new edition. But for reasons which remain unclear (though a deteriorating relationship between Basedow and Trapp would be a good bet), Trapp did not complete the editing, and eventually Basedow decided to prepare the second edition himself. The second edition is a bit shorter than the first edition, consisting only of three volumes rather than the initial four. The final tenth book ("*Das Nötigste der Grammatik und von der Wohlredenheit*" / The Essentials of Grammar and Rhetoric) was deleted, and many changes in Books 3 (on logic), 4 (religion), and 5 (ethics) were also made. A third "emended and improved" edition was also published in Stuttgart in 1849, nearly sixty years after Basedow's death. But because it is a revision (*Überarbeitung*) of the original text made without Basedow's approval, it is seldom used by scholars today.

The first edition of the *Elementarwerk* also appeared in simultaneous Latin and French translations. The Latin translation was prepared by Carl Ehregott Mangelsdorf; the French, primarily by a Mr. Huber (whose name does not even appear on the title page). However, because even the translators themselves were not particularly pleased with their efforts,[3] neither translation has been used much.

The original edition contains over 1,600 pages of text, and because of its multi-volume format and the inclusion of Chodowiecki's copper engravings, it was a very costly book—"to date ... undoubtedly the most ambitious and expensive educational publication" (Landschoof 1933: 177), initially priced at twelve *Reichsthalers*. On the opening page the following short poem appears:

> Lord, our God, increase
> Our knowledge and contentment!
> Destroy the power of sin,
> And reform this corrupt age!
>
> Fritzsch 1972: I: XXX

A second poem is printed on the second page, followed by dedications to Holy Roman Emperor Joseph II, Catherine II of Russia, his Danish Majesty Christian VII, the Russian Prince Paul Petrowitz, his new sponsor Leopold Friedrich Franz, Prince of Anhalt-Dessau, and finally the general public, "which trustingly sent over 15,000 *Reichsthalers* in advance for the *Elementarwerk*" (Fritzsch 1972: I: XXXI).

The four volumes of written text in the first edition are divided into ten books, which are then further subdivided into multiple chapters and sections. The titles of the ten Books are as follows:

Vol. I
1. Only for Adult Friends of Children
2. Of Diverse Topics, Particularly Concerning the Human Being and the Soul
3. Introductory [*Gemeinnützige*] Logic

Vol. II
4. Concerning Religion
5. Ethics
6. Of the Occupations and Classes [*Stände*] of Human Beings

Vol. III
7. Elements of History
8. Natural Science

Vol. IV
9. Continuation of Natural Science
10. The Essentials of Grammar and Style [*Wohlredenheit*]

There are not a lot of surprises in the lengthy written text—again, one of the most common complaints made by commentators about Basedow's writings is their repetitiveness. His main goal is an ambitious and perhaps impossible one: to provide young students with all the knowledge and information they need to find their way successfully in the world. Nevertheless, the encyclopedic scope of the *Elementarwerk* is extremely impressive. A secondary (and more readily achievable) goal is to offer readers a "comprehensive explanation of the goals of philanthropic education" (Overhoff 2010: 62). At the beginning of the Preface to the first edition, Basedow strikes a strong chord for religious pluralism that must have shocked many contemporary readers:

> The *Elementarwerk* is concerned only with nontheological sciences, therefore not with Christian religion but merely with natural religion. It can be used by a

heretical church group, but is equally useful for Catholic, Greek Orthodox, Protestant, Mennonite, Jewish, and naturalistic [*naturalistischen*] families and organizations.

E: I: XL

In Book 1, Basedow presents his initial advice to parents and teachers concerning the education of young children, with special emphases on the key role of games in early education and on devising educational methods that are consistent with children's natural development. "One must give children the freedom to play safely according to their pleasure"—though he of course also encourages adults to channel children's natural love of play into games specifically designed to "promote the skills of the body, certain concepts of the understanding, learning necessary future memorization-work, and the facilitation of future virtues" (Bk. 1.III.b; E: I: 23–4).

Book 2, its title ("Of Diverse Topics, Particularly Concerning the Human Being and the Soul") notwithstanding, continues the discussion of educational games, and here much of Basedow's discussion is linked to Chodowiecki's famous copper engravings. He prefaces Book 2 with the warning: "*Show children no copper engravings until they can read*" (E: I: 61), and then offers numerous dialogues for parents to read with older children concerning human customs regarding (e.g.) eating and drinking (engravings I–II), clothing (III), and housing (IV). But many of these dialogues are also designed to inculcate basic moral norms as well as to encourage reflection on them. For instance, one section entitled "Of Food and Work. First Concepts of Justice and Injustice" begins as follows:

> *Tutor*: Now something about the hungry man in the second engraving. Some human beings live in such circumstances that they cannot get enough food, clothing, and other necessary things for life and health, unless they are given them freely by others out of compassion. These are called poor people. They must now and then go around and ask others to give them sometimes this, sometimes that, which they lack, or money, so that they can buy things. Then they are called beggars. Sometimes they do not even have a hut, but sleep under the open sky or here or there, where someone permits them to do so.
>
> *Detlev* [the tutor's student]: From where do the others, who are not poor, receive food, clothing, housing, household appliances, and whatever else they need?
>
> *Tutor*: Most of them receive these things through work.
>
> *Detlev*: This I don't understand.

Bk. 2.I.i; E: I: 77

Later sections in Book 2 (which is 150 pages long in Fritzsch's edition) do focus on "the human being and the soul," and many of the discussions here are also linked to Chodowiecki's copper engravings. For instance, a section entitled "Of Reason and Madness. Engraving XXVI" begins as follows:

> Animals indeed have certain mechanical instincts [*Kunsttriebe*] and ways of knowing that are absent in humans and which we do not all know. One can also truthfully say that humans are as little capable of the animal way of thinking as animals are of the human. But from the use of innate reason in humans or the missing powers of understanding in animals it follows that we have this advantage: animals are much more in our power than we are in theirs ... Look (in the first of the four pictures) at the lion locked in a cage in a wagon. He has been captured through the skill of humans and brought to this condition.
>
> Bk. 2.IV.n; E: I: 152–3

Basedow opens Book 3, on logic, by warning readers that "this third book is not for the first years of childhood" (Bk. 3.I.a; E: I: 213n.). And much of his discussion is not confined to logic as currently conceived, but rather involves issues in epistemology and psychology. Here too, much of the discussion makes reference to Chodowiecki's engravings. For instance, a section entitled "Of Belief, Supposition [*Vermuten*], Doubt, and Knowledge. Engraving XXV" begins as follows:

> Concerning the judgments of our understanding we note a number of differences ... Some are joined with conviction, with a complete, certain belief and free from all doubt, from all change between belief and doubt. The small boy shows such conviction to his benevolent father (in the first of the four pictures). *However, the ground or cause of our certainty is of various sorts. 1. The use of the senses* often gives us certainty of that which we experience from them. When we see the figure and color of a tree and at the same time feel it, we cannot doubt that it is a tree, because the senses instruct us. 2. But next to the five external senses we have an inner sense or the power to experience what is in our soul. This convinces us when we believe or doubt something happily or sadly, when we feel love or disgust.
>
> Bk. 3. I.b; E: I: 218–19

In Book 4 ("Concerning Religion") Basedow immediately reveals his Enlightenment credentials in the opening chapter when he criticizes popular religious tracts written for children: "In many catechisms the question, *how do you come to know that God exists?* is simply answered under the headings: this I know 1) from His works, 2) from my conscience, 3) from the agreement of all people, 4) from the Holy Scripture. These are, I say, titles of proofs [*Titel von Beweisen*], but not proofs themselves" (Bk. 4.I; E: I: 316). Later in Chapter IV he does claim to present a "proof, that God exists" (Bk. 4.IV; E: I: 335). The argument here is a version of the venerable cosmological argument traditionally associated with Aquinas ["the world certainly took its beginning through a sufficient cause, which itself did not have a cause, and therefore this ... from eternity was the real immeasurable original being" (Bk. 4.IV; E: I: 335–6)].[4] However, unlike Aquinas and many other defenders of the cosmological argument, Basedow does not claim that this attempt to prove God's existence has the status of certainty. We do not know the truth of the conclusion with absolute certainty. Rather, it is something "you must believe, that there exists and remains a single, perfect God" (Bk. 4.IV; E: I: 338). In other words, the *Glaubenspflicht* also stands behind this "proof." It is morally incumbent on us to believe in God, because this belief has an essential bearing on our life and conduct.

In Book 4 Basedow also illustrates some of his religious teachings for children through Chodowiecki's copper engravings. For instance, in Chapter XIII ("Concerning Benevolence and God's Love. Engraving XLIX"), he writes:

> Now then! This picture (engraving XLIX) gives you, as often as you look at it, a vivid memory of many of God's good deeds and consequently His immeasurable good. You see presented the benevolent sunshine and some of the best of humans and animals (between mountains and valleys, water and land, meadows and fields, developed and undeveloped parts) in alternate regions of the earth. You see in the garden pleasures of taste in food and drink, of faces in color, symmetry, and beauty.
>
> Bk. 4.XIII; E: I: 368

The final chapter of Book 4 is entitled "Differences of Human Beings in Religion," and includes brief discussions of not only numerous Christian sects and Judaism but also "Muslims [*Mahomedanern*], Naturalists, Skeptics, and Atheists" (Bk. 4.XXII.e; E: I: 439). In his concluding paragraph Basedow again emphasizes one of his core religious themes—the common ground between the world religions:

> And so I have given you, dearest youth and dearest reader, a short description of the opinions on God and religion ... But in this *Elementarwerk* I prove nothing other than the *natural religion* or the doctrines of the one God and his providence, the immorality of the soul, and the future requital [*künftigen Vergeltung*] of good and evil, as they could be proved to a carefully instructed and reflective human being, without prior faith in revelation, simply through a consideration of

ourselves and the whole of nature, with reasonable exercise of the duty to believe [*Glaubenspflicht*]. Deists, Jews, Christians, and Muslims agree on this.

Bk. 4.XXII.e; E: I: 443

Book 5 (Ethics) is concerned in part with "the cultivation of character and mores" (Bk. 5.III; E: I: 480). In comparison with other liberal Enlightenment moral theorists, particularly Kant, Basedow advocates a much more religion-based approach to ethics. For instance, the opening sentence in a section entitled "Very General Doctrine of Virtue" reads as follows:

> My child, follow the *light*, which illuminates to you the higher grades of knowledge and the obedient love of God.[5] And keep away from the possibility of all *objections* and *doubts* against divine providence, against the immortality of the soul, and against the paramount requital [*Vergeltung*] of good and evil after this life. The *firmest faith* is the surest path to your own happiness and to that of your brothers.
>
> Bk. 5.III.a; E, I: 480

Toward the end of his nearly 100-page discussion of the cultivation of virtue, Basedow summarizes his doctrine in ten points, the first and last of which read as follows:

> *a) Explanation*. Ethics [*Die Sittenlehre*] is a convincing [*überzeugende*] doctrine of the conformity of human action with beneficial rules [*gemeinnützigen Regeln*] or, in short, of virtue (Bk. 5.IX; E, I: 537).
>
> *k) Ethics* [*Die Ethik*] is called the doctrine of the promotion of virtue in ourselves and others.
>
> Bk. 5.IX; E: I: 541

In Chapter X ("Continuation and Conception of Practical Philosophy"), he brings Book 5 to a close by offering readers the following "reminder," which again illustrates his conviction that religion and ethics are tightly interconnected:

> Here one has the ethics of the *Elementarwerk*. What is useful for young children in it is obvious to the eye. This chapter comes to the aid of each of the previous parts of the *Elementarwerk*, particularly the chapter on religion ... Here one finds a number of other ethical principles that are joined together without special proof, namely those that need no special proof if one *believes in God, the duty of beneficence, and common experience*.
>
> Bk. 5.X; E: I: 543

Book 6 ("Of the Occupations and Classes of Human Beings") leads off Volume II in Fritzsch's edition, and is a kind of primer on applied social philosophy and economics. It contains discussions of numerous human occupations, often made with reference to Chodowiecki's copper engravings, and includes separate chapters on "Gardeners, Farmers, Cleaning Women, Cobblers, Tailors. Engraving XIX" (Bk. 6.V; E: II: 25), "The Blacksmith, Wagon Repairman, Cook, and Freight Hauler. Engraving XX" (Bk. 6.VI; E: 30), and "The Foundry Worker, Metal Worker, Coin Maker, and Wirepuller. Engraving LVI" (Bk. 6.IX; E: II: 49).

In Book 6 Basedow in effect functions as a kind of professional guidance counselor to students—his main goal is to provide young readers with information and advice about future career options. But (surprisingly for an educational reformer renowned for emphasizing the importance of play), in this part of the *Elementarwerk* he also makes a strong distinction between work and play, clearly placing a much higher value on the latter:

> Not every deliberate occupation can be called *work*. If you are merely busy in order to have the pleasure of movement or diversion, then your occupation is not work but merely a game. For with work one must have the intention either to achieve something good or the promise of good [*Gutscheinendes*], or to prepare oneself for future useful occupations, or finally to act in accordance with the will, to which one owes obedience and approval. Play and delight are good things, but they bring neither honor nor lasting pleasure. He who plays too often or for too long will soon regret it. Work, however, has lasting usefulness.
>
> Bk. 6.III; E: II: 12

The last chapter in Book 6—appropriately enough for a moralist's overview of human occupations—is entitled "Of Deception in Commerce" (Bk. 6.XX; E: II: 89). It opens on the following stern note, which anticipates Kant's famous discussion of false promises in the *Groundwork of the Metaphysics of Morals*: "*Keeping one's word is one of the most noble duties* in the industry of human beings. For without confidence in promises there can be but little industry, and through each deviation from keeping one's word confidence is diminished" (Bk. 6.XX; E: II: 89).[6]

Book 7 ("Elements of History") fills another 100 pages in Fritzsch's edition, and opens (via reference to engraving XXXI) with a very brief account of humanity's transition from savagery to civilization:

> In the *upper half of the engraving* is the condition of a region in the time of the greatest savagery [*Wildheit*] of its inhabitants; however in the *lower half* the condition of the same region is presented, in which they have moved up through the industriousness [*Fleiß*] and art of numerous inhabitants. Here and there one sees exactly the same valleys, hills, mountains, and rivers.
>
> Bk. 7.I.a; E: II: 95

Some peoples remain in a state of *Wildheit*; others slowly become "more or less civilized." But all of our distant ancestors started out in a savage condition:

> Some peoples are savage, without agriculture, without craftsmen and artists, without orderly authority; others are more or less civilized [*gesittet*]. But even the civilized nations almost always know that they have descended from wild or half-wild ancestors who went around naked or clothed only in animal skins, and who merely lived off of herbs, acorns, other fruits from trees and roots, or from wild game and fish or livestock breeding. At that time there were no buildings, no paved paths or bridges, no cultivated fields or meadows. Many regions that are now very fertile were then inaccessible forests, marshes and swamps or moors and deserts, a dwelling place merely for some wild and half-wild human beings, for a few tame animals, and for an even greater number of wild animals.
>
> Bk. 7.I.a; E: II: 93–4

After a brief tour of the Dark Ages up to the new era (*die Neue*), Basedow adds another discussion of the Jewish people, now highlighting some of their valuable contributions to European culture and philosophy:

> [U]nder this nation reasonable, upright, and very learned men have also been known. Among others, in the twelfth century was *Moses Maimonides*, in whose writings one amazingly finds God's providence and the perfection of the world, the same truths which in our century have been extended among Christians through the great men Leibniz and Wolff. An equally praiseworthy man of our time is *Moses Mendelssohn*, whose philosophical and critical writings are read with equally great approval by Jews and Christians of all sects.
>
> Bk. 7.V.a; E: II: 233

Engraving LXXX includes a portrait of Mendelssohn, a native son of Dessau, the same city in which Basedow was living when the *Elementarwerk* was first published in 1774, and where the Philanthropin would soon first open its doors to students. As noted earlier, Mendelssohn himself was a strong supporter of the school, and he and Basedow occasionally corresponded with each other.

Basedow concludes Book 7 with an overview of various kinds of history (universal history, church history, art history, natural history, etc.), along with a warning that he has intentionally focused only on core issues. (Again, the *Elementarwerk* aims only to present "all necessary knowledge"): "What I have not touched on regarding these historical sciences (except for natural history, which follows below) is not beneficial for most readers" (Bk. 7.VIII; E: II: 271).

Book 8 is the first of two books devoted to the natural sciences, broadly construed. Book 8 focuses primarily on the life sciences; Book 9, on the physical sciences. Wolke, Basedow's first assistant, made substantial contributions to this part of the *Elementarwerk*. Book 8 opens with a survey of human knowledge of other animals, "with the help of" (E: II: vi) a number of different copper engravings. Basedow begins by drawing attention to a bee depicted in engraving VIII: "Their way of living is either wild in hollow trees and other hollow spaces together with a great number of others, or they are brought together through the effort of human beings in beehives, as one sees under the roof there" (Bk. 8.I.a; E: II: 275). In a later section entitled "Of the Skill of Animals. Engraving LXXXVI," he writes:

> He who knows his own soul can also *not deny the souls of animals*. However, it may please him to call them something else rather than souls. I think it is exactly the same with the understanding of human beings and the *understanding of animals*. Animals do not have human souls and human understanding. Something is missing in animal understanding that is present in human understanding. Because of this lack in animals, one does not call the capacity of their understanding reason: rather, *by "reason" one refers only to the capacity of human understanding or of a still higher understanding*.
>
> Bk. 8.I.e; E: II: 295

However, Book 8 is not confined to the life sciences. After the opening discussions of insects, plants, and animals, Basedow moves on—rather disjointedly—to discuss "noteworthy tools" (Ch. V), shipping (Ch. VI), as well as mills and clocks (Ch. VII), before concluding with some remarks about architecture (Ch. IX). The discussion of tools is conducted with reference to engraving LXXXVIII, and includes advice about how to move heavy objects onto wagons using wedges, ropes, and pulleys, as well as brief descriptions of a number of basic mechanical devices such as thermometers, water pumps, and fire hoses. This particular chapter of the *Elementarwerk* is a good example of the more practical, applied side of Philanthropininist education, criticized by both conservatives and neohumanists for its allegedly secular and utilitarian leanings.

Book 9 continues the overview of science and technology, focusing now on physics. This discussion certainly constitutes one of the more difficult sections of the *Elementarwerk*, as Basedow himself admits in a note ["only for very proficient men"] (Bk. 9.I.b.note; E: II: 373 n.). He begins Book 9 with a discussion of bodies and motion, principles of statics and dynamics, and the principles of motion and equilibrium, before moving on to discourses on other physical phenomena such as air, the effects of electrical and magnetic phenomena, light, and the measurement of time. Book 9 illustrates another core progressive feature of the Philanthropinist curriculum: its emphasis on science education, made possible in part by its restriction to "nontheological sciences" (E: I: XL).

In the final Chapter in Book 9 Basedow turns to an overview of philosophy in general:

> Every rational human being philosophizes to a certain extent, that is, he thinks for himself, either to discover new knowledge or to search both for the truth as well as the usefulness of knowledge imparted to him.
>
> But some philosophize more and better than others. Some are by nature *philosophical geniuses* or have acquired a *philosophical spirit* through superior practice.
>
> Bk. 9.XII; E: II: 469

He then discusses different branches of philosophy, following the traditional division of theoretical and practical philosophy, and concludes on the following note:

> Many *textbooks of philosophy* and their parts are *difficult* and *long-winded* to such a degree that the time and effort which their use demands makes them unhelpful ...
>
> One will see from the above that, except for the discussion of the mathematical sciences, *the Elementarwerk contains all of the philosophy* that is of benefit to most readers, to think through, from time to time to reiterate, and in certain circumstances to refer to.
>
> Bk. 9.XII; E: II: 472

As noted earlier, Book 10—"The Essentials of Grammar and Style"—was deleted from the second edition of 1785, "probably as a result of Mangelsdorf's objections" (E: II: 474).[7] At the same time, however, this particular part of the *Elementarwerk* was often singled out for praise in some of the earliest reviews. Iselin, for instance, in a lengthy review first published in the *Allgemeine deutsche Bibliothek*, writes:

> The tenth book contains the essentials of grammar and style. Young people will not easily find such correct and clear concepts of the essentials of general as well as German grammar in another work intended for them, and grown men will also encounter a great many things here that will be informative for them ... As short as the section on style in the *Elementarwerk* is, it nevertheless contains more good and more that is useful than all of the other rhetoric books known to us which have tormented young people in elementary and secondary schools.
>
> In E: II: 558

Examples of Basedow's professional interests in grammar and style are already on display in some of his very earliest publications. For instance, during his tenure at Sorø in the 1750s he published two books on these topics: *A Textbook of Prose and Poetry Style in Different Writing Styles and Works, Arranged in Academic Lectures* (see Basedow 1756) and *The New Art of Teaching and Practice in the Regularity of the German Language* (see Basedow 1759).

After some brief preparatory remarks on grammar in general ("Everything which is spoken and written consists of *sentences* or judgments which are expressed through words and characters [*Zeichen*]"—Bk. 10.I; E: II: 475), Basedow continues with two longer chapters dealing with German grammar as well as style and issues related to reading. The former chapter covers standard topics such as pronunciation and spelling, declensions and conjugations, different uses of cases and verbs, as well as word order, concluding with some exercises; while the latter includes sections on expression and writing style, exercises in translation, remarks on writing letters, and the art of cultivating readers ("*Von der vernünftigen Art, Leser zu bilden*"—Bk. 10.III.e; E: II: 526). In the final section of the third chapter, Basedow offers his "Conclusion of the Entire Work:"

> Here, dearest and most honorable reader, do I come to the end of my long road (God knows with what effort and danger). Herein lie the tools for improving education, instruction, and the school system, and thereby of making our beloved descendants better and more content [*besser und zufriedener*] than we ourselves have been. Out of love for these important things and out of gratitude for the confidence in me manifested by the public, I shall devote the rest of my life to making this work more useful through addenda, remarks, explanations, improvements, and investigations ... and to impart all of this ... to the world through supplements or special writings. If the method of teaching [*Lehrart*], whose tools I have offered and wish to improve, does not come into practice in our own time, posterity will marvel over it so long as this work endures.
>
> Bk. 10.III.f; E: II: 530

The fact that Basedow here defines the remainder of his life in terms of the *Elementarwerk* ("I shall devote the rest of my life to making this work more useful") strongly suggests that he himself regarded it as his single greatest achievement. But how did his contemporaries assess the book, and how did later generations view it? Meier, as usual, can be counted on for negative comments. In the first volume of his 1791 biography he writes:

> The famous *Elementarwerk* deserves a special description in Basedow's biography. One must acknowledge that Basedow worked with all the powers of

his soul, and I might also add with all the powers of his body, on the continuation and completion of this so often pompously announced *Elementarwerk*. Admittedly, I could not constrain my laughter when I heard in 1772 that he had made a public apology to his readers because the work ... had not yet appeared ... Finally in 1774 he completed this important work. Truly a very short and too short a duration for such an important work ... Basedow's inconsistencies and shortcomings are here once again not to be denied ... Only very few school people could afford this book ... Does it contain very little or almost nothing new? Does it contain more errors than perfections, or is the reverse true? Did Basedow possess sufficiently broad knowledge and scholarship to complete such an important work in such a short time?

M: I: 337–41

And in Volume II, which contains his summaries and appraisals of each of Basedow's publications, Meier adds:

I have already said something about this ninth wonder of the world in the first part ... In the entire luxurious and expensive work, which is a mere tumbled-together chaos, I find nothing new, nothing special, nothing striking, and nothing excellent. Most of it has already been far better stated before.

M: II: 300–1

On the other hand, the book was reviewed widely when it first appeared, and most of the reviewers were extremely positive. For instance, an anonymous reviewer in a 1775 issue of the *Allgemeine Bibliothek für das Schul- und Erziehungswesen in Deutschland* writes:

The *Elementarwerk* contains much that is good, useful, and reasonable for the instruction of youth—and has also here and there the clarity and tone that one rightfully expects in a book that is written with this aim. In the hands of a wise and prudent father or tutor it can therefore be of very good service in order to teach children such useful knowledge and moral dispositions which otherwise in education, as it generally exists, have not been thought of.

In E: II: 561

Similarly, another anonymous reviewer in the January 14, 1774 issue of the *Frankfurter gelehrte Anzeigen* remarks:

With manifold benefits and happy intimation [*vielfachem Nutzen und froher Ahndung*] for our descendants we have read through the first three volumes of this newly worked-out *Elementarwerk*, and with heartfelt gratitude toward the author we must recommend it to our readers, for whom the improvement of the educational system is a matter of genuine seriousness.

In E: II: 560–1

Later judgments made with the benefit of hindsight are even more glowing. Göring, in his 1880 anthology of Basedow's writings, calls the *Elementarwerk* "epoch-making for its time, indeed, superb" (G: 242). And Fritzsch opens the Introduction to his 1909 edition of *The Elementary Book* with the following proclamation: "The *Elementarwerk* takes us 'into the time of the greatest and most successful reform efforts in the area of education and the school system which the peoples of Europe experienced' in the time of the Enlightenment" (Fritzsch 1972/1909: I: V).[8] More recent assessments are equally positive. For instance, Overhoff, in a 2010 article, notes that "both the *Elementarwerk* and the school in Dessau were to exert a great influence on German pedagogy until well into the nineteenth century" (Overhoff 2010: 62).

But, again, for readers who were familiar with Basedow's earlier publications, the long-winded written text of the *Elementarwerk* does not contain too many surprises. Over the course of their writing careers, prolific authors often develop the habit of repeating themselves in their works, and Basedow is an extreme example of this annoying tendency. And the assumption that any single-authored book (even a massive four-volume work) could somehow be sufficient for anyone's education is fallacious on multiple fronts. On this point, critic Schlözer was right: a universal *Elementarbuch* is simply not possible. But this overstatement on Basedow's part can be traced primarily to his well-documented "boastful" character (Reble 1999: 161). And while there is nothing groundbreaking in the book's philosophical orientation, the sheer scope of the work is extremely impressive. Judged within the context of eighteenth-century Germany, Basedow did indeed come close to offering his readers "a stock of all necessary knowledge." And for those who could afford the hefty sale price of twelve Thalers, the *Elementarwerk* definitely does offer readers a comprehensive overview of the chief theoretical commitments and goals of what would soon be widely known as Philanthropinist pedagogy.

But what is at least quasi-novel about Basedow's *Elementarwerk* is Chodowiecki's copper engravings. None of Basedow's previous publications (with the exception of the 1770 *Elementarbuch*, which in effect is a prototype of the longer and more elaborate 1774 *Elementarwerk*) contain any pictures. As Reble notes, the *Elementarwerk* is "a true picture-book of man and the world" (Reble 1965: 260). However, as other commentators have noted (see, e.g.,

Schmidt 1861: 544), even this added pictorial dimension of the work is certainly not entirely new, for in many respects it is highly reminiscent of Johann Amos Comenius's influential 1657 *Orbis Pictus*, which also claimed to offer readers "pictures of all the chief things that are in the world" (Comenius 1887: title page).

Assessments of the copper-engraving portion of the *Elementarwerk* also vary considerably. Göring, as we saw earlier, views them as the book's chief weakness:

> The engravings, as would be expected from so skilled a hand, are in general well executed. However, in many cases they contain astonishing trivialities, [and] in the area of the natural sciences so defined there are errors that are in fact not insignificant. For our time therefore this part of the book is no more of any use.
>
> G: 242

Meier, of course, is also critical: "In the copperplates there are many things that are highly unnecessary to represent in engravings, things which children eager to learn could be better shown from common life" (M: II: 301). And Goethe complained about what he felt was the artificiality and disjointed nature of many of the engravings:

> It displeased me that the drawings of his *Elementarwerk*, even more than the subject matter, do not represent actual life conditions, for impossible elements are associated. In nature all things, in spite of their many-sidedness and apparent disorder, always have something orderly and settled. However, this *Elementarwerk* disarranges them completely, so that things never found together in actual experience stand next to one another for the sake of a relationship of concepts. Thus it lacks the orderly, methodical arrangement which we must confer to the works of Amos Comenius.
>
> In G: 242–3

On the other hand, Basedow's contemporary, Karl Abraham von Zedlitz (1731–93), who, in his capacity as Prussian Minister of Education exerted a tremendous impact on German educational policy during the Enlightenment,[9] reached a very different conclusion: "The Basedowian engravings for the *Elementarwerk* ought to be the handbook for all educators. They present a true picture gallery, and teach children the clearest concepts in the matter of education" (in G: 242). And Hermann Gilow, in his Introduction to volume III of Fritzsch's edition of the *Elementarwerk*, renders a verdict similar to Zedlitz's:

> One can frankly ask: What would the *Elementarwerk* be without these engravings? ... It is universally acknowledged what incomparable value

these pictures possess for our knowledge of middle-class [*bürgerlichen*] culture of the eighteenth century, but their harmonious relationship with the text also deserves praise.

Gilow 1972; in E: III: 6

Many of the criticisms of the engravings stem from misunderstandings of Basedow's intentions. Consider, for instance, Meier's complaint that in many cases it would be better to dispense with the pictures and get children in direct contact with real life. This is an extremely paradoxical charge to issue against Philanthropinist pedagogy, which was a forerunner in emphasizing extracurricular activities such as field trips, hikes, student apprenticeships with adult skilled workers, etc. As Basedow emphasizes in Book I of the *Elementarwerk*, teachers must leave time for "preliminary exercises in actual adult living. To some extent the student must learn the tools of carpenters, the tradesman, of the cabinet-maker, the thresher, the blacksmith, the mason, and the gardener, some small use of which one often needs in the household" (Bk 1.IV; E: I: 35). The copperplates were certainly not meant as a substitute for real life, but merely as an introduction to the world outside the classroom. Meier seems to also overlook the basic pedagogical intent of the engravings. They were not meant to be a mere source of amusement. As Basedow explicitly states in his short "Instructions for the Use of the Collection of Copperplates:" "In the beginning children must not be permitted to have the collection of copperplates outside of the lesson period, and not even then, if the teacher does not wish to present them" (E: III: 22). And Göring's charge that some of the plates contain "astonishing trivialities" ignores Basedow's explicit remark that one of the chief goals of the engravings was to familiarize students with "mundane [*alltägliche*] things" (MB V.8; in G: 107) and scenes from daily life. The plates were not intended as a mere collection of esoterica. As for Goethe's frequently cited criticism of the allegedly unnatural and disjointed quality of some of the scenes depicted in the plates (he does not provide any specific examples), this seems to reflect underlying assumptions within his own proto-romantic philosophy of nature, which stands in opposition to Enlightenment scientific theories. Basedow, though by no means an expert in the natural sciences (as noted earlier, he received extensive help from Wolke on this particular part of the *Elementarwerk* project), is closer to the dominant Newtonian science of his day. Finally, several of the criticisms, though they contain true statements, are also the products of a limited perspective. Göring, for instance, is certainly correct in pointing out that some of the science depicted in the plates contains "errors that are in fact not insignificant." But it does not follow from this that the plates are "no more of any use." As Gilow and others rightly observe, even though some of the science depicted in the plates is out of date, they continue to serve as invaluable historical documents ("it is universally acknowledged that these pictures possess an incomparable value for our knowledge of middle-class culture of the eighteenth century").

Underneath at least some of the frequent references to Comenius's *Orbis Pictus* is the insinuation that, here as well (as with the Rousseau issue), Basedow is simply not an original thinker. But Basedow was certainly well aware of Comenius's famous work, and he was not trying to plagiarize it. Over the years, many commentators have offered detailed comparative analyses of these two collections of engravings. Earlier we cited Bollnow's observation that "while Comenius begins with God and from there unfolded the world in great objective order ... Basedow enters in with the children's environment: the family at the dinner table, food, clothing, and the home" (Bollnow 1952: 619). More recently, Dietrich Benner and Herwart Kemper, in their multi-volume work, *Theorie und Geschichte der Reformpädagogik*, reach a similar conclusion when they write:

> The order which Basedow introduces to the observer is completely different than the *Orbis Pictus* of Comenius. Comenius looked at the world from the teleological-cosmological view of a Christian creator-god who has fixed a world order, to which the observer is introduced so that he will learn how to think, judge, and act reasonably. Against this, Basedow begins not with a symbol of the all-powerful God, but rather with a table, which shows the expansion of needs in modern middle-class [*bürgerlichen*] society from the perspective of a child, where a fullness of spread-out foods stands before his eyes, which he must learn about and enjoy.
>
> Benner and Kemper 2009: 102

Contemporary readers of the *Elementarwerk* should therefore endorse the same conclusion that Basedow himself reached about the book: even if the ambitious program of educational reform laid out in this multi-volume work could not be fully realized in his own lifetime (or, indeed, in anyone's lifetime), nevertheless "posterity will marvel over it so long as this work endures" (Bk. 10. III.f; E: II: 530).

Figure 4 The first Philanthropin building in Dessau (on the right—destroyed in the Second World War). By permission of the Stadtarchiv Dessau-Roßlau.

9

Back to School

With the publication of the mammoth *Elementarwerk* finally behind him, Basedow's next goal was to realize the ideals of the book by opening his own experimental school in Dessau. As usual, this important event in his life was marked by yet another publication with a long title: *The Philanthropinum founded in Dessau: A School of Human Friendship and Good Knowledge for Learners and Young Teachers, Poor and Rich; A Public Necessity for the Improvement of the School System in all Regions according to the Plan of the Elementarwerk. For Explorers and Doers of the Good among Princes, Philanthropic Societies, and Private Persons, recommended by J. B. Basedow* (see Basedow 1774a).

The school officially opened on December 27, 1774 (timed to coincide with the birthday of his chief patron, Prince Leopold of Dessau), with an enrollment of only three students, two of whom were Basedow's own children: Emilie, born in Altona on March 18, 1769; her younger brother Friedrich (Fritz), born in Altona in 1771;[1] and Abel Anton Schwarz,[2] whom Wolke had previously tutored. In addition to Wolke, Basedow had by now also hired a second assistant to help him at the school: Friedrich August Benzler,[3] a talented twenty-two-year-old clerk from Lemgo (a town further west in North Rhine Westphalia, about fifteen miles east of Bielefeld) who first came to Basedow "without formal education, except writing, counting, and a little French. He had not once enjoyed proper instruction" (ES: 91–2). However, within the space of only one year, by applying the natural method of his new employer, Benzler somehow managed to "make himself sufficiently proficient in Latin to explain the philosophical essays of Cicero, of Nepos, and Eutropius" (Landschoof 1933: 226; cf. Schmid 1898: 191) and had also learned "so many concepts from philosophy and mathematics that one could not put an intelligible question before him without his knowing which specially designated part of philosophy and mathematics it belonged to" (DEP: 63).

We began this study by examining some key features of Basedow's famous Philanthropin, focusing primarily on the Public Examination of the school held on May 13–15, 1776 and some of the novel features of the institution that attracted popular attention. At this point there were nineteen students enrolled, and by December of 1776, student enrollment (which, along with the related matter of financing, was a constant challenge at the Philanthropin) had increased to an impressive twenty-nine students. By 1779, fifty students were enrolled at the school, and "in 1782, there were fifty-three, from as widely scattered places as Lisbon and Riga" (Landschoof 1933: 237). But what was daily life like for students and teachers at the school, and what were the chief causes for its closing? How could a school that Kant praised for being "the greatest phenomenon which has appeared in this century for the improvement of the perfection of humanity" (V-Anth/Fried 25: 722) shut its doors so quickly?

Despite Basedow's core emphasis on the importance of play in education as a strategy for recapturing the joy of learning, the daily routine for students enrolled at the Philanthropin was by no means all fun and games. On the contrary, all pupils were required to adhere to a very strict and demanding daily schedule. Somewhat surprisingly, there was a strong emphasis on *Ordnung und Disziplin*. Basedow himself, in the second issue of *Pedagogical Negotiations, or Philanthropinist Journal and Reader* (1778)[4] offers the following description, in a section entitled "House Rules and Curriculum of the Philanthropinum in Dessau:"

> At five o'clock in the morning a servant wakes one of the famulants,[5] who then wakes a teacher and the remaining famulants. Then the teacher inspects the famulants' rooms to see if things are in good order and all business properly carried out. At a quarter before six reveille is sounded by a servant or famulant. Then all the teachers and the remaining Philanthropin students get up. The teacher who is the inspector then visits all pupils in their rooms and takes note of which ones he finds guilty of carelessness in anything. After all students, under supervision [*unter Aufsicht*], have dressed and washed, they assemble in the fourth auditorium for morning prayers. After prayers are concluded they all go to breakfast, and then—during winter at eight, during summer at seven—to lessons.[6]

And what happened to students who transgressed these norms of school conduct? Basedow's policies here are somewhat inconsistent. On the one hand, as noted earlier, yet another innovation of the Philanthropin was its de-emphasis on corporal punishment. As he writes in his 1768 *Vorstellung an Menschenfreunde*: "physical beatings ... are very seldom necessary in good schools" (VM §46; in R: 56). And even more forcefully, in the *Methodenbuch*: "With regard to instruction and while it is taking place, I must advise against all *compulsion*, in order to promote *diligence in school*, as something very harmful" (MB V.2; in G: 95). In a 1776 publication which describes curriculum policies at the Philanthropin in some detail, he also writes: "Intellectual studies [*Geistesstudien*] will all be made pleasant, through alleviation and avoidance of all [*aller*] punishment, fear, threat, and reprimand" (ES: 53).

On the other hand, students at the Philanthropin by no means enjoyed unrestricted freedom, and despite the above pronouncements, corporal punishment was employed as a last resort. In a 1774 work announcing the opening of his school, Basedow assures parents that their children will be kept in line in the following note:

> Obedience will also be enforced through *corporal punishment* [*Leibesstrafen*] when it no longer appears possible through more human means [*menschlichere Mittel*]. And if this does not succeed, after a *Pensionist* has been here for a year (for some souls are so depraved that one cannot improve them in a communitarian educational setting without damage to the whole), then the parents have the free choice, if they wish to keep their son here, either to employ a special disciplinarian [*besonderen Zuchtmeister*] so that he can participate in instruction, or to take him out of the school. Under obedience is also included abstaining from forbidden places, *slanderous* lying (note well), intentional or habitual violence toward persons and useful things, etc.
>
> DEP: 16

The day-to-day life of Philanthropin students was also strictly regulated in a number of different ways. In a chapter in the earlier-mentioned *Philanthropinum* booklet of 1774 entitled "Something of the Conduct for the *Pensionisten*," Basedow writes:

> 1) Within the Philanthropinum we permit only attire in the official school *uniform* . . .
>
> 2) The *Pensionisten* eat two dishes for *lunch* and only one in the *evening* . . .
>
> 3) Our week (excluding Sunday) has two *merit days*, two *patrons' days* [*Reichtumstage*] and two *caste-days* [*Standestage*] . . .[7]
>
> 4) Each month has a *casual day* [*Kasualtag*] of twenty-four hours. The *Pensionisten* . . . fast until two pm, and then enjoy cold food and water in the evening in cold rooms or under unpleasant skies, sleeping at night on the floor or on straw . . . For education must prepare one for the hazards of life.
>
> 5) Each *Pensionist* knows at each hour and for each activity to whom he owes *obedience*. Blind or absolute [*klostermäßige*] obedience will be enforced up to the twelfth year. . .

9) The daily schedule for each student, with the exception of sleep time, is calculated to be seventeen hours, and is divided as follows: *six* hours for eating, drinking, dressing, and the student's own recreation. *One* hour for the strictest order of the room, clothing, tools, paying bills, and writing letters. *Five* hours for studies. *Three* hours for orderly recreation in movement, such as dancing, riding, fencing, music, etc. *Two* hours for such *manual work* as is somewhat difficult but not dirty... There will be a rule: *you must do either seven hours of studies or seven hours of manual work. At all times you have the choice of the latter instead of the former*...

10) The customary *punishments* for mistakes and vices [*Laster*] are a decrease in merit points, the exchange of a study hour for an hour of manual labor, boredom in a completely solitary room where one cannot see out the window and in the vicinity can hear the pleasant sounds of young people enjoying themselves or studying,... [or] a transfer for some time into the situation of a *Famulant*...

12) 10 pm is bedtime in summer; in winter, 11, because students rise at 5 am in summer and at 6 in winter...

13) All *Pensionisten*, likewise also the *Famulanten*, when there is a sufficient number of the appropriate age, will become proficient in all military movements and positions through an experienced person... In this way we can offer a great deal of what we wish to do in order to perfect the entire human nature and not merely the soul of a future man...

DEP: 13–19

Basedow also designed a rather elaborate system of rewards to encourage Philanthropin students to strive for extra diligence and order, *Fleiß und Ordnung*. In the *Reliquiae Philanthropini* (Remains of the Philanthropinum), there is a section entitled "Set-Up of the Merit Board (*Meritentafel*)," which reads in part as follows:

Tickets will be given for special diligence, for excellent attentiveness and good behavior, for order in one's preparations, and for the effects of special diligence. A golden point on the merit board comes with fifty such tickets, which will be posted after worship services... Fifty points gives a Philanthropinist the Order of Diligence, which consists of a ribbon and a silver medal, and which the student may wear during certain ceremonies.

Reliquiae Philanthropini I/1; in Benner and Kemper 2000: 153

All of this is likely to strike most contemporary readers as an extremely authoritarian expression of over-regulation and rigidity, particularly when viewed within the context of what was supposed to be a progressive boarding school that emphasized learning as play. And it is. However, when compared to the policies and practices of other late eighteenth-century European schools—where, as Raumer reminds us, "instruction was hard and heartlessly severe," and "grammar was beaten into the memory" (Raumer 1843: 278)—it was not. And all of the ornate minutiae of these rules and regulations regarding conduct need (somehow!) to be made consistent with the much more liberal-sounding core principles (*Grundsätze*) that Basedow promised his readers served as a guide for all instruction at the Philanthropin:

> Our core principles of instruction ... are as follows: 1) Young people must also be happy young people during school days. 2) We promote more practice in virtue and less in dispensable science [*entbehrliche Wissenschaft*]. 3) We exercise students' memory primarily in order to retain the ordering of ideas [*Vorstellungen*] and things, not of words. 4) The rest of the necessarily remaining memorization work is made easier by means of music and by hanging very readable tables or paintings and copper engravings or outlines on the walls in the school. 5) ... *No direct instruction [unmittelbare Unterricht] in religion may be given at the Philanthropinum* ... We repeat the assurance that no word or action will occur in the gatherings of the Philanthropinum that cannot be approved by every worshipper of God (be he Christian, Jew, Muslim, or deist) ... Every teacher or student of pedagogy or *Pensionist* or *Famulant* or scholarship student is therefore equally welcome to us ... Further, all Philanthropinist lessons and instruction books ... must be *free of theological verdicts* for Christians against Jews, Muslims, and deists or for this or that church against so-called dissidents, who in some places are called heretics. We mean that such verdicts must not occur even in passing or in examples. For *cosmopolitan instruction* must be universal [*allgemein*], and cannot advise against clergy of any denomination.
>
> ES: 62–5

These guiding principles of the Philanthropin—especially the emphases on returning joy to learning, deemphasizing the role of rote memorization in instruction, and, above all, the promise of a nondenominational learning environment open to students of all religious backgrounds (but in a setting that nevertheless stressed "practice in virtue"), are what attracted students, parents, and liberal intellectuals to Basedow's school—not the arcane merit points, silver medals, and stringent food regulations.

After the enrollment figures at the school had increased a bit, Basedow gradually introduced four distinct grades or levels for the *Pensionisten* students. Depending on their chronological age and previous academic achievements, these students were divided into juniors and seniors (or what Basedow called

Figure 5 The second Philanthropin building in Dessau (Palais Dietrich). By permission of the Stadtarchiv Dessau-Roßlau.

"bigger" and "smaller," *größere* and *kleinere*), and each of these two grades were then subdivided into higher and lower (or first and second, *erste* and *zweite*) levels. A separate curriculum was designed for the *Famulanten*. In the 1778 issue of the *Pedagogical Negotiations* journal referred to earlier, Basedow also offers the following detailed description of the curriculum for each group:

For the first class of senior Pensionisten:

From 8–9. Formation [*Bildung*] of taste and German style from Professor *Trapp*,[8] over selected sections from *Ramler's*[9] *Balleur*, from *Schütz's*[10] *Textbook for the Education of Taste and Understanding*, and from *Sulzer's Preparatory Exercises*. This is only for the first three days of the week. In the following three days natural religion and ethics will be taught by Professor *Trapp*, over *Basedow's Natürliche Weisheit im Privatstande*.[11]

From 9–10. Dancing with *dancers*, riding with equestrian *Schrödter*, under the supervision of *Feder*[12] and *Hauber*,[13] alternating for the entire week except Wednesday and Saturday. The former takes place in the fourth auditorium, the latter in the Prince's riding arena.

10–12. *Basedow* teaches Latin in his house, either ancient history (with an adjunct) or practical philosophy according to *Cicero's De Officiis*.

12–1. Mealtime.

1–2. Moderate physical exercise, such as threshing, planing, and carpentry in one of the accommodating rooms of our sovereign prince at the Palais *Dietrich*.[14]

From 2–3. Monday and Tuesday: Geography by *Hauber* over Pfennig's *Geography*.[15] Wednesday: knowledge of the human body and some chemistry with Privy Councilor and court physician *Kretzschmar*[16] in his house, where the anatomical specimens and instruments are available. For the last three days of the week exercise in mathematical drawing with Professor *Wolke*.

3–5. Practice in the French language and in world history by Professor *Trapp*, over Schröckh's *Universalhistorie* and Méllot's *Histoire universelle*,[17] for five days. On Saturday *Hauber* presents a newspaper colloquium during this time period, in order to make the national constitutions and noteworthy events of adults gradually known.

5–6. Mathematics by *Buße*,[18] over Ebert's *Nähere Anweisung zu den philosophischen und mathematischen Wisenschaften*[19] in the first three days of the week; in the last three days physics according to Erxleben's *Naturlehre*.[20]

6–7. Some knowledge of the heavens and the earth with *Wolke* according to Schmid's *Buche von den Weltkörpern*,[21] two times in the week; ancient Greek four times a week with *Damer*, over Principal Stroth's *chrestomathia graeca*,[22] over *Luciani Timo* and Xenophon's *memorabilia Socratis*.[23]

This is an impressive and rigorous curriculum plan, and it is good to see that at least the advanced students at the Philanthropin were not merely studying Basedow's *Elementarwerk* (even it was a "well-ordered stock of all necessary knowledge"). Rather, they were learning from some of the best European textbooks available at the time, works written by a number of different authors. Texts written by classical authors (e.g., Cicero, Xenophon) were also assigned, though not as many as one would find in more traditional schools. Several of the teachers working with this advanced group of students were themselves also highly accomplished individuals. However, with the exception of the "moderate physical exercise" via "threshing, planing, and carpentry" scheduled daily between 1 and 2 pm, nothing in this curriculum plan appears too far outside the educational mainstream of late eighteenth-century Germany. One could easily envision this same curriculum being used at any number of other academically challenging German gymnasia of the time—including Basedow's own alma mater in Hamburg. As the Philanthropin matured, did its curriculum become more mainstream (perhaps in an attempt to convince more conventional parents to send their children to a no-longer-radical

Philanthropin)? Were the innovative features of his school confined only to the lower levels of instruction? Or were the Philanthropin's more novel characteristics primarily extracurricular—qualities that did not pose explicit challenges to traditional curricular assumptions, but which were intended to peacefully coexist alongside of them?

Basedow's description of the curriculum for the next group of students runs as follows:

> *For the second class of senior Pensionisten*:
>
> From 8–9. Same instruction as the first class, with Professor *Trapp*.
>
> 9–10. Riding and dancing, alternating with the first class, that is, those who ride today dance tomorrow, and those who dance today ride tomorrow. Practice in arithmetic for some with Professor *Trapp*.
>
> 10–12. Latin by *Hauber* over authors in Basedow's *Chrestomathia hist. antiq*.[24]
>
> 1–2. Threshing and planing, alternating with the first class.
>
> 2–3. Drawing with Doctor *Samson*.[25] Some participate in instruction with the first class, some have practice in arithmetic with *Buße*.
>
> 3–5. Same activity as the first class.
>
> 5–6. Mathematics with *Damer* for three days, for the remaining days some participate in instruction with the first class, and some have private activity.
>
> 6–7. English with Professor *Trapp* over the *Vicar of Wakefield*.[26]

There are not too many surprises here. Because the size of each class was so small, and also because of the modest number of faculty members, students from different grades often met together. One might think it odd that the senior class did not also receive instruction in English. But for German students in the late eighteenth century, English was still less important than French and Latin.

Basedow's description of the curriculum for the first group of younger or smaller (*kleinere*) Pensionisten reads as follows:

> *For the first Class of junior Philanthropisten*:
>
> From 8–9. Practice in German with *Jahn*.[27] The readers are *von Rochow's* and *Weiße's Kinderfreund*,[28] *Campe's Sittenbüchlein für Kinder in gesitteten Ständen*,[29] *Feddersen's Beyspiele der Weisheit und Tugend*,[30] *Funk's Kleine Beschäftigungen für Kinder, erste Nahrung für den gesunden Menschenverstand*.[31]
>
> 9–10. Practice in writing with *Vogel*,[32] alternating with the second class through the entire week. Instructive association [*Lehrreicher Umgang*] with Principal *Neuendorf*[33] in his room or on walks.

10–11. Latin with *Feder* over *Büsching's Phaedri Fabulae* and *liber latinus*[34] and over selected passages from *Basedow's liber elementaris* and *Chrestomathia Colloquiorum Erasmi*.[35]

11–12. French with *Jasperson*.[36]

1–2. Music and free period under *Feder's* supervision.

2–3. Practice in drawing with Dr. *Samson*, under the alternating supervision of *Jasperson*, *Vogel*, and *Spener*.[37]

3–4. Practice in dancing with *dancers*, under *Vogel's* supervision.

4–5. French with *Spener* over selected passages from *Basedow's Manuel d'éducation*.[38]

5–6. Latin with *Feder* over selected passages from the Latin *Elementarbuch*.[39]

6–7. A free period for social contact under *Hauendorf's* supervision. (See above.)[40]

Of particular note in the curriculum plan for this group is the greater attention devoted to German instruction as well as the use of several of Basedow's own works as texts—including the French translation of his *Elementarwerk* for French class and the Latin translations of both the *Elementarbuch* and *Elementarwerk* for Latin classes.

The curriculum for the fourth group of students (aka the freshman class) reads as follows:

For the second Class of Philanthropinists:

8–9. Practice in writing with *Vogel*.

8–10. Spelling and free period for social contact, alternating with the first class. (See first class.)

10–12. Latin with *Wolke*.

1–2. As with the first class.

2–3. Drawing, as above [with the first class].

3–4. Dancing, as above [with the first class].

4–5. French with *Jasperson* over selected passages from the *Manuel d'éducation*.[41]

5–6. Practice in reading instructive books with *John* [*Jahn?*], in his room.

6–7. Free period for conversation with *Neuendorf*. On the first and fifteenth day of each month the smaller Philanthropinists practice letter writing. Walks, two afternoons a week.

In Pinloche 1896: 467

Finally, the curriculum for the *Famulanten*, those students enrolled at the Philanthropin who paid a reduced tuition:

For the Class of Famulanten:

5–7. After getting dressed, servants' activities [*Bedientengeschäfte*] for the teachers and *Pensionisten*.

7–8. Morning prayers and breakfast.

8–9. Practice in counting, 3 hours with *Buße* and 3 hours with *Danner*.

9–10. Practice in the French language with *Spener*.

10–11. Various sorts of information [*Allerlei Kentnisse*], with Prof. *Wolke*. (See above.)

11–12. Time for setting the tables [*Decken der Tische*] of the *Pensionisten* and to eat, under *Jahn's* supervision.

1–2. Time for clearing the tables.

2–3. Practice in carpentry, with a master carpenter under *Jahn's* supervision.

3–4. Free period for appropriate work.

4–5. Practice in style, in grammar, in essays, that is to say in receipts, etc., in the layout of bills, with *Feder*.

5–6. Practice in mathematics with *Buße*.

6–7. Time, to set the tables for the *Pensionisten*, and for themselves to eat.

7–8. Waiting at table for the *Pensionisten* who are dining.

8–10. Clearing the tables and then some more servants' activities.[42]

The Philanthropin—as Basedow proclaims in the title of one of the eight different books he published in 1774—was intended to be "a school ... for learners and young teachers, poor and rich" (DEP: title page). And his goal of making education more accessible to people of limited means was a very progressive one in late eighteenth-century Germany. Schools routinely charged for tuition in this era, and while a few had regulations that enabled poorer students to attend (such as the Johanneum in Hamburg, where Basedow was a student), his policy of charging a higher tuition rate for students from wealthy families and a lower one for students of more modest means was a novel one.

However, as noted earlier, there were actually very few students enrolled at the Philanthropin on the *Famulanten* track. According to Hanno Schmitt, approximately 40 percent of the Philanthropin students "had aristocratic backgrounds, and the remaining students were sons of businesspeople, wealthy famers, and scholars" (Schmitt 2008: 176–7). A large part of the explanation is certainly economic. Then, as now, private educational institutions with meager endowments (and the Philanthropin essentially had no endowment during its entire existence) are often forced to accept more full tuition-paying wealthy students than they would like. And the reduced tuition fees for poorer students that such institutions are able to offer are often still more than their families are able to pay.

But let us leave economics aside for a moment. Judging from Basedow's own description of the curriculum designed for the *Famulanten*, they were at best second-class citizens at the Philanthropin—"a school of human friendship" (DEP: title page). Only one step (and not a very big one) removed from household servants, all of the *Famulanten* were required to wait on the wealthier *Pensionisten* at mealtimes as well as to perform daily "servants' activities [*Bedientengeschäfte*]" for the teachers.

Furthermore, the kind of education *Famulanten* were offered at the Philanthropin was much less challenging than the curriculum of the *Pensionisten*. It was essentially a kind of vocational training rather than a liberal arts education. Instead of mathematics, "practice in counting"; instead of the formation of taste and style via German poetry, training in the down-to-earth business of writing bills and receipts. A little French, but no English, Latin, or Greek. And of course no education in the arts. Rather than seeking to ameliorate class antagonisms, the Philanthropin curriculum seems designed to reinforce and strengthen them. Rather than creating an educational climate that would make it possible for talented individuals from working-class backgrounds to have more options in adult life, the Philanthropin sought to keep them in their place. All of this—especially when viewed in the context of Basedow's own life story and working-class background—is deeply ironic and sad.

Staff turnover at the Philanthropin was high, and little or nothing is known at present about many of the faculty members. But by 1778–9, probably the Philanthropin's high point, the teaching staff (most of whose names are mentioned in the above curriculum plans) had grown to a respectable nineteen:

Basedow: Director (Latin, Ancient History, Practical Philosophy)
Wolke: (Mathematical drawing, Astronomy, Latin)
Salzmann, a Protestant minister who left in 1784 to found his own Philanthropin Institute near Gotha.
Olivier: from Lausanne, worked primarily with the junior classes.
Trapp: Natural Religion and Ethics, proper German "taste and style," French, and English.
Buße: Mathematics.

Danner: Latin, Greek.
Feder: Latin and French for the junior class.
Hauber: Geography, Current Events.
Jahn: German for the junior classes.
Jasperson: French for the junior classes.
Kretzchmar. Chemistry, Anatomy and "medical knowledge" (ES: 93).
Neuendorf: Conversation and hiking with the junior classes. (Neuendorf left the Philanthropin in 1780, but was called back by the Prince in 1784 to become director of the troubled school.)
Samson: Drawing.
Spence: French.
Schrödter: Riding (Schrödter was also employed by Prince Leopold in his riding stables.)
Vogel: Dancing. (See Landschoof 1933: 238)[43]

The above descriptions of conduct and curriculum policies at the Philanthropin show that it was not quite the utopia that Basedow often described it as being. Nevertheless, this was a special school where fathers would regard "every day that their sons spend outside the Philanthropinum as sheer deprivation [*reinen Verlust*];"[44] where grateful students would write effusive letters to their former teachers, thanking them for "the greatest influence on our happiness," noting that they "missed the friendly encounters" and "wished now that we were back in a time when we were treated more generously;"[45] and where intellectuals would praise Basedow for his "noble undertaking" which "could be perpetuated not only for our own century, but something far more, could deliver the foundation-stone for a not yet anticipated broadening and strengthening of the happiness of the human race."[46]

However, despite the glowing reports and increased publicity that followed the Public Examination of the school held on May 13–15, 1776, Basedow was still not happy. According to Göring,

> Despite all the recognition ... Basedow himself was very unsatisfied with the results of the Examination. He was so discouraged over the nonappearance of subsidies that had been expected with certainty that as early as June 11, 1776 he appealed to Iselin in Basel to be director of the Philanthropin.
>
> Göring 1880: LXXVII

Göring suggests here that lack of funding was the chief cause for the school's ongoing problems. But most biographers point to issues within Basedow himself—to his character and temperament. Diestelmann, for instance, writes:

Difficulties soon appeared; however, they certainly consisted no more in lack of funds, for money again began to flow in abundantly; they showed themselves no more in the lack of numbers who visited the school in order to apply, for these now came in such abundance that one could inspect and reject them; they were also not due to lack of praise for Basedow's ideas ... The difficulties lay much more in Basedow himself. The longer he was there, the more it became apparent that it was not possible for him to work together with others, due to his entire character. His unsteadiness, extreme ferocity, incompetence ... his overestimation of his own merit and underestimation of others' merit, all these and so many other weaknesses which more noble natures living together with him had to suffer for the duration, made him unsuited to be the leader of an exemplary educational institution.

Diestelmann 1897: 83

Similarly, Reble laments over "what could have happened at the Dessau Philanthropin if Basedow had had a more skillful hand in leadership and above all in collaborative work. For only in his time at Dessau did the root difficulties in him take their full effect, in particular the lack of sociability [*Mangel an Verträglichkeit*]" (Reble 1965: 262). Pinloche also points to "the instability and capriciousness of his character" and Basedow's "incapacity for leadership of the Philanthropin" (Pinloche 1896: 118, 119) as the chief grounds for the school's troubles. Surprisingly, Meier, who can almost always be counted on for some disparaging remarks about Basedow, offers nothing terribly negative here, noting only that Basedow "was much too weak in soul and body to be able to carry out such a colossal undertaking, or even to have the hope of experiencing its carrying out" (M: I: 389). But a page later he confirms a key weakness in Basedow's character that most biographers point to: that "to stand in joint association with Basedow for long in order to carry out an undertaking was almost impossible" (M: I: 390). Certainly better funding and more robust enrollment figures might have helped the school for a while, but given "the human inadequacy of its leader" (Reble 1999: 162), they would have served only to paper over a much deeper problem.

However, Diestelmann, after reciting the litany of character defects that in many biographers' views prevented Basedow from doing a credible job as director of the Philanthropin, then adds: "It is probable that Basedow himself came to this insight, and in part from this knowledge endeavored to win for himself a co-director position for the leadership of the Philanthropin, a set-up, which because of its internal disadvantage [*inneren Unzuträglichkeit*], certainly had to fail" (Diestelmann 1897: 83). In other words, Basedow voluntarily stepped down from the directorship of the Philanthropin. He was not fired, and despite his many personal shortcomings, he possessed a greater than average amount of self-knowledge. He knew that his main talents lay in writing and teaching rather than in administration and committee work. But the problem was that he had invested an immense amount of time, energy, and money in creating the Philanthropin. He was its sole parent, and he would not give up his child easily.

Iselin declined to accept Basedow's offer to assume the directorship position, despite the hiring committee's "wishes and hopes for a resolute yes" from him and their conviction that accepting their offer would be "the true best for the world."[47] Instead, Campe was chosen as the new director, and on December 15, 1776 Basedow officially resigned from the directorship and supposedly withdrew from the Philanthropin. For a while, things looked promising. At the beginning of 1777 there were thirty-six pupils enrolled at the school, including twelve *Famulanten*. And Prince Leopold, "who appeared to have more trust in the new director than in the old, quickly arranged for a part of the Palais Dietrich to be used by the Institute, next to a chapel for worship services and a garden for the recreation of the students" (Pinloche 1896: 120). Many believed that Campe "was in actuality the right man to bring the Philanthropinum into bloom, if he had become independent leader of the school. However, this was not the case" (Diestelmann 1897: 84). Despite his resignation, Basedow unfortunately was not able to keep his hands out of school affairs, and his new unofficial executive role—a position that "had no name" but which "allowed him to retain all rights and assume no obligations"—soon became "an inexhaustible source of conflict of all sorts" (Pinloche 1896: 120, 123). For instance, the earlier-mentioned quarrel with Mangelsdorf, which had begun four years earlier when Mangelsdorf was working on the Latin translation of the *Elementarwerk*, now rose to a head. Basedow had promised to pay Mangelsdorf a fixed sum for the translation work, but Mangelsdorf never received the money. He appealed to Campe to resolve the matter, but "the new director lacked sufficient heft to correct the mistakes of the old director" (Pinloche 1896: 122).

After less than a year in office, Campe, weary from numerous quarrels with Basedow, suddenly left for Hamburg in September 1777. Basedow appealed to him to return ("I am your brother ... Come back into our arms, into the arms of your family"),[48] but it was no use. On October 20, 1777, Campe officially resigned. Simon and Schweighäuser also resigned from the school at this point, leaving for Strasbourg to found a girls' school. Kant, in a letter to Campe of October 31, 1777, expressed his disappointment, but also indicated that he understood Campe's reasons for resigning: "With the greatest regret I have heard of the decision that the concern for your self-preservation has wrung from you, to leave the Philanthropin to its fate and to escape with your life before its downfall [*vor dem Untergange*]" (Br 10: 216).

After Campe's departure,

> Basedow again assumed leadership as 'Director of Teaching', that is, he determined by which method and in what order the sciences should be taught, and he demanded that each teacher carry out his advice and regulations, while he alone assumed all responsibility. Wolke, as deputy director [*Vicecurator*], looked after correspondence, bookkeeping, greeted visitors, and consulted with Basedow over the hiring of new teachers, whose confirmation of appointment was dependent on the Prince.
>
> Göring 1880: LXXVIII; cf. Schmid 1898: 242

At first, this seemed like a prudent solution. Let Wolke (whom Basedow had earlier praised as "the teacher and friend of my children ... an upright man, a virtuous Christian, an educative friend of children out of warm-hearted love and a strong natural instinct for youth, experienced and practiced in three languages, familiar with all areas of instruction"—DEP: 41) handle the day-to-day details of running the school, but still grant founder Basedow some official executive authority. But as many of his earlier biographers have noted, Basedow was temperamentally unsuited for collaborative work. He grew increasingly jealous of Wolke, and on Easter Day, 1778 resigned from this new position as well, announcing now that he would "never again take part in the leadership" of the Philanthropin—a decision that Wolke later called "decisive infanticide from the father" (in Diestelmann 1897: 86).[49] However, after this point Basedow still continued to offer courses in religious instruction, and he retained the title of school liturgist.

Wolke struggled on after Basedow's second resignation, but the situation grew from bad to worse. Johann Gottlieb Karl Spazier, an instructor at the school during Wolke's tenure, later published an anonymous autobiography in which he describes the school in Hobbesian terms—it had become "a total war of all against all ... complete anarchy," to which the Prince could only respond: "I am very sorry that things are this way. You cannot believe what I have suffered. You know how much I have loved this Institute. Do me the favor and reconcile with each other!"[50] Kant, who had been kept abreast of the deteriorating situation in Dessau through several local contacts, supported both Campe's and Wolke's leadership efforts, but at the same time grew increasingly eager to extricate himself from the uncomfortable role he had taken on as an unofficial fundraiser for the school. In a letter to Königsberg court chaplain Wilhelm Crichton (1735–1805) of July 29, 1778, in which he successfully appealed to the clergyman's vanity to take over this job ("I am heartily ready and willing to continue, but I think that the influence would be much greater if Your Reverence would be willing to take an interest in this cause and lend your name and pen to its furtherance"), Kant nevertheless once again expresses extremely high hopes and admiration for the Philanthropin:

> The world at present strongly feels the necessity of better education, but various attempts have not been successful. Those of F. v. Salis and Bahrdt[51] have stopped. And now the Dessau Institute stands alone; certainly simply because the humble and indescribably active *Wolke*, as its head, is not deterred by any hindrances, and moreover has the rare nature to remain true to his plan without obstinacy—under his supervision [the Philanthropin] will with time become the mother [*Stammmutter*] of all good schools in the world, if one merely in the beginning lends external support and encouragement.
>
> Br 10: 234[52]

And less then a week later, Kant wrote to Wolke, informing him that the influential clergyman Crichton would now be taking over the fundraising and recruitment efforts for the school in the Königsberg area, but also adding: "You are the last anchor of a matter whose idea alone makes the heart swell up, and on whom all hope of the participants rests." (Kant to Wolke, August 4, 1778; Br 10: 236–7).

Wolke struggled to keep the sinking ship afloat after Basedow's second departure in 1778, but relations between the two former friends continued to deteriorate. "In 1781 Basedow accused Wolke of having intended to embezzle a sum of 300 Thaler which had been designated for him (Basedow)" (Pinloche, 1896: 128), but this was only part of the story behind their increasingly acrimonious relationship. The Prince eventually intervened in 1783 to force a reconciliation between them, and Basedow, in his usual manner, published several short books defending his position regarding both the quarrel and the enforced truce.[53] Fueling Basedow's bad behavior throughout this entire time period, of course, was his excessive alcohol consumption. Pinloche is particularly blunt on this point: "It was no secret that the author of *Praktische Moral*[54] only too often sought immoderate enjoyment in wine and spirits as consolation for his sorrows and bad temper" (Pinloche 1896: 127).

In February 1784, deciding that he had finally had enough, Wolke left Dessau and headed for St. Petersburg, Russia, where he had been invited by Catherine the Great to become director of a cadet school. Carl Gottfried Neuendorf, who had left the Philanthropin in 1780, was now called back by the Prince to become the new director. Neuendorf reorganized the curriculum (due in part to complaints from parents that their children were not learning anything), and even dropped the word "Philanthropin" from the school's official name. It now had the bland and inoffensive title of "Educational Institute at Dessau." And the new director made it clear that in doing so he was trying to sever the school's ties with any radical pedagogical theories that might scare off potential students: "The former method, in which one mixes games and instruction with one another, we employ only in the beginning and with the greatest caution" (as cited by Pinloche 1896: 149).[55]

But all of this proved to be too little, too late—"the extent of decadence was far too strongly marked for a sound rehabilitation of the school" (Landschoof 1933: 255). After nineteen years of stormy and stressful existence, Basedow's "school of human friendship" finally closed its doors for good in 1793.

10

After School

After resigning from the Philanthropin's directorship position for the second time in 1778, Basedow still retained a smaller post as school liturgist. But he would soon resign from this job as well. According to Diestelmann,

> he also gave up this position in 1780, due in part to his loss of vision and difficulty of speaking with the loss of his front teeth, but primarily because (as he himself felt) his life sometimes deviated from the external dignity [*äusserlichen Würde*] that a Christian liturgist must always and everywhere observe.
>
> Diestelmann 1897: 87[1]

Christian Gotthilf Salzmann, who had worked previously as a pastor in Erfurt, would soon take over Basedow's liturgist duties at the school, remaining in this capacity until 1784, when he left Dessau to found his own Philanthropinist institute at Schnepfenthal, near Gotha.

Biographers are often extremely dismissive toward Basedow's post-Philanthropin years. Pinloche, for instance, opens his chapter on "Basedow's Final Years" by proclaiming that the history of the last years of his life "offers little that is interesting" (Pinloche 1896: 150; cf. Schmid 1898: 243–4). However, there are at least two noteworthy features of the last stage of Basedow's professional life. The first is his continued literary activity, which remained prodigious by any measure. "Basedow had to write, as Salzmann says, 'until his final breath.'"[2] Reble lists twenty-two separate publications from the last decade of Basedow's life, which include both theological and pedagogical works. Included in the first group are the following:

- *Doctrines of Christian Wisdom and Contentment for Searching Self-Thinkers* (see Basedow 1780).
- *Universal Christian Hymnbook for all Churches and Sects* (see Basedow 1781a).
- *Paraphrased Extracts from the New Testament, Arranged According to the Needs of our Time by a Christian Researcher of Many Years* (see Basedow 1781b).

- *Jesus Christ, the Great World of Christianity and the Small Choice* (see Basedow 1784a).
- *An Examination of the Most Natural Religion and Other Practical Doctrines of Civil Duty, Tolerance and Virtue, likewise Reason and its Knowledge of God* (see Basedow 1784b).
- *A Society of Brotherly Love Hymnbook for Christians and for Philosophical Companions of Jesus* (see Basedow 1784c).

Diestelmann (himself a pastor by profession) may be right when he notes that "Basedow's role here was played out, and none of the ten theological works that he still published [after retirement] have lasting value" (Diestelmann 1897: 87). Similarly, Vorbrodt remarks that Basedow's theological writings of his final years "are useless [*wertlos*] for us, they also contain little that is new" (Vorbrodt 1920: I: 30), and Meier complains that they are often merely "changed [versions]—or as one says—improved revisions" of earlier publications (M: II: 334). But these are unduly harsh verdicts: books on tolerance and peace are still being published at present, and given human nature there will always be a need for them. And ecumenical hymnbooks (even if Basedow had published one before—see Basedow 1767b) were still something of a novelty in the late eighteenth century. Even if one does accept Diestelmann's, Vorbrodt's, and Meier's verdicts regarding the quality and originality of these final theological works, their sheer quantity—particularly when judged in light of Basedow's deteriorating health—remains impressive.

Missing from Reble's list of twenty-two publications after Basedow's final departure from the Philanthropin in 1780 is the second edition of the *Elementarwerk*, published in 1785. As noted earlier, Basedow did all of the editing for the second edition of this colossal work on his own, after Trapp declined to carry out his initial plan to prepare the new edition. In his Preface to the second edition, Basedow writes:

> my understanding and my heart have not renounced this school matter [*dieser Schulsache*] quite yet. I did and do, visibly and invisibly, with loss of bodily strength and a part of my personal assets, all that was and is possible in order to secure a successor, one who has or will reach concurring insight with me in this important concern of humanity and who lives in happier circumstances, to prepare and make easier the new beginning and unbroken progress of undertakings like this.
>
> E: I: LIV

Basedow is alluding here, at least in part, to an earlier job position for a prospective teacher at the Philanthropin that he himself posted in the 1778 issue of the *Pädagogische Unterhandlungen*. The lengthy and demanding job description reads in part as follows:

> It is assumed that those who apply will have at least read Basedow's *Methodenbuch* and Chapter XI, Sections 6-8 of his new *Practische Philosophie*[3] and the *Pädagogische Unterhandlungen* ... They must, I say, be so eager for improvement in schools that, if they can find sufficient honor and remuneration in it, they will wish to be of use here for the rest of their lives ... We seek a man who, as concerns the entire teaching style of the Institute, in the beginning wants to and can work in company with *Basedow*, through invention—through consultation, through the production of extracts and school books, through attention to younger writers at the Institute, through advances in teaching practices with younger teachers—and through management of our liturgy ... No area of study must be foreign to him ... In German he must belong to the most worthy authors. He must at least understand French, however he must be able to read and write Latin with some skill ... He must know philosophy more than the other sciences, in order to teach how to decrease and shorten the horrible difficulties of the theoretical parts and to handle well the practical parts. He must be able to truthfully say that he believes in the sayings of the New Testament, and in the crucified, resurrected Jesus Christ ... whatever church or private opinion concerning different doctrines he may prefer ... In addition, because Basedow must decrease [*abnehmen*] his role, his must increase [*zunehmen*], and in a few years he must learn to oversee [the school] ... Very desirable qualities of the candidate are also that he at least sing well in choir (however, excellent declamation is necessary), and at least be able to compose good, edifying, moral, and spiritual German verses. Also desired, though not necessary, is that he be unmarried and be willing to remain so for several years.[4]

Given the multiple high demands packed into this job description, it should come as no surprise that the initial job search proved unsuccessful. And so Basedow ran the ad again in 1780—this time "without the enumeration of conditions which were placed on the capability of the candidate" (Pinloche 1896: 131). The second search was eventually successful: Salzmann, a young pastor from Erfurt, was hired to fill the position. But while Salzmann soon gained the respect and love of colleagues and students at the Philanthropin, he also grew increasingly uncomfortable with the bickering between Basedow and Wolke and the overall deteriorating situation at the school. Reflecting on the matter later in his 1784 *Ankündigung einer Erziehungsanstalt* (*Announcement of an Educational Institute*—viz., the school that he founded in Schnepfenthal), Salzmann predicted accurately that "it was not entirely improbable that the sad quarrel would destroy and knock over the entire [Philanthropin] Institute" (Salzmann 1784: 76). And so, in February 1784 he decided "to leave the Institute, in order to find a place where he himself could realize his ideas" (Salzmann 1784: 73). In less than a year, Salzmann opened his own Philanthropinist Institute in Schnepfenthal—an extremely successful and influential school that is still in operation today (albeit one that has undergone many changes in direction over the years).

Basedow's earlier-cited remark in the Preface to the 1785 edition of his *Elementarwerk* that he had "not renounced this school matter quite yet" also points to the second noteworthy feature in the last period of his professional career: his renewed work in education. His pedagogical pursuits during his post-Philanthropin years took two forms: publications and classroom teaching. His post-1780 books on educational method include the following:

- *For Reflection and Investigation. Of the Method of Teaching Latin through Knowledge of Facts. With a Description and Offer of a Pre-Academy of Latin Studies for those who begin late and wish to finish soon* (see Basedow 1785a).
- *An Unexpected, Important Improvement in the Art of Teaching Reading, together with a Booklet on Spelling* (see Basedow 1785b).

Pinloche reports that Basedow "regarded this [second] book as so useful that he wished to make a gift to the working classes, and allowed 500 free copies to be distributed to various elementary schools" (Pinloche 1896: 151).

- *A New Tool [Neues Werkzeug] for Teaching Reading, in which the Particular Part for Learners Provides for the Beginning of Knowledge of Facts, Ethics, Knowledge of God and Grammatical Correctness, by Johann Bernhard Basedow, and One for the Enlightenment of Working Society* (see Basedow 1787).

As Meier notes, the *Neues Werkzeug* "is not only Basedow's final pedagogical work, but also his last publication" (M: II: 340). It is item number 108 in Reble's extensive and imposing list of Basedow's *Schriften* (R: 274).

But more impressive still is the fact that Basedow's return to pedagogical writing at the end of his life also led to a renewed interest in testing his theories through practice—he returned to classroom teaching. Rathmann writes:

> He hoped that through the use of his method the unavoidable difficulties for the millions of children who each year must learn to read would not only be made easier, but that they would also learn to read more quickly and more correctly, and that he could also thereby lead them to more know-how than had occurred

previously. In view of this, he justifiably regarded his own ventures as very important and meritorious ... After he finished a trip to Braunschweig, Altona, and Leipzig, he arrived in Magdeburg in fall 1785. Here he not only recommended his teaching methods to many fathers, mothers, and schoolteachers among his friends, but he also chose one from among the many excellent primary schools there, in order to offer instruction in the correct application of his method. This was the school of *Frau Inspektorin Kalisky* in Magdeburg.

Ra: 151–2

Unfortunately, very little is known at present about *Frau Inspektorin Kalisky* or her school. In the Preface to his final publication, the *Neues Werkzeug zum Lesenlehren* (1787), Basedow writes:

> About twenty months ago I traveled through Magdeburg and spoke with Councilor *Funk*,[5] my dear friend of thirty years who has learned to know me well in all situations of my life. Our helpful conversation also passed on to *learning how to read*, of which I boasted to him without blushing that I could introduce an unbelievably better method, if I had only one or two advice-loving female teachers [*rathliebende Lehrerinnen*] who of course themselves must also read very well ... He named a widow, *Frau Inspektorin Kalisky* who, helpless after the death of her husband, had determination, industry, thrift, and luck, and through this manner of work was able to maintain herself and her five children decently.

Basedow 1787: VI

Basedow adds later that "her school belonged to the best" (Basedow 1787: VII) in Magdeburg, but he provides few other details. Kalisky was probably Russian (some sources spell her name 'Kaliski'), and the academy she founded was a school for girls. Most of her students did not come from wealthy families, and Basedow worked primarily with the youngest ones (ages five and six). Rathmann also notes that Basedow worked at Kalisky's school "from 1785 on for several years, and each year for several months, daily for three to four hours" (Ra: 153).

Several biographers emphasize that Basedow volunteered his time at the school, and that he was very popular with the students. Pinloche, for instance, writes:

> He wanted to prove the superiority of his method. Therefore in fall 1785 he set out for Magdeburg, where he himself gave lessons in beginning reading to small children in the school led by a lady (*Kalisky*), without taking any remuneration for it, and he did this at an age when others devoted themselves to rest. His instruction had such a success, and his selflessness drew him such sympathy,

that he found the residency in Magdeburg extremely enjoyable and fixed on the plan to settle down there permanently.

Pinloche 1896: 151

Similarly, in Göring we read:

> Despite his age and his illness, he dedicated part of his time to the practical application of his theory, and from his own initiative took part in instruction at a school in Magdeburg. He spent several months each year in this city, partly because participating in the instruction of children brought him the greatest joy, partly because by doing this he could withdraw from the oppressive atmosphere of Dessau. This activity led him to the attempt to produce a simple method of reading.
>
> Göring 1880: CI

Although Basedow's "simple" method for learning how to read was in fact quite sophisticated and detailed, the part of it that no doubt endeared him most to Kalisky's young female students was his recommendation that cookies in the form of each letter be baked as an aid to learning the alphabet and improving one's spelling. In the *Neues Werkzeug zum Lesenlehren* he defends this novel practice as follows:

> What will this baking cost? At most, little. The children must have breakfast. One needs only to bake the letters to a modestly tastier degree than the normal breakfast, although they can also be prepared from ordinary bread dough. In our experience, after more than four weeks no child needs to eat the letters anymore.
>
> Basedow 1787: 33

In his impressive volunteer work at Kalisky's school for girls in Magdeburg during the final years of his life, there is a sense in which Basedow's tempestuous life has come full circle—back to his first teaching experience as a young tutor in the von Qualen family home in Borghorst and back to his first attempt to write about pedagogical methods in his 1752 Kiel dissertation. It is almost as though the difficult years in Dessau as Director of the Philanthropin—certainly the most famous chapter of his life—were merely an unfortunate tangent that took him away from his most important work. Basedow was most at home and most himself when he was working with young students in the classroom and reflecting on his teaching experiences in his writing about educational methodology.

It is clear that Basedow enjoyed his time in Magdeburg immensely (in part because of the welcome respite from the chaos in Dessau which it provided), and as a result he began making plans to move there permanently. His daughter Emilie had already moved to Magdeburg some years earlier, in order to continue her education under the tutorship of a pastor (see Landschoof 1933: 260). But his wife's health was failing, and this made the move impossible. Gertrude Elisabeth died in Dessau on May 23, 1788, after thirty-three years with Basedow. Few details of their married life are available, but it is safe to assume that she had put up with a lot over the years. As the anonymous author of the 1790 "Fragmente über Basedow" remarks: "*He was married to the public.*—He therefore lived less for his family, than he himself perhaps wished" ("Fragmente über Basedow" 1790: 301). And given Basedow's mood swings, heavy drinking, frequent fundraising and publicity trips, demanding writing schedule, and generally quarrelsome nature, he could not have been the easiest person to live with.[6] But his own health was also in serious decline at this point, and he too needed help at home. And so Emilie returned to Dessau to "manage her father's household for a while, until 1789 when she married a worthy pastor from Bernburg, Herr [Emanuel] *Cautius*" (Ra: 161)—a marriage which, according to Basedow's great grandson Max Müller, "was unhappy, though so far as I know, it did not lead to any public scandal."[7]

But Basedow and Gertrude also had a second child together who survived infancy—their son Ludwig, born on October 2, 1774 and now 14 years old.[8] As the sole surviving parent, after his wife's death Basedow assumed the duty to care for their son, and his top priority was to make sure that Ludwig received a good education—the son's "instruction, education, and culture was almost his only concern in the last years of his life" (Ra: 161; cf. Pinloche 1896: 152).[9] And according to Neuendorf, caring for his son after his wife's death now "gave his activity a more peaceful and more definite direction, which was so beneficial for him that he enjoyed more domestic peace and happiness than ever before" (as cited by Schmid 1898: 244). In July 1790 Basedow returned to Magdeburg with Ludwig with the intent of finally moving there. "A small apartment had already been rented near his friend Funk, whom he had appointed guardian in the event of his own demise" (Diestelmann 1897: 88). But the father and son had also planned another short trip together to Halle, Leipzig, and Dessau before moving into their new apartment, intending to leave on July 26. However, on July 24 Basedow fell ill, "seized by dizziness and nausea, and had to retire to bed, which he was never able to leave again" (Pinloche 1896: 152). On July 25 at two in the afternoon he died at the age of sixty-six, after suffering a severe hemorrhage. His final words, recorded by nearly all of his biographers, were: "*I wish to be dissected [seciret] for the good of my fellow human beings*" (Ra: 168; cf. Pinloche 1896: 152; Diestelmann 1897: 88; Göring 1880: CI; Schmid 1898: 244–5).

Needless to say, this was by no means a typical deathbed request in late eighteenth-century Germany, particularly for a religious man. At any rate, because "the wish could not be carried out, due to the heat" (Pinloche 1896: 152), burial plans were made immediately. Although some townspeople protested that "Basedow is not worthy to be buried in the churchyard,"[10] on July 27 he was buried at the church cemetery of the Holy Spirit Church in Magdeburg, a congregation dating back to 1214, where composer and native son Georg Philipp Telemann had been baptized in 1681. In 1796 a small memorial was added to Basedow's gravesite, which his friend Funk helped arrange. The marble was furnished by Prince Karl Wilhelm Ferdinand von Braunschweig-Wolfenbüttel (1735–1806). Unfortunately, the original memorial no longer exists (though several replacements have been erected over the years), and the wording of its inscription was not recorded. Diestelmann notes that it was paid for by "true admirers and students of the man who, in spite of all of his weaknesses, worked tirelessly for the welfare of his fellow human beings" (Diestelmann 1897: 89).

11

"The Mother of All Good Schools in the World"

Time and politics have not been particularly kind to two of the most tangible physical markers of Basedow's life. Dessau, home of the Philanthropin, was almost completely destroyed toward the end of the Second World War. On March 7, 1945, 520 allied aircraft bombed the city—eighty-four percent of Dessau was destroyed, and 1,136 civilians lost their lives. The original site of Basedow's school—the Rautenstockschen Haus on Neumarkt Straße—was among the many buildings reduced to rubble. After the war Dessau was rebuilt in typical GDR *Plattenbau* style (prefabricated concrete slab architecture). Fortunately, the Palais Dietrich, where the Philanthropin moved part of its operations in 1777 after Basedow's first resignation as Director, and where it was housed entirely from 1780 until the school's final closing in 1793, was not destroyed. But when one visits this building today—an impressive, yellow eighteenth-century structure in what remains of the *Altstadt*—there are few visible traces of Basedow or the Philanthropin. Although the Museum für Stadtgeschichte in Dessau does contain a few items relating to the early history of the Philanthropin, at present there is no public museum dedicated exclusively to either Basedow or his school inside the Palais Dietrich or anywhere else in Dessau—one cannot even purchase picture postcards of the Philanthropin or its founder in the palace gift shop.

The name "Philanthropinum," however, has fared much better in Dessau. In 1945 the Hauptmann-Loeper-Gymnasium moved into the Palais Dietrich, and in 1947 it adopted both the name "Philanthropinum" and, at least at first, the progressive tradition of Basedow's pedagogy. Due to increased enrollment, in 1950 the school moved to a larger building on Mauerstraße, and in 1961 it relocated yet again to the former Städtischen Handels-Realschule on Friedrich-Naumann-Straße. During the 1960s, after further reorganization of the city school system, the school became known as the Erweitere Oberschule "Philanthropinum." After the *Wende*, the school again became a gymnasium and the campus on Friedrich-Naumann-Straße was extensively renovated. At one point there were more than 1,000 enrolled students and over 100 teachers and assistants working at the school, though in recent years Dessau's population has declined a bit. At present, the Gymnasium Philanthropinum in Dessau has about 800 students and 60 teachers. But it is a Philanthropinum more in name than in content. Although the school's official website does pay homage to several of Basedow's key ideas in its "Schulprogramm" section,[1] for the most part the present-day Philanthropinum has been mainstreamed into the German public school system, and the extent to which it adheres to and actively promotes the progressive ideals of Basedow's original school is negligible.

Magdeburg, the city where Basedow was buried, taught reading to beginning students at Frau Kalisky's school for girls after he left the Philanthropin, and where he had also intended to take up residence toward the end of his life, was also nearly completely destroyed during the war. On January 16, 1945, the British Royal Air Force (with U.S. support) bombed the city. About ninety percent of the inner city was obliterated (including fifteen churches)—at least 200,000 civilians lost their lives, and 190,000 people lost their homes. The church where Basedow's grave was located—the Heilige-Geist-Kirche—was severely damaged, but after the war it was rebuilt and services were once again held there beginning in 1950. However, the newly rebuilt church did not fit in with the socialist

Figure 6 Robert B. Louden at the new Basedow Memorial in Magdeburg, July 2018. By permission of Hiroko Fogarty.

government's plans for the reconstruction of the city, and in 1959 the GDR government itself blew up the church again—along with the church cemetery, where Basedow was buried. Most of Basedow's modest memorial, which itself had undergone several modifications over the years, was destroyed. Fortunately, in 2015 a new Basedow *Denkmal* was unveiled in Magdeburg.[2] Composed in part out of remnants of the 1897 version of the original 1797 memorial, the new monument consists of a pedestal of Greek marble, a portrait of Basedow cast in round, white stone, and a broken marble column, underneath which is some printed information about the Philanthropin and its founder, the construction of the new memorial, and the sponsors who funded the reconstruction. Although centrally located on Regierungstraβe in the *Altstadt* (not far from the site of the original monument), it sits awkwardly next to a government office building, and few city residents seem to even be aware of its location.

But the most enduring aspects of some human beings' lives are not physical buildings and gravestones, but rather the ideas and principles that they advocated. What is Basedow's intellectual legacy today? The most obvious place to look is within the progressive education movement in the U.S. and elsewhere.[3] The roots of many of the core principles commonly associated with this movement definitely lie in Basedow's pioneering work. Chief among these principles are the following:

- The need to educate the whole child—i.e., to attend to physical and emotional growth as well as intellectual.
- Learning through doing—"active learning."
- The importance of creative and manual arts in the curriculum, particularly the teaching of vocational skills to children.
- The responsibility of schools to take the lead in restructuring society.
- The need to prepare students to function successfully as adults, both in their capacities as democratic citizens in the world at large and as productive members of society.
- The need to restore joy in learning, so that "children like, or love, to come to school" (Dewey 1900a: 128).

It should come as no surprise that the standard criticisms of progressive education—criticisms which eventually led to the movement's demise in the mid-1950s: that it treated classical literature and languages too cavalierly, that it was grounded in an objectionable naturalism, that its orientation was anti-intellectual and utilitarian, that it was subversive and counter to traditional values—are also quite similar to criticisms that political conservatives, neohumanists, and traditional Lutherans made of Basedow and the Philanthropinists back in the 1770s and following. But this also adds further support to the claim that Basedow is the true father of progressive education.

Unfortunately, standard accounts of the progressive education movement seldom even mention Basedow, preferring instead to proclaim Rousseau as the movement's intellectual father. The following passage is typical of this tendency:

> The seminal text of the child-centered movement was Rousseau's *Émile*. Since its publication in 1762, it has inspired educational reformers in Europe and the United States who sought alternatives to routinized and formal schooling ... Rousseau's belief in education was an important influence on the American progressive education movement ... Like Rousseau, Dewey rejected the rote learning and formalism of public schools, especially the common belief that what was taught should be disagreeable so as to teach children to exercise their willpower and self-discipline.
>
> Ravitch 2000: 169–71[4]

And in the rare cases where Basedow's name is cited in discussions of progressive education, he is too often portrayed as a merely derivative thinker whose chief ideas are borrowed from Rousseau's *Émile*—an error, as we saw earlier, that one also finds in many earlier accounts of Basedow's work. The following passage (taken from the entry on "Progressive Education" in the *New Encyclopedia Britannica*) is a representative example:

> The sources of the progressive education movement lay partly in European pedagogical reforms from the 17th through the 19th centuries, ultimately stemming from Jean-Jacques Rousseau's *Émile* ... In the late 18th and early 19th centuries, Rousseau's theories were given practical application in a number of experimental schools. In Germany, Johann Friedrich Basedow established the Philanthropinum at Dessau (1774), and Friedrich Froebel founded the first kindergarten at Keilhau (1837). In Switzerland, Johann Pestalozzi dedicated himself, in a succession of schools, to the education of poor and orphaned children.
>
> "Progressive Education" 2002: 9: 722

These failures to accord Basedow his rightful place in the history of progressive education are perhaps partly explainable due to the fact that John Dewey, the most influential theorist of the progressive education movement, makes no explicit references to either Basedow or the Philanthropin in any of his voluminous writings.[5] Nevertheless, establishing clear links between the Philanthropinist and progressive education movements is not hard to do. For anyone familiar with these two educational reform groups, the connections are evident.[6]

But what are we to make of Kant's much bolder assertion that the Philanthropin is "the mother of all good schools in the world" (Kant to Crichton, July 29, 1778; Br 10: 234)? Was Kant (as Raumer holds) simply "inspired by amiable good will to hope for too much" (Raumer 1857: 291), or does the claim possess plausibility? What features of the Philanthropin led Kant to speak of the school in such superlative terms?[7]

It must be admitted at the start that in making this remark Kant is working with a somewhat idealized conception of the school. He never visited Dessau, and the day-to-day situation at the Philanthropin was sometimes quite different than what he envisaged. But if we keep this proviso in mind, it is possible to establish the truth of his claim. In his *Lectures on Pedagogy*, Kant states:

> We must establish experimental schools before we can establish normal schools ... It is often imagined that experiments in education are not necessary, and that one can just judge from reason [*aus der Vernunft*] whether something will be good or not. However, this is a great error ... We see, therefore, that since it is a question of experiments [*auf Experimente ankommt*], no one generation can present a complete plan of education. The only experimental school which to an extent made a beginning in blazing a trail [*die Bahn zu brechen*] was the Dessau Institute. We must let it keep this glory regardless of the many mistakes of which one could accuse it ... It was in a sense the only school in which teachers had the freedom to work according to their own methods and plans, and where they were in contact with each other as well as with all scholars in Germany.
>
> Päd 9: 451[8]

As we have seen, Kant strongly endorsed Basedow's naturalism. The Philanthropin is superior to other schools because its "educational method ... is wisely derived from nature itself and not slavishly copied from old habit and inexperienced ages" (AP 2: 449). Good schools are schools that work with rather than against nature (cf. AP 2: 447). Friedrich Paulsen also stresses the importance of Basedow's naturalism when he notes that Basedow's principal aim in founding the Philanthropin "was to make room ... for an education that was in touch with real life and in accordance with human nature ... The life of the pupils was arranged with a view to conformity with Nature."[9] But in the above passage from the *Lectures on Pedagogy*, Kant draws attention to several additional distinctive features of the Philanthropin. Part of his strong praise and support for the school stems from its experimentalist orientation. According to Kant's idealized conception of the Philanthropin, the school was committed to testing its educational ideas in practice and was continually guided by experimentation.

The Philanthropin's curriculum was not set in stone, and the school regularly evaluated its practices by examining empirically whether its goals were being met. If the evidence showed that things were not working as expected, then appropriate changes would be introduced. Unfortunately, the actual level of experimentation at the Dessau Philanthropin was much lower than Kant suggests. For the most part, teachers at the school were simply expected to implement the curricular policies that Basedow had laid out in his earlier publications. And we know that Basedow himself was not a team player—he was not sufficiently open to the suggestions and criticisms of colleagues. Additionally, there is no clear evidence that he himself adopted an experimental attitude toward educational policies after the Philanthropin first opened in 1774. But part of what Kant means in calling the Philanthropin the mother of all good schools in the world is that good schools are experimental schools where ideas are tested. Good schools acknowledge that they are not perfect, and they continually test their theories in practice in an effort to improve themselves.

A second feature that Kant draws attention to in the above passage is that the Philanthropin was also intended to be a gathering place for young teachers to work with more experienced educators, as well as a site for scholars to engage in and share their research on educational methods. The Philanthropin was designed, as Basedow himself stressed in the title of a 1774 publication, as "a school of human friendship and good knowledge for students and young teachers" (DEP: title page). In other words, the Dessau Institute was envisioned as a teacher-training institute, something novel at the time—"it alone would be a planting center [*Pflanzort*] of teachers for everyone" (DEP: XVI).

In this respect as well, Kant's conception of the school is somewhat overidealized. In fact there was much more infighting among faculty at the school than mutual cooperation and sharing of ideas, and a large part of the blame must be placed on Basedow's own crankiness and unsociability. Nevertheless, the Philanthropin did succeed in attracting many excellent teacher-scholars to its doors. Granted, many of them soon left after finding Basedow too much to bear, but in the process of doing so they also went on to found their own Philanthropin-inspired schools in other regions. In this manner, the *Pflanzort* aspect of the Philanthropin program succeeded admirably, albeit in a somewhat different way than originally intended. Raumer and others, as noted earlier, have also singled out this missionary dimension of the school, praising its success:

> From the Dessau Philanthropin a great pedagogical initiative and excitement spread out over Germany and Switzerland, indeed, over a great part of Europe...

Educational institutions, on the model of the Philanthropin, soon arose in all quarters ... However, the Philanthropin school had an influence not only through these institutions but also through a heap of writings for young and old, with which Germany was inundated.

Raumer 1857: 2: 307

Kant's second point can be summarized as follows: Like the Philanthropin, good schools are schools that attract aspiring teachers. They are ongoing communities of learning and research—for students, teachers, and scholars alike.

Yet another feature of Basedow's Philanthropin that led Kant to call it the mother of all good schools is that, at least for a while, it was propelled by an unparalleled level of energy and enthusiasm. Like many other Enlightenment intellectuals,[10] Basedow and Kant were both convinced that education is the single most decisive factor in human beings' lives. As Basedow writes in his *Methodenbuch*: "Education is the most important thing in human life" (MB IV.5; in G: 50)—a conviction echoed in the following passage from one of Kant's moral philosophy lectures: "the final destiny of the human race is moral perfection ... How then are we to seek this perfection, and from where is it to be hoped for? From nowhere else but education" (V-Mo/Collins 27: 470, 471). But Basedow (unlike Locke, Rousseau, Kant, and many other philosophers of education with whom he is often compared) was not just a theorist on this topic. He took the additional (and in his case, more precarious) step of founding a new type of school in order to realize the ideals advocated in his writings. And his project struck a resounding chord far and wide. Financial and literary support streamed in from many quarters of Europe as well as Russia, and this is partly what led Kant to proclaim in yet another classroom lecture that the Philanthropin was "the greatest phenomenon which has appeared in this century for the improvement of the perfection of humanity. Through it all schools in the world will receive another form" (V-Anth/Fried 25: 722). Christian Garve too, as we saw earlier, singled out Basedow's unflinching devotion to the cause of human progress through education as his most admirable quality: "There are perhaps many people among us who are just as profound," he noted, but those within this select group who are also working "entirely on the improvement and happiness of human beings, and ... the means of promoting moral perfection in all classes, are much more rare." And finally, among those in this extremely select second group, "there are perhaps none except" Basedow who have managed to combine their intellect and commitment to moral improvement "with such a great enthusiasm, so much activity, so much hardening against dangers and difficulties, so much persistence against opposition and hindrances" (Garve 1771:

322; reprinted in E: II: 548). This last point can perhaps be summarized as follows: Like the Philanthropin, good schools are institutions that are nourished and propelled by an infectious level of human energy and enthusiasm, one that itself grows out of an awareness of the central importance of education in human life, one that is still able to sustain itself and inspire others when confronted by counterforces.

Last but definitely not least, the Philanthropin was a school that sought to be a welcoming place for students of all religious faiths, nationalities, and economic backgrounds. As we have seen, the Dessasu Institute opened its doors both "for poor and rich" (DEP: title page), and all texts used at the school were "*free of theological verdicts* for Christianity against Jews, Muslims, and deists" (ES: 65)—Basedow's chief aim was to use religious faith as a means of connecting people with each other rather than as a weapon for dividing them from one another. And this too was a project dear to Kant's heart. As he remarks toward the end of his *Lectures on Pedagogy* (perhaps with the Philanthropin in mind): "Despite the variety of religions there is nevertheless overall unity of religions" (Päd 9: 496).[11] Students at the Philanthropin were also taught to see that "we are citizens of the world" (ES: V), and this need for schools to foster a cosmopolitan orientation is yet another central point on which Basedow and Kant agree. On the last page of his *Lectures* Kant emphasizes: "Cosmopolitan sentiments should be developed ... Children must rejoice over the highest good in the world [*das Weltbeste*], even if it is not to the advantage of their fatherland or to their own advantage" (Päd 9: 499).

Granted, gender is one weak point in Basedow's (not to mention Kant's) cosmopolitan impulse toward the moral equality of all human beings—he should have done better here. But the extensive education his daughter Emilie received at the Philanthropin as well as his *pro bono* classroom teaching during his final years at Frau Kalisky's school for girls in Magdeburg show that he did make some substantial efforts in this area as well.

The vital role that schools can and should play in overcoming hate has yet to be properly harnessed, and here as elsewhere, Basedow was a pioneer whose message needs to be recovered. As Rodgers and Hammerstein correctly note in their 1949 song, "You've Got to Be Carefully Taught" (from the Broadway musical *South Pacific*):

You've got to be taught to hate and fear,
You've got to be taught from year to year ...
You've got to be taught before it's too late
Before you are six or seven or eight.

To hate all the people your relatives hate,
You've got to be carefully taught.[12]

South Pacific 1949

Our schools still have a long way to go in this area. Rather than reinforcing hate, they can and should act as a corrective to the multiple forms of hatred that many children still learn from their parents and other segments of society (including, unfortunately, a large number of religious institutions).

So, when interpreted in the above manner, we can see that there is much truth in Kant's striking claim that the Philanthropin is the mother of all good schools in the world. For it was a new type of school, grounded not only on the principle that educational methods should be in accordance with human nature, but also on the premises that ongoing experimentation is vital to schools, that teacher training as well as persistent research and publication are central to their mission, that schools must be continually motivated by an understanding of the overriding significance of education in human life, and that they need to serve vigilantly on the forefront of the continual battle against hatred. And this is certainly at least part of what good schools everywhere (whether they call themselves "progressive" or not) should aspire to.

And when we add to this inspiring set of ideals the fact that the man behind the Philanthropin and the influential reform movement it generated was himself a tragicomic figure with a much higher than average number of character flaws and personal weaknesses, who somehow managed to persevere and even flourish in the face of great adversity, the story becomes still more poignant and inspiring. Basedow was not quite the "prophet" that Goethe sarcastically described him as being (*Dichtung und Wahrheit* XIV; in R: 244), but he was clearly no ordinary mortal. On this point, Garve was much closer to the truth: "there are perhaps none" like him.

Notes

Introduction

1. Cf. Reble (1965: 253).
2. However, there is one very good English-language PhD dissertation on Basedow—see Landschoof (1933). Although I have benefited greatly from Landschoof's (1894–1965) pioneering work, my project also incorporates much new material that was not available to him. Lang (1892) is merely a short (29 pp.) and unoriginal pamphlet.
3. One of the most influential examples here is Barnard (1863)—an English translation of parts of Raumer (1843). Later English-language works on the history of education that include coverage of Basedow—e.g., Quick (1896) and Graves (1912)—are largely derivative on Barnard.
4. This tendency to demote Basedow to an unoriginal German Rousseau pervades many earlier discussions. See, e.g., Pinloche (1896: 60–61) and Blankertz (1982: 80).
5. Sahlberg and Doyle, in *Let the Children Play*, bemoan the fact that "play is an increasingly endangered experience for many of the world's children" (Sahlberg and Doyle 2019: 5). But nowhere in their 445-page book is Basedow's name even mentioned.

1 A New School for a New Age

1. Lauchkard (1848: 93). A strong supporter of the Enlightenment, Leopold III Friedrich Franz, Duke of Anhalt-Dessau (1740–1817), the "Prince of Dessau" was the chief patron of Basedow's school. In 1771 he invited Basedow and his family to move to Dessau, providing both a building for the future school and a salary for Basedow.
2. "Friends of Humanity" (from the Greek *philia*, friendship + *anthropôs*, man). In some texts the name is spelled "Philanthropinum;" in others, "Philanthropin." I prefer the shorter spelling.
3. But can "a general, Christian, Philanthropinist liturgy" always be "*free from theological verdicts* against Jews, Muslims, Deists," etc.? There is often a tension between Basedow's desire to find common ground between different religious faiths and his own Christian commitments.

4 Raumer (1843: 2: 256). Parts of Raumer's influential book have been translated by into English by Henry Barnard. See Barnard (1863).
5 Jewish philosopher Moses Mendelssohn (1729–86), a central figure in the German Enlightenment, was born in Dessau, the city where Basedow's Philanthropin was established. He and Basedow personally corresponded with each other, and Mendelssohn encouraged Jewish students to attend the Philanthropin. And while the two philosophers disagreed with each other on many issues, Mendelssohn was also in frequent dialogue with Kant.
6 The 119th Psalm consists of 176 stanzas, and is by far the longest of the 150 Psalms in the Bible.
7 Schummel (1748–1813) studied theology in Halle from 1767 to 1769 and worked subsequently as a teacher in Magdeburg, Liegnitz, and Breslau. He was the author of a number of sentimental and satirical novels.
8 Christian Heinrich Wolke (1741–1825), the first assistant teacher Basedow hired at his school. For discussion, see Wolf (2004).
9 "Higher faculties" refers to the three most popular professional programs of the time: law, medicine, and theology. The sole lower faculty was philosophy—which essentially consisted of all of the arts and sciences. Kant, in his *Conflict of the Faculties*, writes:

> One can call the lower faculty that rank in the university that occupies itself with teachings which are not adopted by order of a superior ... So the philosophy faculty, because it must answer for the *truth* of the teachings it is to adopt or even allow, must be conceived as free and subject only to laws given by reason, not by the government.
>
> But a department of this kind, too, must be established at a university; in other words, a university must have a faculty of philosophy. Its function in relation to the three higher faculties is to control them and, in this way, be useful to them, since *truth* (the essential and first condition of learning in general) is what matters most [*auf Wahrheit ... alles ankommt*], whereas the *utility* [*Nützlichkeit*] the higher faculties promise the government is only a consideration of secondary importance.
>
> SF 7: 27–28

Then, as now, students' parents often tried to steer their children into one of the professional programs, in hopes that they would be better remunerated after graduation.
10 A. S. Neill's influential Summerhill School (founded in Sussex, England in 1921) would seem to also owe an unacknowledged debt to Basedow's emphasis on learning as play. In *Summerhill: A Radical Approach to Child Rearing*, Neill writes: "Summerhill might be defined as a school in which play is of the greatest

importance" (Neill 1960: 62). Summerhill's advocacy of "sex instruction" (Neill 1960: 218–22), as we will see later, reveals a second Basedowian debt.

11 Cf. Meier, who, in his 1791-2 two-volume biography of Basedow—a work which in Göring's judgment "belongs to the most downright bigoted products of biographical literature" (Göring 1880, XVII)—claims that Basedow "is definitely not the inventor of his teaching method in languages, because it was used for a long time before him" (M: I: 216).

12 Kant used this book as his text when he first taught his pedagogy seminar at the University of Königsberg in winter semester 1776-7, and the contents of his own *Lectures on Pedagogy* (first published in 1803, but based on earlier classroom lectures) reveal many Basedowian influences. However, it is not clear which edition he used. For discussion, see Weisskopf (1970: 119–35).

13 This is one of the many innovative curricular features of the Philanthropin that impressed Kant. In his *Lectures on Pedagogy*, he writes: "One should be able to walk on narrow footbridges, on steep heights where one faces an abyss, or on a shaky support. If a human being cannot do these things, he is not completely what he could be. Since the Dessau Philanthropin has led the way here with its example, many experiments of this sort have been made with children in other institutes" (Päd 9: 467).

14 For further discussion of the importance of physical exercise in the Philanthropin curriculum, see Borkman (1993: esp. 28–60).

15 Bollnow (1952: I: 619). In the Preface to the second edition of the *Critique of Pure Reason*, Kant famously compares his epistemological revolution in philosophy to Copernicus's revolution in astronomy. Previous astronomers assumed that the sun circled the earth rather than vice versa. Philosophers prior to Kant assumed that the mind is passive rather than active in experience—that knowledge consists merely in representations of objects in the world. On Kant's view, the human mind plays a much more active role in the constitution of knowledge. Instead of our representations conforming to objects, Kant holds that in knowledge objects must conform to our representations. Objects must conform to our cognition, rather than vice versa. See KrV B xvi–xviii.

16 In his *Autobiography*, Mill writes: "I have no remembrance of the time when I began to learn Greek. I have been told that it was when I was three years old ... The only thing besides Greek, that I learnt as a lesson in this part of my childhood, was arithmetic: ... it was the task of the evenings ... In my eighth year I commenced learning Latin" (in Mill 1961: 13–15).

17 Holst (1984: 57). For further discussion, see Louden (forthcoming) and Steinhauben (2008). Article V of Basedow's *Zweites Stück des philanthropischen Archivs* (Dessau, 1776) is entitled "Of a Catherineum, or Female Institute, in Connection with and Separation from the Philanthropin." Named in honor of Catherine the Great of

Russia, a generous supporter of Basedow's *Elementarwerk*, the proposed school would be housed "in a separate building" where the students would receive "instruction in German, French, all ladies' studies [*Damenstudien*], also singing, music, dancing, and sewing." At the same time, "some classes of both institutions will be held in common," and "with the religions of different churches it shall be the same in the Catherineum as it is in the Philanthropin." "With God's help," Basedow wrote, the Catherineum "will officially open on June 11, 1777" [reprinted in Benner and Kemper 2000: I: 123–4]. The school never opened.

18 Barnard (1863: 516–17). The *Salzmannschule Schnepfenthal* is still operating at present, and is currently rated as one of the top schools in Germany for the study of foreign languages. For further information, see http:::// salzmannschule.de. The school was founded by Christian Gotthilf Salzmann (1744–1811), who taught at the Philanthropin from 1780 to 1784.

19 For detailed discussion, see Thalhofer (1907: esp. 8–16).

20 In this section I borrow a little from my discussion of Kantian naturalism in Louden (2017). This is yet another area where Kant's intellectual debt to Basedow is substantial.

21 Christoph Friedrich Nicolai (1733–1811), writer and bookseller, a key figure in the Berlin Enlightenment.

22 Christian Gottfried Struensee (1717–80), educator and author.

23 Ernst Platner (1744–1818), one of the founders of modern anthropology. Kant's pragmatic anthropology is developed partly in opposition to Platner's physiological study of human nature. In a letter to former student Marcus Herz written toward the end of 1773, Kant states emphatically that his own plan for anthropology is "quite different" than Platner's (Br 10: 145).

24 Georg Joachim Zollikofer (1730–88), a liberal theologian who was well known for his promotion of Enlightenment values.

25 Friedrich Gabriel Resewitz (1729–1806), author of *Die Erziehung des Bürgers* (1773), in which he advocates teaching methods aimed at improving the lives of the working class.

26 Johann Gottlieb Schummel (1748–1813), author of *Fritzens Reise nach Dessau* (1776, cited above) and other works on education.

27 Joachim Heinrich Campe (1746–1818), prolific author and reviewer who later (October 1776–September 1777) served briefly as Director of the Philanthropin.

28 Friedrich Andreas Stroth (1750–85), appointed principal of the gymnasium in Quedlinburg in 1774; died of pulmonary disease at age 35.

29 Johann Joachim Christoph Bode (1731–93), well-known translator of English and French literary works into German.

30 Friedrich Eberhard von Rochow (1734–1805), author of the popular two-volume reader *Der Kinderfreund* (1776–9) and founder of a school in Rekahn that became a model for schools in rural areas.

31 Wilhelm Abraham Teller (1734–1804), Enlightenment theologian, author of *Lehrbuch des christlichen Glaubens* (1764).
32 Oberlin College in the US was named in honor of Oberlin upon its founding in 1833.
33 Oberlin to Simon, March 16, 1777 (reprinted in Pinloche 1896: 110).
34 These lecture notes are a transcription of Kant's anthropology course from winter semester 1775–6. In winter semester 1776–7, he offered his pedagogy course for the first time—a "Scholastico-practicum über Basedow's *Methodenbuch.*"
35 Garve (1771: 322–3; reprinted in G: 11).
36 A shorter version of this opening chapter was presented (in German) as an invited talk at the *Interdisziplinäres Zentrum für die Erforschung der Europäischen Aufklärung* (IZEA) in Halle and at *Ludwigs-Maximilians-Universität* in Munich in June 2018. I would like to thank Daniel Fulda and Ansgar Lyssy for the invitations to present my work, Christian Mueller for help with the translation, and Andrea Thiele for help in preparing my presentation.

2 Blame It on the Parents?

1 See, e.g., Göring (1880: CII–CXII). See also Chapter 2 ("His Talents. His Character") of the anonymously published "Fragmente über Basedow," which appeared shortly after Basedow's death in the *Deutsche Monatschrift* ("Fragmente über Basedow" 1790: 287–96).
2 As one author remarks: "It is sufficient to say of him personally that he was vulgar, immoral, intemperate, given to the vices of the peasantry from which he sprang without possessing their fundamental virtues; above all it cannot be doubted that he was in some respects an imposter and a mountebank" (Monroe 1907: 580).
3 Johann Kaspar Lavater (1741–1801), liberal Enlightenment theologian, philosopher, and poet based in Zurich.
4 Johann Georg Hamann (1730–88). A strong critic of Kant's philosophy, Hamann is often viewed as "the pioneer of anti-rationalism" (Berlin 1993: 4), but he is more accurately described as being "as much a student of the Enlightenment as its critic" (Dahlstrom 2018: 239). Johann Gottfried Herder (1744–1803). A student of Kant's in Königsberg, he too (like his friend Hamann) later became a strong critic of Kant's philosophy. Herder made major contributions to many areas of philosophy, including philosophy of language and the philosophy of history.
5 This particular passage in vol. 25 of *Kants gesammelte Schriften* is taken from the *Dohna* transcription of 1791–2. See Kowalewski (1924: 35). Malaga is a sweet, fortified wine made from Pedro Ximénez and Moscatel grapes in Málaga, Spain—Picasso's hometown. Wine has been produced in this region for nearly 3,000 years. I

would like to thank Lucinda Baker for mailing me a bottle of red Malaga. (It is also available in white and rosé—I'm not sure which variety Basedow favored, but I suspect red.)

6 See M: I: 160; Ra: 25; Göring (1880, XX); Müller (1967: II: 113). Max Müller (1823–1900), Oxford University's first Professor of Comparative Philology and one of the founders of Indology (Indian Studies), was a prolific scholar and translator. In 1881 he published an English translation of the first edition (traditionally referred to as the "A edition") of Kant's *Critique of Pure Reason*. Toward the end of his "Translator's Preface," he writes: "The bridge of thoughts and sighs that spans the whole history of the Aryan world has its first arch in the Veda, its last in Kant's Critique ... While in the Veda we may study the childhood, we may study in Kant's Critique of Pure Reason the perfect manhood of the Aryan mind" (Müller 1922: lxxvii).

7 As cited by Armin Basedow (AB: 7). Basedow wrote his vita in Latin. Armin Basedow (who informs readers on p. 5 that he is a "direct descendant" of Johann Bernhard Basedow) reprints the entire document on pp. 7–9, along with a German translation. Landschoof includes a photostatic copy of the original handwritten Latin vita along with an English translation (Landschoof 1933: Appendix).

8 See Landschoof (1933: Appendix, VI), who provides a photostatic copy of the Title Page of Basedow's Kiel thesis.

9 Cf. Max Müller: "His grandfather was a traveler of East Indies, of whom it was said that he became three times rich and three times poor. His great-grandfather was supposed to be a baron and because of great losses sold the name and estate 'Basedow'" (Müller 1967: 114).

10 Reble lists 108 different works in his list of Basedow's writings (R: 267–74); Vorbrodt, 100 (Vorbrodt 1920: II: 120–7); Göring, 91 (G: 513–19).

11 If Basedow were to be examined by contemporary healthcare professionals, would he receive a diagnosis of attention deficit hyperactivity disorder (ADHD)? Bipolar disorder? Narcissistic personality disorder (NPD)? ... Quite possibly. But unfortunately, there is not enough reliable information at present to make a well-informed diagnosis.

12 Johannes Bugenhagen (1458–1558), also called *Doktor Pomeranus* by Martin Luther, introduced the Protestant Reformation in the Duchy of Pomerania and Denmark in the sixteenth century. In 1521 he went to Wittenberg, where he developed a lasting friendship with Luther.

13 Johann Samuel Müller (1701–73), born in Braunschweig and died in Hamburg, educator and author, was a close friend of Lessing's.

14 According to Schmid (1898: 4: 29) "assistant Rector Ludwig Hake."

15 Christoph Heinrich Dornemann (1682–1753), mathematician and educator.

16 Basedow (1746: 34, stanza 4; as cited by Swet 1898: 25 n. 2).

17 Basedow (1750; as cited by Swet 1898: 26 n. 2). Swet claims that the poem was "unknown until 1890" and surmises that the actual publication date was 1749 rather than 1750 (Swet 1898: 25 n. 5).
18 Basedow 1761; as cited by AB, 38. This title does not appear in either Göring's or Reble's list of Basedow's publications. Armin Basedow notes that it was "printed once only for private use" and "no doubt has previously remained completely unknown" (AB, 38 n.1).
19 In his typically churlish style, Meier adds, after citing the above remark from the review: "I have reason to doubt the accuracy [of this remark]. They would have said: 'Basedow could [*könnte*] become a charitable and thoughtful man.' That sounds more correct" (M: I: 184 n.) As Diestelmann notes, in his own footnote on this comment, Meier's biography is "influenced by an irritable partiality against Basedow" (Diestelmann 1897: 102 n. 12).
20 Basedow 1771b: I: 4; as cited by Landschoof 1933: 35 n. 1.
21 Mönckeberg 1867: 40; as cited by AB: 36. The quoted phrase at the end of this passage is taken from correspondence between Basedow and Reimarus which, according to Armin Basedow, has been lost (AB: 36 n.1).
22 August Pfeiffer (1640–98), German Lutheran theologian, orientalist, writer, and superintendent of the city of Lübeck. Pfeiffer was also an alumnus of the Hamburg Johanneum.
23 Reimarus, *Concerning the Intention of Jesus and His Teaching*, in Reimarus (1970: 269).
24 See also Overhoff (2004: esp. 17–48), who argues that Basedow's *pedagogical theory* also owes serious debts to both Richey and Reimarus. In Overhoff's view, Basedow was not the lone inventor of a new Enlightenment philosophy of education, but was in fact building on the insights of his two favorite Hamburg gymnasium teachers. As he indicates in his title (see Overhoff 2004), there is an "early history of Philanthropinism" that goes back at least as far as 1715—over thirty years before Basedow's first publication. Overhoff documents his thesis well, but the primary focus of the present study is Basedow's own life and works—not his gymnasium teachers' influences on his thought. Additionally, it is well known that Basedow owes serious debts to still earlier authors. See, e.g., Locke (1693/1996).

3 College Days

1 This saga probably also played a role in Basedow's short-lived desire to visit India after he ran away from home at age sixteen.
2 Viz., Basedow (1760).
3 Unfortunately, the addressee of this letter is not named. Diestelmann (1897: 15) speculates that it is Richey, but according to Armin Basedow "this patron is not

Richey, as Diestelmann, p. 15, assumes" (AB: 42 n.1) The letter is addressed to a "Herr Doktor," which Richey was not, and this leads Armin Basedow to conclude that the recipient is "Dr. *Matthäus Arnold Wilckens* in Hamburg" (AB: 42 n.1; see also Pinloche 1896: 29 n.1). Wilckens (1710–59), a well-known jurist and poet, had studied law at the University of Leipzig.

4 Pinloche (1896: 458—Pinloche reprints the complete letter on 457–9.)
5 Christian August Crusius (1715–75), professor of philosophy and theology at the University of Leipzig. A strong critic of Leibniz and Wolff, Crusius was a major influence on Basedow's intellectual development. As Overhoff notes, it was Crusius "who showed him the way to a new interpretation of the Bible and to the rapprochement of theology and philosophy" (Overhoff 2010: 59). Kant was also deeply influenced by Crusius.
6 "This society of experienced writers" consisted of a group of young poets, some of whom Basedow had met in his gymnasium days at Hamburg, working under the guidance of Johann Christoph Gottsched (1700–66). Gottsched was a professor of poetry at Leipzig, and Basedow also attended some of his lectures. In 1744 the group began publishing a journal in Bremen, known as the *Bremen Beiträger* (short for *Beiträge zum Vergnügen des Verstandes und des Witzes*). For further discussion, see AB: 43, 45 and Specht (1999: 10, 78).
7 August Friedrich Walther (1688–1746), professor of anatomy, pathology, and therapy at Leipzig. In 1737 he was appointed rector at the university.
8 Presumably Daniel William Triller (1695–1782). However, Triller did not go to Leipzig in 1746, settling instead in Dresden. In 1749 he accepted a professorship at the University of Wittenberg, where he remained until his death.
9 Alexander Gottlieb Baumgarten (1714–62), philosophy professor at Halle (and later at Frankfurt an der Oder). Baumgarten played a formative role in the development of modern aesthetics. His *Metaphysica* (4th ed., 1757) has recently been translated into English for the first time. See Baumgarten (2014/1757). Kant used Baumgarten's *Metaphysica* as his text when he began lecturing on metaphysics in 1755, and he also used the chapter on "Empirical Psychology" for his text when he began lecturing on anthropology in 1772.
10 Christian Gottlieb Jöcher (1694–1758), professor of history and university librarian at the University of Leipzig.
11 Salomon Deyling (1677–1755), Lutheran theologian and professor of theology at the University of Leipzig from 1722 to 1755.
12 Basedow (1771b: 5, 6). Cf. Diestelmann (1897: 14) and Basedow (1764a: I: 472–4).
13 A degree below that of a PhD given by universities in some countries. Cf. the recent US college admissions scandal involving wealthy parents who tried to buy their children's admission into elite universities. For discussion, see Taylor (2019).
14 Basedow (1750), as cited by Swet (1898: 27). See also AB: 54.

4 A New Way of Teaching

1. Meier (M: I: 209), Rathmann (Ra: 10) and other early biographers spell the name "Quaalen," but I follow Göring (1880: XXX), Armin Basedow (AB: 53)—as well as Basedow himself (MB VI.2; in G: 111)—in spelling the name as "Qualen."
2. In philosophy, this emphasis on the fundamental role of play in human life is traditionally associated with Friedrich Schiller. In his 1795 work, *On the Aesthetic Education of Man*, he writes: "To mince matters no longer, the human being only plays when he is in the fullest sense of the word a human being, and *he is only fully a human being when he plays*" (Schiller 1967: 106). Was Schiller influenced by Basedow on this point? The editors Wilkinson and Willoughby refer briefly to Basedow in their discussion of a passage where Schiller discusses "praktische Philanthropie" and "Erziehung" (Schiller 1967: 248, 88, 90), but it is not clear to me that Schiller is alluding to Basedow's school here.
3. See Basedow (1774b). See also Basedow (1774c, 1774d, and 1763).
4. Benjamin Hedericus (1675-1748), German lexicographer. Best known for his Greek–Latin lexicon [*Graecum Lexicon Manuale* (London, 1810)].
5. Basedow (1752b): § 3 (unpaginated); as cited by Swet (1898: 37–8)).
6. Swet (1898: 39). Swet has taken the two quoted passages near the end from Basedow's *Nachricht*, §6 (see Basedow 1752b). The rest of this citation is a paraphrase of §6.
7. In the manner of Aristotle (from the Greek *peripatetikos*: "walking up and down").
8. Swet (1898: 39). Here Swet paraphrases §7 of Basedow's *Nachricht*.
9. See Basedow (1750).
10. Basedow (1750: 19); as cited by Swet (1898: 29).
11. For related discussion, see Schmid's discussion of Basedow's "natural method of instruction" (Schmid 1898: 47–52).
12. See also the more recent criticism that Basedow and other Enlightenment educational reformers are advocates of "dark pedagogy" (*schwarze Pädagogik*), on the ground that they seek to discipline the body and spirit of the human being merely to serve the goal of economic productivity. This criticism also rests on a misreading of Basedow's pedagogy. Basedow and the other Philanthropinists who followed in his wake sought to modernize education and make it more practically efficacious, but molding students into economically productive tools of capitalism was by no means their goal. For readings and discussion, see Rutschky (1977).
13. British Enlightenment author Joseph Priestley, in his *Miscellaneous Observations Relating to Education* (1778), would later defend a reformist position that is surprisingly close to Basedow's. For instance, at the end of his Preface he complains that the existing plan of instruction "was too scholastic, consisting of those studies which were originally thought requisite to form the *divine*, and *philosopher* only, and

had no direct view to *civil and active life*; and yet the greater part of our pupils were not intended for any of the learned professions" (Priestley 2013: xx).
14 Rousseau (1979: 107; cf. 37–8). In his Preface, Rousseau alludes to Locke's *Some Thoughts Concerning Education* in the following remark: "After Locke's book, my subject was still entirely fresh" (Rousseau 1979: 33). But the pre-1762 publication date of a number of Basedow's own works falsifies this claim as well.
15 Cf. Swrakoff: "Without denying Rousseau's stimulating influence on Basedow, we must also assert that the spiritual creator and father of the new direction in pedagogy was Johann Bernhard Basedow and no one else" (Swrakoff 1898: 9; see also 58).
16 Rousseau's position on education in *Émile* is also strongly gendered: because "woman is made specially to please man," "it follows that they ought not to have the same education" (Rousseau 1979: 358, 363).
17 The title page of the Kiel dissertation is reprinted in Landschoof (1933: Appendix, vi). See also AB: 61.

5 The Professor

1 Basedow (1752a: paragraphs 1–2; as translated and cited by Landschoof 1933: 72–3). *Note*: I have not been able to obtain a copy of Basedow's thesis, and in the following summary I rely primarily on Landschoof's account. Landschoof often includes Basedow's original Latin in his footnotes. I have occasionally made minor modifications in Landschoof's translations.
2 Basedow (1752a: Ch. 1, para. 1; as cited and translated by Landschoof 1933: 75).
3 Basedow (1752a: Ch. 1, para. 2–3; as cited and translated by Landschoof 1933: 76–7).
4 Basedow (1752a: Ch. 1, para. 4–5; as cited and translated by Landschoof 1933: 78–9).
5 Basedow (1752a: Ch. 1, par. 10; as translated and cited by Landschoof 1933: 80).
6 Basedow (1752a: Ch. 1, par. 12; as translated and cited by Landschoof 1933: 80).
7 Basedow (1752a, Ch. 2, par. 16; as translated and cited by Landschoof 1933: 82).
8 Basedow (1752a: Ch. 2, par. 18; as translated and cited by Landschoof 1933: 83–4).
9 Basedow (1752a: Ch. 2, par. 20; as translated and cited by Landschoof 1933: 84–5).
10 Basedow (1752a: Ch. 2, par. 22; as translated and cited by Landschoof 1933: 86).
11 Basedow (1752a: Ch. 4, par. 39; as translated and cited by Landschoof 1933: 87).
12 Daniel Georg Morhof (1639–91), professor at the University of Rostock and later at the University of Kiel. His *Unterricht von der deutschen Sprache und Poesie* (1682) is the first attempt in German at a systematic survey of European literature.
13 Desiderius Erasmus (c. 1469–1536), Dutch humanist and Renaissance scholar. His satires on the Catholic Church paved the way for the Reformation.

14 Johann Matthias Gesner (1691–1761), pedagogue, classical philologist, and librarian. From 1730 to 1734 he served as Rector of the *Thomasschule* in Leipzig, and in 1734 he was appointed Professor of Rhetoric (and subsequently Librarian) at the newly opened university in Göttingen.

15 Basedow (1752a: Ch. 4, par. 42; as translated and cited by Landschoof 1933: 88).

16 This emphasis on the importance of distinguishing the probable from the improbable is most likely a reflection of Basedow's earlier work with Crusius at the University of Leipzig. As Overhoff notes, it was Crusius who had first drawn Basedow's "'attention to the Wolffian error' of accepting nothing but 'mathematical demonstration' as the proper scientific methodology even in the field of theology (Basedow 1764a: 1: 472). Much in philosophy and theology, as Crusius had emphasized, could only be known with probability and it was one of the most frequent mistakes of philosophers to be too certain about things that could not be known with mathematical certainty" (Overhoff 2010: 60).

17 Armin Basedow is paraphrasing his ancestor's lecture in most of this passage, but quotes directly from § 7 at the very end.

18 Basedow (1753b). Landschoof mistakenly translates "*Freigeisterei*" as "freedom of the will" (Landschoof 1933: 92).

19 Basedow [1758b: Preface (unpaginated)]. In a later publication, Basedow remarks that "even in the forty-seventh year of his life, 1771" he still regards the *Praktische Philosophie* as one of his best writings (Basedow 1771b: 7). A second edition of the book, in which the phrase "a cosmopolitan book without offense toward any nation, form of government, and church" is added at the end of the original title, was published in Dessau in 1777 by Siegfried Lebrecht Crusius. The contents of the two editions often vary.

20 Hugo Grotius (1583–1645), Dutch jurist and diplomat.

21 Samuel Pufendorf (1632–94), German jurist, political philosopher, economist, and historian. For discussion, see Louden (2007a: 112–15).

22 "And God blessed them, and God said unto them, Be fruitful, and multiply, and replenish the earth, and subdue it: and have dominion over the fish of the sea, and over the fowl of the air, and over every living thing that moveth upon the earth. And God said, Behold, I have given you every herb bearing seed, which is upon the face of all the earth, and every tree, in which is the fruit of a tree yielding seed; to you it shall be for meat" (*Genesis* 1: 28–9).

6 That Old-Time Religion

1 Johann Melchior Goeze (1717–86), Lutheran pastor and theologian; Basedow's primary theological opponent.

2 Presumably Johann Dietrich Winckler (1711–84), Lutheran theologian active in Hamburg and Hildesheim.
3 Gottfried Profe (1712–70), professor of mathematics at the Altona gymnasium. For discussion, see AB: 77 f.
4 Ludwig Harboe (1709–83); Danish theologian. He served as Bishop of Seeland from 1757 to 1783.
5 Johann Andreas Cramer (1723–88); German Court Preacher to King Frederick V of Denmark, professor of theology at the University of Copenhagen and (later) at the University of Kiel.
6 Friedrich Gottlieb Klopstock (1724–1803); German poet, classmate and friend of Basedow's at the University of Leipzig.
7 Gottfried Benedikt Funk (1734–1814); German educator. Funk worked as tutor for Cramer's family in Copenhagen, and taught later at the Cathedral School in Magdeburg.
8 Johann Elias Schlegel (1719–49); critic and poet, law student at the University of Leipzig. Schlegel, like Basedow, was a contributor to the *Bremen Beiträge*.
9 Johann Hartwig Ernst von Bernstorff (1712–72); German-Danish statesman and member of the Bernstorff noble family in Mecklenburg.
10 However, Basedow was "threatened with stoning" during this time. According to Overhoff, Basedow's "house was attacked once by a mob of angry Altona shoemakers" who were apparently motivated by Goeze's remark during a sermon that "one must stone [*steinigen*] the guy" (Overhoff 2004: 166). Unfortunately, Overhoff does not offer further details concerning the attack. But as another commentator notes: "He who comes too early is punished by life. Basedow was ahead of his time" (Kegler, 1994: 21).
11 I believe Göring is referring to Basedow (1764b) here.
12 Overhoff claims that "Basedow's transfer to the Gymnasium in Altona was therefore under no circumstances [*keinesfalls*] ... a demotion" (Overhoff 2004: 159). But being transferred from a *Ritterakademie* to a *Gymnasium* is roughly equivalent to moving from a liberal arts college to a high school. When one adds to this the new restrictions placed on his public lecturing (not to mention his family's excommunication from church and their public ostracism), the transfer to Altona is indeed best described as a demotion. Basedow's earlier biographers all agree on this point.
13 See Basedow (1761). Neither Göring nor Reble list this work in their extensive bibliographies of Basedow's writings. Armin Basedow notes that it was "only printed once for private use" (AB: 38 n.1).
14 Stern (1912: 73). Kegler, on the other hand, summarizes Basedow's outlook as follows: "Before 1768, Basedow became well known with a series of religious writings in which he was shown to be a defender of natural religion. This led to

Basedow's persecution by the Protestant orthodoxy. His books were burned, in many regions they could not be sold anymore, Basedow was threatened" (Kegler 1994: 20). Kegler's description of Basedow's religious position is incorrect. Throughout his career, Basedow sought to reconcile natural religion with Protestant orthodoxy. Similarly, Tonelli's remark that "Basedow's theological ideas, inspired by the English and French deists, aimed at a natural religion ... rejecting every kind of orthodox Christianity" (Tonelli 1967: 251) also underplays Basedow's desire to remain faithful to biblical Christianity.

15 Both Basedow's *Methodischer Unterricht* and *Philalethie* were published in 1764, and it is quite possible (though not certain) that Kant had Basedow's theological "middle position" in mind when he made this remark. Stern's conclusion that "Basedow was a philosophical and theological eclectic ... [and] his philosophical and theological views are not sufficiently clarified" is also not far from Kant's charge of syncretism (Stern 1912: 87).

16 Needless to say, Basedow is by no means the first religious reformer to criticize clergy for their frequent efforts to cram abstruse theological doctrines down congregants' throats when they are not in an epistemic position to understand the message. Basedow's main target was the orthodox Lutherans of his era, but Luther himself had earlier issued similar criticisms against Catholic priests. For instance, in his 1527 pamphlet concerning the duties of Christians during a plague, *Ob man vor dem Sterben fliegen möge* (Whether One May Flee From a Deadly Plague), Luther encourages pastors to visit the afflicted while they are still in their right minds, before the illness overwhelms them. To teach the gospel at the last minute, he adds, is like life "under the papacy when nobody asked whether they believed or understood the gospel but just stuffed the sacrament down their throats as if into a bread bag" (Luther 1999: 43: 135).

17 For critical discussion of Kant's conception of enlightenment and references to secondary literature, see Louden (2016b). Kant's definition of enlightenment also echoes Descartes' proclamation at the beginning of the *Meditations on First Philosophy* (1641) that it is necessary "to demolish everything completely and start again right from the foundations" if one wants "to establish anything at all in the sciences that ... [is] stable and likely to last" (Descartes 1984: II: 12). Basedow's motto thus fits well with the strong stress on intellectual autonomy that is a hallmark of modern European philosophy.

18 Goeze, as cited by Overhoff (2004: 164.) I would like to thank Friedemann Stengel for helpful discussion of this issue.

19 Goeze, as cited by Overhoff (2004: 164–5). It should be emphasized Goeze's animus against Basedow was not merely expressed in written form. Indeed, his most effective medium of communication may well have been his Sunday sermons. As noted earlier, Overhoff reports that "once at the end of one of his sermons

concerning the Altona professor he said: 'People need to stone the guy'" (Overhoff 2004: 166; cf. Göring 1880: XXXVIII).

20 Basedow (1764a: I: 404). Basedow defines a "politically good religion," in part, as one "that commands no external action which disturbs the public peace" (Basedow 1764a: I: 404).

21 Another way that Basedow often tried to summarize his position, particularly regarding religious instruction in school, was to emphasize that religion and theology must be kept separate from one another (cf. Bessler 1900: 18). As he states in the *Methodenbuch*: "Still one more thing, which many will understand. *Religion and theology are different*. The former, if it is true, must be short, must be simple, must be entirely practical" (MB IIIa; in G: 40).

22 I am indebted here to conversation with Thea Sumalvico, and also to Sumalvico (2018).

23 Basedow (1764c: 85). See also Basedow (1764a: I: 24).

24 "The thesis I defend is, briefly stated, this: *Our passional nature not only lawfully may, but must, decide an option between propositions, whenever it is a genuine option that cannot by its nature be decided on intellectual grounds*" (James 1897: 11).

25 Chance (2019: 377). I am indebted to Chance's analysis of Basedow and the duty to believe in the above discussion. Although Kant may not have read Basedow's *Theoretisches System der gesunden Vernunft*, he was quite familiar with the *Methodenbuch*, and Basedow also discusses the *Glaubenspflicht* in this latter work (see MB VII.14; in G: 143). For Kant's discussion of the postulates, see KpV 5: 122–34.

26 Basedow (1901: § 24; in R: 28). See also Egerland (1994).

27 The 1761 date of this letter is important for two interrelated reasons: First, it offers further evidence that Basedow's pedagogical theory is not merely a copy of Rousseau's. Second, it shows that Basedow's pedagogical interests were by no means an attempt to capitalize on the popularity of Rousseau's *Émile*. For *Émile* was not published until 1762.

28 One indication of its popularity and influence is that for many years Reclam included a very affordable version of this work in its famous "Universal-Bibliothek" series [# 4663, edited by Theodor Fritzsch—see Basedow (1901/1768)]. Fritzsch begins his Introduction with the following proclamation: "Since Luther's *Epistle* to the mayors and councilmen of all cities in Germany, no work has aroused such a universal and dynamic pedagogical interest as the following *Vorstellung an Menschenfreunde*. Its appearance signifies the beginning of a new epoch in the history of pedagogy ... which is still of great importance for today" (Fritzsch 1901: 1).

29 For further discussion, see Louden (2016a).

30 Meier, in the synopsis of Basedow's publications included in volume II of his biography, writes: "This small brochure was dictated at the time with much ado

when I was still in close contact with Basedow, and I had the opportunity to hear and judge that the whole thing was reheated cabbage which he had already served up 110 times, particularly in his *Vorbereitung der Jugend zur Moralität*" (Preparation of Youth for Morality). In Basedow one must expect the same repetitions, since he has a very short and weak memory" (M: II: 294). (The *Vorbereitung*, first published in 1766, was yet another work written during Basedow's prolific Altona period. See Basedow 1766b.) Unfortunately, Meier's "reheated cabbage" charge also applies to many of Basedow's other publications as well. He was an extremely repetitive author.

31 Meier observes: "The adjective '*unkirklich*' ['secular', literally 'unchurchly'] is here in this position and connection of great significance. The orthodox should have been assured and comforted by it: for Basedow's aim was not at all to erect this moral improvement on the destruction of doctrines and statutes of churchdom. As he himself understood, this language was written for Lutherans, Catholics, and members of the Reformed Church, and also for other greater and smaller sects and parties, yes, even for the Jews" (M: I: 303).

32 Johann Joachim Spalding (1714–1804), German theologian and philosopher of Scottish ancestry. Spalding's 1748 book, *Betrachtungen über die Bestimmung des Menschen*, is a key text of German Enlightenment theology.

33 Johann Georg Sulzer (1720–99), Wolffian philosopher and director of the philosophical section of the Berlin Academy of Sciences. In 1755 Sulzer translated Hume's *Enquiry Concerning the Principles of Morals* into German. A polymath, his best-known work is *Allgemeine Theorie der schönen Künste*, 4 vols. (1792–4). In the *Critique of Pure Reason*, Kant offers the following rebuke to Sulzer's metaphysical hopes: "I am not, to be sure, of the opinion that excellent and thoughtful men (e.g., Sulzer), aware of the weakness of previous proofs, have so often expressed, that one can still hope someday to find self-evident demonstrations of the two cardinal propositions of our pure reason: there is a God, and there is a future life. Rather, I am certain that this will never happen" (KrV A 741–2/B 769–70).

34 Fritzsch (1901: 5). Fritzsch does not indicate where Basedow reports this.

7 "For Fathers and Mothers of Families and Nations:" The *Methodenbuch*

1 Electronic versions of some (though by no means all) of Basedow's better-known writings (as well as some of the early biographies) are available through Google Books.

2 I am citing from the 3rd edition (1773), as reprinted in Göring. The Table of Contents and text for the 1st edition (1770) differ slightly from the 3rd edition.

3 Joseph II (1741–90), Holy Roman Emperor from 1765 and sole ruler of the Austrian Habsburg dominions until his death. Joseph has been ranked with Catherine the Great of Russia and Frederick the Great of Prussia as one of the three great Enlightenment monarchs.

4 However, it is by no means the case that this chapter of the *Methodenbuch* is an unvarnished obsequious plea to princes. Earlier in his discussion Basedow inserts a poem, which reads in part: "Could princes exist without farmers? / I think not. / Can farmers exist without princes? / I think so" (MB IIIa; in G: 31). As Hirsch notes: "a radical was called into public service—where else did this happen in the Germany of that period?" (Hirsch 2008: 24).

5 Kant later echoes much of this advice in his *Lectures on Pedagogy*: "In particular one should observe not to give children anything piquant, such as wine, spice, salt, etc. . . . [C]hildren must not be kept too warm . . . That is why the child should receive a cool and hard bed. Cold baths are good too" (Päd 9: 457–58). Kant used Basedow's *Methodenbuch* (probably the first edition of 1770, though this is not certain) as the text for his first pedagogy seminar at the University of Königsberg in winter semester 1776–77. For discussion, see Weisskopf (1970: 119–35).

6 Kant uses this same example in the *Lectures on Pedagogy* in his discussion of physical education: "One should be able to walk on narrow footbridges" (Päd 9: 467). Cf. Weisskopf (1970: 599).

7 Kant's brief discussion of sex education toward the end of his *Lectures on Pedagogy* may also owe a debt to Basedow's *Methodenbuch*: "Children now and then put inquisitive questions to grownups about it [i.e., procreation]; for example: 'Where do children come from?' . . . [S]ilence only makes things go from bad to worse. One sees this in the education of our ancestors. In the education of more recent times it is correctly assumed that one must speak openly, clearly, and decidedly" (Päd 9: 496–97).

8 Opposition to employing fables to explain natural phenomena is another hallmark of Enlightenment thought. Kant, for instance, begins a 1757 essay about his physical geography course by announcing that "the rational taste of our enlightened times" has brought us to a point where we are "no longer in danger of losing ourselves in a world of fables [*Welt von Fabeln*] instead of attaining a correct science of natural curiosities [*natürliche Merkwürdigkeiten*]" (EACG 2: 3).

9 Cf. Basedow's later introduction of the "merit board" (*Meritentafel*) at the Philanthropin, on which teachers would publicly record their students' moral and cognitive achievements, in order to encourage character development through competition. For discussion, see Chapter 9, below.

10 As we will see later when we turn to the *Elementarwerk*, copperplates were also a prominent feature of Philanthropinist education. Basedow's views about when to use copperplates in instruction seem to have changed over time.

11 Göring's text reads "*die vorzügliche*," which doesn't really make sense. Here I am following the first edition of the *Methodenbuch*, which reads "*die vorzüglichste*" (Basedow 1979: 218).
12 Cf. Proverbs 9:10. As Georg Cavallar notes, here one does see a sharp contrast between Kant and Basedow: "Basedow was clearly less radical than Kant in terms of the relationship between religion and morality ... For Basedow, morality could not be independent from religion, free-standing or autonomous in a Kantian sense" (Cavallar 2015: 100). At the same time, however, Basedow's claim that one must understand the passage from Proverbs in a way that "does not contradict experience" is another example of his basic theological position: correctly interpreted, the truths of natural religion and the Bible are consistent with each other.
13 This too is quite unKantian. For Kant (or at least for the "critical" Kant), "*empirical principles* are not fit to be the foundation of moral laws at all" (GMS 4: 442) and "all moral philosophy rests entirely on its pure [viz., nonempirical] part" (GMS 4: 389). However, the pre-critical Kant is not always so insistent on the need for a nonempirical grounding of ethics. For instance, in a 1765 publication he writes: "In the doctrine of virtue I shall always begin by considering historically and philosophically what *happens* before specifying what *ought to happen*" (NEV 2: 311). Kant's strong enthusiasm for Basedow is limited to the latter's philosophy of education and parts of his philosophy of religion and history—it does not extend to Basedow's epistemology and ethical theory.
14 Here as elsewhere, the influence of Basedow's *Methodenbuch* on Kant's *Lectures on Pedagogy* is apparent: "As concerns the education of children with a view to religion, the first question is whether it is feasible to teach religious concepts to children at an early age" (Päd 9: 493). "Children cannot grasp all religious concepts, but nevertheless there are some that one must teach them" (Päd 9: 495).
15 Frederick Beiser, for instance, writes: "There is a patent similarity between Basedow's position and Kant's and Jacobi's; thus in criticizing Basedow, Mendelssohn was probably criticizing Kant and Jacobi as well" (Beiser 1987: 97).
16 In the first edition of 1770, this chapter is entitled "Of the Education of Daughters." It appears as Chapter IX, and its contents are quite different from the contents of Chapter VIII in the third edition of 1773, from which I am citing.
17 See Rousseau (1979: 365).
18 This is how the title reads in the Table of Contents in Göring's version of the third edition. However, at the beginning of Chapter IX, the title reads: "Of State Supervision over Morality, Education, Schools, Studies, and of some Errors Therein" (G: 185).
19 Keeping colleges and universities away from the allegedly contaminating influence of urban centers was a popular sentiment in the late eighteenth century. For instance, "when eight Maine towns were contending for the location of Bowdoin

[College], North Yarmouth argued in its own behalf that it was 'not so much exposed to many Temptations to Dissipation, Extravagance, Vanity and Various vices as great seaport towns frequently are.' The antipathy to towns as college sites was so strong in North Carolina that the charter for the University of North Carolina in 1789 provided that it could not be located within five miles of any seat of government or any place where law or equity courts met" (Rudolph 1962: 92).
20 See Basedow (1771a).
21 Although he did later publish several edited anthologies of Latin texts (see, e.g., Basedow 1776b), the other projects in this wishlist of future publications were never completed.

8 "A Well-Ordered Stock of All Necessary Knowledge:" The *Elementarwerk*

1 Dohm (1751–1820), son of a Lutheran pastor and author of the two-volume *Ueber die bürgerliche Verbesserung der Juden* (1781—On the Civil Improvement of the Jews).
2 Lauchstädt (Bad Lauchstädt)—a small town (present population around 5,000) about nine miles southwest of Halle. Iselin (1728–82) studied law and philosophy at the University of Basel and the University of Göttingen. His best-known work is *Ueber die Geschichte der Menschheit* (1764—On the History of Humanity).
3 Mangelsdorf writes: "Because I was supposed to work under the supervision [of Klotz in Halle] and then received other instructions from Altona at the last moment, the work turned out poorly" (as cited by Fritzsch 1972: I: XXXI). Mangelsdorf (1748–1802) also worked later as a teacher at the Philanthropin, but—as happened all too frequently with Basedow—a quarrel between the two soon developed. And here too, Basedow defended his position on the matter by publishing yet another book—*To the Public, Concerning Mangelsdorf's Diatribe against the Dessau Educational Institute and Prof. Basedow* (see Basedow 1777b).
4 Basedow's argument is quite similar to Aquinas's "second way" of proving God's existence—viz., "the argument from causation." See Aquinas (1945: I: 22).
5 Kant, on the other hand, in his discussion of religious education in the *Lectures on Pedagogy*, advises: "One must not begin with theology ... Morality must ... come first" (Päd 9: 494–5).
6 As Kant remarks: if everyone were to make false promises, then "there would actually be no promises at all, since it would be futile to pretend my will to others with regard to my future actions, who would not believe this pretense; or, if they rashly did so, would pay me back in like coin, and thus my maxim, as soon as it were made a universal law, would have to destroy itself" (GMS 4: 403).

7   See note 3, above.
8   The source of Fritzsch's quotation is not clear. On the other hand, French author Pinloche, in the 1896 German translation of his work on the history of the Philanthropinist movement, is extremely dismissive of the *Elementarwerk*, labeling it a mere "synthesis of some ... general ideas which were still scattered about, and because of this needed to be fused together in order to pass over to the realm of practice" (Pinloche 1896: 61). However, Pinloche's verdict is tainted by his own misguided desire to paint Basedow simply as a German Rousseau. As he writes a paragraph earlier: "The influence of Rousseau's *Émile* was so important that without it—this is our deepest conviction—Basedow's entire work , the theoretical as well as the practical part, could never have come about" (Pinloche 1896: 60–1). See Chapter 1 for a refutation of this popular criticism of Basedow.
9   Kant dedicated the first *Critique* to "His Excellency, the Royal Minister of State, Baron von Zedlitz" (KrV A iii/B iii).

9 Back to School

1   Fritz would soon die in 1777 at age six in Diesdorf, a small town about 120 miles west of Dessau. Schmid notes that "in the first three years he was always sickly" (1898: 189), and Basedow, in a letter to Klopstock written in 1774, states that Fritz "has only half the aptitude [*Fähigkeit*]" of his sister Emilie (in G: 503).
2   Schwarz was the son of the mayor of Magdeburg, who is described by Basedow as "the father of a very large and impressive family, friend and supporter of the *Elementarwerk*" (DEP: 54; cf. Göring 1880: LXIV).
3   Benzler (1752–1810) later served as principal of the Gymnasium in Bückeburg, a town in Lower Saxony. Before being hired as an assistant at the Philanthropin, he worked as a "writer and amanuensis" (DEP: 59) for Basedow and also accompanied him on his summer 1774 trip along the Rhine with Goethe and Lavater. Benzler wrote a report of this famous excursion, portions of which are reprinted in Bach (1923). Benzler's first entry in Bach reads: "In summer 1774 we again took a long trip ... The intention was to travel to Switzerland, in order to speak with Iselin, Lavater, [and] other friends, above all on pedagogical and religious topics. The journey went over Halle, where we visited Semler, Naumburg, past Roßbach, Weimar, where we visited Wieland, Gotha, Eisenach, Erfurt, where we spoke with Meusel, Frosing and Frankfurt (Bach 1923: 80–1).
4   See Basedow (1777c). This journal was published between 1777 and 1784. Reble (R: 272) and Göring (G: 519) both include this work in their lengthy lists of Basedow's writings. However, the title page of the first issue (1777) reads "edited by

J. B. Basedow and J. H. Campe," and the title pages of later issues read "edited by the Dessau Education Institute."

5 As noted in Chapter 1, two different groups of students were enrolled at the Philanthropin: "*Pensionisten*" (boarding students who paid full tuition and came from wealthier families), and "*Famulanten*," who were charged a reduced fee. *Pensionisten* paid an annual tuition of 250 *Reichsthalers*; *Famulanten*, 100. In exchange for their reduced tuition (and also because of their lower social status), *Famulanten* were also given extra chores to perform at the school.

6 Reprinted in Pinloche (1896: 465). Reble also reprints this material in his anthology (R: 220–3), as does Göring in his introductory essay on "Basedow's Life and Works" (1880: LXXXII–IV).

7 On caste-days *Famulanten* who had distinguished themselves "through their service" were given the first seat at the table, ahead of all the *Pensionisten*. On patrons' days special honor was given to students whose parents (through extra donations) made it possible for the *Famulanten* to attend the school. And on merit-days, those students who had accumulated sufficient merit points—regardless of whether they were poor or rich, *Pensionisten* or *Famulanten*—sat side by side at the table.

8 As noted earlier, Trapp taught briefly at the Philanthropin from 1778 to 1779, before leaving for Halle to assume the first professorship in pedagogy at a German university. For discussion, see Schmidt (1861: 571–81), Herrmann (1979: 151–3), and Reble (1999: 168).

9 Karl Wilhelm Ramler (1725–98), German poet.

10 Christian Gottfried Schütz (1747–1832), German classical scholar and humanist. A professor of philosophy at Halle and later Jena, Schütz was also a defender of Kant's philosophy. In a letter to Kant of May 22, 1800, he refers to "the pleasant business, which I had taken on, of attending to the final proofreading of the second edition of your *Anthropology*" (Br 12: 307).

11 The full title of Basedow's book is: *Die ganze natürliche Weisheit im Privatstande gesitteter Bürger* (see Basedow 1768c)—*Complete Natural Wisdom for Well-mannered Citizens in Private Life*.

12 Christoph Friedrich Feder, born in 1752 in Asch, a town currently in the Czech Republic. He died in 1807.

13 Christoph Immanuel Hauber, born in 1754 in Emmendingen, a town in Baden-Württemberg, Germany. He died in 1827.

14 The Palais Dietrich in Dessau (unlike the building where Philanthropin classes were initially held) was not destroyed during the Second World War, and still stands today. Beginning in 1777, the Prince made parts of the palace available for certain school activities. From 1780 to 1793, all school functions were held at the palace.

15 Johann Christoph Pfenning (1724–1804) studied theology and philosophy at the University of Halle. Basedow is probably referring to Pfenning's 1765 book, *Anleitung zur Kenntnis der physikalischen Geographie*.
16 Samuel Friedrich Kretzschmar (1730–93). "Court physician", i.e., personal physician to Basedow's patron, Prince Leopold Friedrich Franz of Dessau.
17 Johann Matthias Schröckh (1733–1808), Austrian–German historian and literary scholar. Basedow is probably referring to his 1757 book, *Einleitung zur Universalhistorie: Umarbeitung von Hilmar Curas* (*Introduction to World History: A Revision of Hilmar Curas*). Jean-Dominique Méllot, author of *Discours sur l'histoire universelle* (1681).
18 Friedrich Gottlieb von Buße, born in 1756 in Gardelegen, a town in Saxony-Anhalt, Germany. Later a professor of mathematics and physics at the University of Freiberg, he died in 1835.
19 Johann Jacob Ebert (1737–1805), German mathematician, poet, astronomer, journalist, and author. *Nähere Anweisung zu den philosophischen und mathematischen Wissenschaften für die obern Classen der Schulen und Gymnasien* (Frankfurt and Leipzig, 1773)—*A More Detailed Introduction to the Philosophical and Mathematical Sciences for the Upper Classes of Schools and Gymnasia*.
20 Johann Christian Polycarp Erxleben (1744–77), German naturalist, professor of physics and veterinary medicine at Göttingen. *Anfangsgründe der Naturlehre* (Göttingen and Gotha, 1772)—*Elements of Physical Science*.
21 Nikolaus Ehrenreich Anton Schmid (1717–85). *Von den Weltkörpern: Zur gemeinnützigen Kenntnis der großen Werke Gottes* (Hannover, 1766)—*Of the Heavenly Bodies: Toward Beneficial Knowledge of the Great Works of God*.
22 Intended is Friedriech Andreas Stroth (1750–85), classical philologist and Protestant theologian, author of *Eklogai sive chrestomathia graeca* (Biesterfeld and Quedlinburg, 1780). Stroth also edited an edition of Xenophon's *Memorabilia Socratis* in 1780. The latter book, an account of Socrates' final days written by an Athenian general, presents a very different portrait of Socrates than one finds in Plato's better-known *Apology*.
23 Reprinted in Pinloche (1896: 465–6).
24 Probably a reference to Basedow (1776b)—one of several edited anthologies of Latin texts that he published.
25 Samson was a part-time instructor, and came from out of town to offer occasional drawing lessons. He is described in one of Basedow's publications as "a medical doctor, Jewish, and a very beloved friend of the young Philanthropinists" (Basedow 1777c: 7. Stück, 598).
26 Reprinted in Pinloche (1896: 466). Oliver Goldsmith, *The Vicar of Wakefield. A Tale, Supposed to be written by Himself*. 2 vols. (London, 1766).

27 Friedrich Georg Willhelm Jahn, born in in 1753 in Bonzenburg, Germany. Jahn died in 1834.
28 Friedrich Eberhard von Rochow (1734–1805), author of *Der Kinderfreund. Ein Lesebuch zum Gebrauch in Landschulen* (Halle, Brandenburg, and Leipzig, 1776)— *The Children's Friend. A Reader for Use in Rural Schools*. Rochow also published an "Authentic Account" of the public examination of the Philanthropin held on May 15, 1776—reprinted in R: 224–8. For discussion of Rochow, see Schmid (1898: 446–76) and Reble (1999: 169–70). Christian Felix Weiße (1726–1804), editor of *Der Kinderfreund. Ein Wochenblatt*, 24 vols. (Reutlingen, 1775–82)—*The Children's Friend. A Weekly Paper*.
29 Joachim Heinrich Campe (1746–1818), *Sittenbüchlein für Kinder in gesitteten Stände* (Dessau, 1777)—*Little Ethics Book for Children in Well-Mannered Classes*. Campe also served briefly as Director of the Philanthropin from 1776 to 1777. For discussion, see Chapter 10, below, as well as Schmidt (1861: 558–62), Schmid (1898: 381–411), and Reble (1999: 167–8).
30 Jakob Friedrich Feddersen (1736–88), *Beyspiele der Weisheit und Tugend aus der Geschichte: mit Erinnerungen für Kinder* (Halle, 1780)—*Examples of Wisdom and Virtue from History: with Memoirs for Children*.
31 *Little Activities for Children, First Nourishment for Sound Understanding*. The author is Basedow's friend Gottfried Benedikt Funk (1734–1814), rector of the *Domgymnasium* in Magdeburg.
32 Vogel is described in one of Basedow's publications as "an escort of the Prince of Schönaich" (Basedow 1777c: 7. Stück, 598).
33 Carl Gottfried Neuendorf (1750–98). Neuendorf was appointed director of the Philanthropin in 1784. For discussion, see Chapter 10.
34 Anton Friedrich Büsching (1724–93). Superintendent of the *Gymanisum zum grauen Kloster* in Berlin as well as editor of the *Wochentliche Nachrichten von neuen Landkarten* (1773–87), Büsching was also an active supporter of the Philanthropin.
35 "*Chrestomathia Colloquiorum Erasmi*" is probably a reference to Basedow (1775)—one of several Latin anthologies that he edited. "*Basedow's liber elementaris*" refers to the Latin translation of the *Elementarwerk* prepared by Mangelsdorf.
36 Johann Jasperson (1744–85), born in Flensburg, a town in Schleswig-Holstein, Germany.
37 Spener offered instruction in languages and other subjects at the Philanthropin for a while, and later became "director of a printing studio in Berlin" (Basedow 1777c: 7. Stück, 598).
38 A reference to the French translation of Basedow's *Elementarwerk* prepared by Huber—*Manuel Élémentaire D'Éducation. Ouvrage Utile A Tout Ordre De Lecteurs en partiulier Aux Parens et Aus Maîtres pour l'education des Enfans & des Adolescens &*

qui renferme une suite de toutes conoissances nécessaires (Berlin and Dessau, 1774). For discussion, see E: I: XXXII.

39 A reference to Carl Ehregott Mangelsdorf's Latin translation of Basedow's *Elementarbuch—Ad Bibliothecam Elementarem. Liber Methodicus scriptus patribus et matribus familiarum et gentium a Joh. Bernh. Basedovio. Interprete Carolo Ehregott Magelsdorfio* (Dessau, 1774). For discussion, see E: I: XXXI-II.

40 Reprinted in Pinloche (1896: 467).

41 See n. 38, above.

42 In Pinloche (1896: 468). For some additional material concerning the curriculum at the Philanthropin, see Rammelt (1929: 27-65).

43 Benner and Kemper (2009: 123), in their list of a Philanthropin course of study from winter 1778-79, also include the names *Du Toit* (dancing and physical exercise) and *Huot* (writing). Basedow, in a section entitled "Of the Teachers at the Philanthropin" in his earlier 1776 *Erstes Stück des Philanthropischen Archivs*, lists himself, Wolke, *Simon* ("25 years old, a young scholar of the French nation"), *Schweighäuser* ("23 years old ... a good teacher and patient in the instruction of youth, who is also superbly competent"), teaching assistant *Friedrich August Benzler* (see above, n. 3), as well as several "fellow Dessau citizens"—*Kretzchmar, Behrisch, Rode*, and "another patriot, *Steinacker*, also completely without self-interest," who taught singing (ES: 90-5). According to several authors, "Behrisch had induced Prince Leopold Friedrich Franz to allow Basedow to found at Dessau an educational institution, called the 'Philanthropinum', which should embody that reformer's ideas" (Graves 1912: 115; cf. Barnard 1863: 459).

44 Letter from Kant to Basedow, June 19, 1776 (Br 10: 194), describing his friend Robert Motherby's intense desire to enroll his son at the school.

45 Letter from former students Meiners, Herrschhoff, Müller, and Helmersen to Feder (no date), in *Reliquiae Philanthropini* III/11; reprinted in Benner and Kemper (2000: 178).

46 Letter of Prof. Mauvillon to Basedow, November 30, 1776, in *Reliquiae Philanthropini* III/11; reprinted in Benner and Kemper (2000: 179).

47 Letter of Basedow, Wolke, Simon, and Schweighäuser to Iselin of June 22, 1776; reprinted in G: 502.

48 Letter of Basedow to Campe of September 20, 1777 (as cited by Pinloche 1896: 124).

49 Shortly thereafter, Basedow also seems to have finally lost the personal support of his main sponsor. Trapp, in a letter of June 16, 1788, reports that the Prince now regarded Basedow as "an insufferable [*unausstehlicher*] man" (in G: 511).

50 Karl Spazier, *Carl Pilger's Roman seines Lebens*, 1792-6, 3: 182; as cited by Pinloche (1896: 129). Spazier (1761-1805) studied theology and philosophy at Halle, and worked at the Philanthropin from 1784 to 1787. "Carl Pilger" was a pseudonym that Spazier used.

51 Karl Ulysses von Salis-Marschlins (1762–1818) renovated his family's castle in Switzerland and opened a Philanthropin school there in 1771, inviting Karl Friedrich Bahrdt (1740–92) to serve as director. The school closed in 1777. For discussion, see Schmidt (1861: 567–9) and Schmid (1898: 326–50).
52 For related discussion, see Louden (2012: 46–9).
53 *Something From the Archive of Basedow's Biography Written by Himself, Concerning the Joint Hostility of Professor Wolke and Mr. Reiche against Him* (see Basedow 1783a); *Basedow and Wolke's Joint Explanation of their Completely Ended Quarrels through their Discovery of many Facts* (see Basedow 1783b).
54 Pinloche is probably referring to the second edition of Basedow's *Practische Philosophie für alle Stände* (see Basedow 1777a). The first edition, published in 1758, became a very popular textbook in moral philosophy (see Basedow 1758b).
55 For further discussion of Neuendorf's directorship of the Institute, see Schmid (1898: 301–5).

10 After School

1 Diestelmann refers to Basedow (1783a) as the source for some of his information here.
2 Pinloche (1896: 150—citing from Salzmann's *Der Bote aus Thüringen*, 1790, Nr. 34, 269).
3 I.e., the second edition of Basedow's *Practische Philosophie für alle Stände*, published in Dessau in 1777. The first edition was published in Copenhagen and Leipzig in 1758.
4 Basedow and Campe, *Pädagogsiche Unterhandlungen*, 1778: 444–46. (See Basedow 1777c.)
5 Gottfried Benedict Funk (1734–1814), author, educator, and city official based in Magdeburg.
6 As Meier remarks, "Because of his moods he was often somewhat unbearable to his own family circle in their domestic life" (M: I: 227).
7 Letter of Müller to Pinloche of March 10, 1888; reprinted in Pinloche (1896: 464). Cf. Schmid (1898: IV.2: 191 n.1). Bernburg, a town on the Saale river, is about thirty miles south of Magdeburg.
8 Ludwig von Basedow went on to study law at Frankfurt and Halle, and later served as mayor (*Regierungspräsident*) of Dessau. He died in 1835. Ludwig's son, Carl Adolph von Basedow (1799–1854—grandson of Johann Bernhard Basedow) studied medicine at Halle and was most famous for reporting the symptoms of what was first dubbed "Basedow's disease," now technically known as exophthalmic goiter. The Carl-von-Basedow-Klinikum in Merseburg, where Basedow died after contracting spotted fever from a corpse he was dissecting, is named after him.

9 In Ludwig's "Sketches From My Life," first printed in Rammelt (1929: 67–84), he writes that in spring 1788 his father decided "to himself complete my education and instruction up to the university, and to dedicate until then all of his time and energy to me" (Rammelt 1929: 80).
10 Wilcker and Scheidhauer (1790); as cited by Göring (1880: CII n.1) and Schmid (1898: 245).

11 "The Mother of All Good Schools in the World"

1 See https://philan.de/schulprogramm/ (accessed on November 19, 2019).
2 For details, see the section on "Aktuelle Projekte" at https://www.mg-90.de/projekte-1/aktuelle-projekte/ (accessed on November 11, 2019). Jürgen Overhoff gave a speech at the unveiling of the new monument—reprinted in Overhoff (2015).
3 Cf. Johnston: "Kant was an enthusiastic supporter of what is now deemed progressive education ... Kant supported Johann Bernhard Basedow's Philanthropinum. Basedow's school was one of the first to trumpet a progressive pedagogy in Germany" (Johnston 2013: 208).
4 Similarly, Kilpatrick, in his entry on "Progressive Education" for *The Encyclopedia of Modern Education*, writes: "It seems historically justifiable to say that this movement began with Rousseau ... But it was Pestalozzi ... who began the significant remaking of the school along the lines here under study" (Kilpatrick 1943: 612).
5 Dewey does occasionally acknowledge his debts to both Froebel (see, e.g., Dewey 1900b) and Pestalozzi. And there are also a few references to American educational reformer Henry Barnard in his writings (see, e.g., Dewey 1987: 3: 230; 1946: 38). As noted earlier, Barnard translated parts of Raumer's *Geschichte der Pädagogik* into English (see Barnard 1863), and Barnard's volume does contain Raumer's substantial chapter on the Philanthropinists. It is hard to believe that Dewey was not familiar with this influential book. And many Americans first became familiar with the names of Basedow, Pestalozzi, and Froebel through Barnard's writings. But the later work of Pestalozzi, Froebel, and other reformers itself builds on Basedow's earlier efforts. As one author notes: "The Philanthropinum introduced many new ideas into all parts of Germany and Switzerland, these were carefully worked out by such reformers as Pestalozzi, Froebel, and Herbart" (Graves 1912: 120). And Dewey was of course well acquainted with Kant—it is also possible that he learned of Basedow's work through his reading of Kant.
6 German author Vorbrodt is perhaps alluding to the American progressive education movement when he writes in 1920 that Basedow is "half noisy town crier, who makes an American advertisement [*eine amerikanische Reklame*] for his plans" (Vorbrodt 1920: II: 2). But he is less cryptic when he writes on the same page that

Basedow is also "half utopian dreamer [*Schwärmer*], who wants to change the entire world through schools" (Vorbrodt 1920: II: 2).

7 Basedow's legacy as the true father of progressive education as well as Kant's unwavering admiration for the Philanthropin give the lie to Ulrich Herrmann's claim that developments after 1789—specifically, "Kant's critical philosophy, Herbart's pedagogy, and the educational philosophy of neohumanism"—"soon handed him [viz., Basedow] over to oblivion" (Herrmann 1979: 146).

8 Frankena, after citing this same passage, notes that what Kant "says here about the theory of education is a strong anticipation of Dewey" (Frankena 1965: 83; cf. 120, 121, 122, 132).

9 See Paulsen (1908: 134). Similarly, Graves writes: "The unifying principle of the school was 'everything according to nature'. The natural instincts and interests of children were only to be directed and not altogether suppressed. They were to be trained as children and not as adults, and the methods of learning were to be adapted to their stage of mentality" (Graves 1912: 116–17).

10 E.g., Locke: "Of all the men we meet with, nine parts of ten are what they are, good or evil, useful or not, by their education. 'Tis that which makes the great difference in mankind" (Locke 1996: §1).

11 For more on the issue of religious unity in the Enlightenment, see Louden (2007a: 15–26).

12 Copyright © 1949 by Richard Rodgers and Oscar Hammerstein II. Williamson Music, a Division of Rodgers & Hammerstein: a Concord Music Company, owner of publication and allied rights throughout the world. International Copyright Secured. All Rights Reserved. Used by Permission of Hal Leonard Europe Limited.

References

Primary Sources

Basedow, Johann Bernhard ([1770] 1979), *Das Methodenbuch für Väter und Mütter der Familien und Völker*, Introduction by Horst M. P. Krause, Vaduz: Topos Verlag. [= MB]

—— ([1774] 1972, 1909), *Elementarwerk mit den Kupfertafeln Chodowieckis u. a.*, ed. Theodor Fritzsch, 3 vols., Hildesheim: Georg Olms. [= E]

—— (1965), *Ausgewählte pädagogische Schriften*, ed. Albert Reble, Paderborn: Ferdinand Schöningh. [= R]

—— ([1768] 1901), *Vorstellung an Menschenfreunde und vermögenden Männer über Schulen und Studien und ihren Einfluß in die öffentliche Wohlfahrt. Mit einen Plane eines Elementarbuchs der menschlichen Erkenntnis*, ed. Theodor Fritzsch, Leipzig: Philipp Reclam. [= VM]

—— (1880), *J. B. Basedow's ausgewählte Schriften. Mit Basedow's Biographie, Einleitungen und Anmerkungen*, ed. Hugo Göring, Langensalza: Hermann Beyer & Söhne. [= G]

—— (1787), *Neues Werkzeug zum Lesenlehren, der für die Lernenenden bestimmte Teil, in welchem zugleich gesorgt ist für den Anfang zur Sachkenntnis, der Sittenlehre, der Gotteserkenntnis und der Sprachrichtigkeit, von J. B. Basedow und einer für Aufklärung arbeitenden Gesellschaft*, 2nd ed., Leipzig: Siegfried Lebrecht Crusius.

—— (1785a), *Zum Nachdenken und Nachforschen. Von der Lehrform der Latinität durch Sachkenntnis. Mit Beschreibung und Anbietung einer Vorakademie der lateinischen Studien, für solche, die sie spät anfangen und bald endigen wollen*, Hamburg: Bohn.

—— (1785b), *Unerwartlich große Verbesserung der Kunst, Lesen zu lehren, nebst einem Buchstabierbüchlein*, Leipzig: Siegfried Lebrecht Crusius.

—— (1784a), *Jesus Christus, die große Christenwelt und die kleine Auswahl*, Leipzig: Siegfried Lebrecht Crusius.

—— (1784b), *Examen in der allernatürlichsten Religion und in andern praktischen Lehren von Bürgerpflicht, Toleranz und Tugend, imgleichen von Vernunft und ihrer Gotteserkenntnis*, Leipzig: Siegfried Lebrecht Crusius.

—— (1784c), *Einer philadelphischen Gesellschaft Gesangbuch für Christen und für philosophische Christgenossen*, Leipzig: Siegfried Lebrecht Crusius.

—— (1783a), *Etwas aus dem Archive der Basedowischen Lebensbeschreibung von ihm selbst, betreffend des Herrn Professor Wolke und des Herrn M. Reichs vereinigte*

Feindschaft gegen ihn. Nebst e. vorgängigen Ankündigung einer Quartalschaft, gennant: Nutzbare Erfahrungen des Basedowischen Lebens, Leipzig: Jublilatemesse.

—— (1783b), *Basedows und Wolkens gemeinschaftliche Erklärung ihrer durch Entdeckung vieler Umstände gänzlich und auf immer geendigten Streitigkeiten*, Leipzig: Siegfried Lebrecht Crusius.

—— (1781a), *Allgemein-christliches Gesangbuch für alle Kirchen und Sekten*, Riga and Altona: Eckhardt.

—— (1781b), *Paraphrastischer Auszug des Neuen Testamentes nach dem Bedürfnisse unsrer Zeiten eingerichtet, von einem vieljährigen christlichen Selbstforscher*, Berlin: Mylius.

—— (1780), *Lehren der christlichen Weisheit und Zufriedenheit für forschende Selbstdenker*, 2 parts, Leipzig: Siefried Lebrecht Crusius.

—— (1777a), *Practische Philosophie für alle Stände. Ein weltburgerlich Buch ohne Anstoß für irgend eine Nation und Kirche*, Dessau: Siegfried Lebrecht Crusius.

—— (1777b), *An das Publikum, die Mageldorfische Schmähschrift wider des Dessauische Edukationsinstitut und den Prof. Basedow begreffend*, Dessau: publisher not identified.

—— (1777c), *Pädagogosche Unterhandlungen oder: Philanthropisches Journal und Lesebuch*, Dessau: Siegfried Lebrecht Crusius.

—— (1776a), *Erstes Stück des philanthropischen Archivs, mitgeteilt von verbrüderten Jugendfreunden an Vormunder der Menschheit, besonders welche eine Schulverbesserung wünschen und beginnen; auch an Väter und Mütter, welche Kinder ins Dessauische Philanthropin senden wollen*, Dessau: Siegfried Lebrecht Crusius. [= ES]

—— (1776b), *Historiae antiquae Chrestomathia Philanthropica, volumina I, II, und III Libri I-VIII. Quibis continentur praeter Geograph. Mythol. Antiq. Rom. U. alia doctoribus prae cognoscenda Eutropius, Iustinus, Florus, Velleius, Nepos, Suetonius, Curtius, utiliter breviati auctore I. B. Basedowis, Phil. Dess. Cur.* Dessau: publisher not identified.

—— (ed.) (1775), *Encyclopaedia Philanthropica colloquiorum Erasmi. Demptis illis partibus, quae erant adolescentum moribus nociuae ordini sacro et militari odiosae. Graecis et Mythologicis implicatae; religionis respecta intemplestinae, erroribus philosophicis mixtae ad nostri seculi genium minus accomodatae. Conscripta in usum non scholarum tantummodo et magistrorum latine loquentium, sed ominium etiam lectorum, qui argumenta ad cujusque aetatis sexus et ordinis prudentiam virtutemque facientia, item nonnulla decenter jocosa et utiliter jucunda, more socratico latioque sermone tractata, legere gestinut. In Philanthropiis Dessauiensi et (N. B.) Rhaetico Helvetiorum*, Dessau: Siegfried Lebrecht Crusius.

—— (1774a), *Das in Dessau errichtete Philanthropinum, eine Schule der Menschenfreundschaft und guter Kenntnisse für Lernende und junge Lehrer, Arme und Reiche; ein Fidei-Kommiß des Publikums, zur Vervollkommnung des Erziehungswesens aller Orten nach dem Plane des Elementarwerks. Den Erforschen und Thätern des*

Guten unter Fürsten, menschenfreundlichen Gesellschaften und Privatpersonen empfohlen von J. B. Basedow, Leipzig: Siegfried Lebrecht Crusius. [= DEP]

—— (1774b), *Arithmetik zum Vergnügen und Nachdenken*, Hamburg: Bohn.

—— (1774c), *Bewiesene Grundsätze der reinen Mathematik*, 2 vols., Leipzig: Siegfried Lebrecht Crusius.

—— (1774d), *Theoretische Mathematik*, Leipzig: Siegfried Lebrecht Crusius.

—— (1774e), *Des Elementarwerks erster, zweiter, dritter, vierter Band. Ein geordneter Vorrat aller nötigen Erkenntnis zum Unterrichte der Jugend von Anfang bis ins akademische Alter, zur Belehrung der Eltern, Schullehrer und Hofmeister, zum Nutzen eines jeden Lehrers, die Erkenntnis zu vervollkommen. Mit kursächsischem gnädigsten Privilegio. In Verbindung mit einer Sammlung von Kupferstichen*, Dessau and Leipzig: Siegfried Lebrecht Crusius.

—— (1771a), *Kleines Buch für Kinder aller Stände* and *Kleines Buch für Eltern und Lehrer aller Stände*, Leipzig: Fritsch.

—— (1771b), *Vierteljährige Nachrichten von Basedows Elementarwerke und von andern Bemühungen, die Erziehung und das Schulwesen zu verbessern*, 1 Stück, Leipzig: Fritsch.

—— (1771c), *Agathokrator oder: Von der Erziehung künftiger Regenten, nebst Anhang und Beilagen*, Leipzig: Fritsch.

—— (1771d), *Dokumentierte Beschreibung der Schlözerischen Taten wider das Elementarwerk, den Verfasser und einige Beförderer desselben nebst Anmerkungen zu des Herrn de las Chalotais' Versuch über den Kinderunterricht*, Leipzig: Fritsch.

—— (1770), *Des Elementarbuchs für die Jugend und für ihre Lehrer und Freunde in gesitteten Ständen erstes, zweites und drittes Stück. Mit dem Zubehör des Methodenbuchs und der Kupfersammlung etc.*, Altona and Bremen: Bohn.

—— (1768a), *Das Nötigste von der Vorstellung an Menschenfreunde und vermögende Männer wegen einer versprochenen Folge von untheologischen Schulbüchern nach dem Bedürfnisse und Geschmacke unsrer Zeiten*, Altona: publisher not identified.

—— (1768b), *Ehrerbietiges Schreiben an diejenigen Menschenfreunde und vermögende Männer, welche um Beförderung der Schulbibliothek und des Elementarbuchs ersucht zu werden verlangen*, Altona: publisher not identified.

—— (1768c), *Die ganze natürliche Weisheit im Privatstände gesitter Bürger*, Altona: Spiering.

—— (1768d), *Vierteljährige Unterhandlungen mit Menschenfreunden über moralische und dennoch unkirchliche Verbesserungen der Erziehung und Studien*, Bremen: Cramer.

—— (1767a), *Hauptprobe der Zeiten in Ansehung der Religion, Wahrheitsliebe und Toleranz*, Berlin and Altona: publisher not identified.

—— (1767b), *Ein Privatgesangbuch zur gesellschaftlichen und unanstößigen Erbauung, auch für solche Christen, welche verschiedenen Glaubens sind*, Berlin and Altona: publisher not identified.

—— (1766a), *Betrachtungen über die wahre Rechtgläubigkeit und die im Staate und in der Kirche notwendige Toleranz*, Altona: David Iversen.

——— (1766b), *Vorbereitung der Jugend zur Moralität und natürlichen Religion*, Berlin and Altona: publisher not identified.

——— (1765), *Theoretisches System der gesunden Vernunft, ein akademisches Lehrbuch*, 2 vols., Altona: David Iversen.

——— (1764a), *Philalethie. Neue Aussichten in die Wahrheiten und Religion der Vernunft bis in die Grenzen der glaubwürdigen Offenbarung, dem denkenden Publiko eröffnet von J. B. Basedow*, 2 vols., Altona: David Iversen.

——— (1764b), *Methodischer Unterricht der Jugend in der Religion und Sittenlehre der Vernunft nach dem in der Philalethie angegebenen Plane*, Altona: David Iversen.

——— (1764c), *Schutzschrift für seine neuesten Bucher gegen den Herrn Göze*, Altona: David Iversen.

——— (1763), *Überzeugende Methode der auf das bürgerliche Leben angewandten Arithmetik, zum Vergnügen der Nachdenkenden und zur Beförderung des guten Unterrichts in den Schulen, erleichtert von J. B. Basedow*, Altona: David Iversen.

——— (1761), *Jo. Bernh. Basedovii oratio auspicalis de vaiis gravissimis circa axiomata moralia questionibus*, Altona: Stanno Burmesteriano.

——— (1760), *Vergleichung der Lehren und Schreibart des moralischen Aufsehers und besonders des Herrn Hofpredigers Cramer, mit dem merkwürdigen Beschuldigungen gegen dieselben in de Briefen: Die neuste Literatur betrffend*, Soroe: Jonas Lindgren.

——— (1759), *Neue Lehrart und Übung in der Regelmäßigkeit der deutschen Sprache*, Copenhagen: Ackermann.

——— (1758a), *Akademische Trauerrede über den Herrn Friedrich von Rosenkranz, Freiherrn, Hofjunker des Königs und Akademisten auf der königlichen Ritterakademie zu Soroe*, Soroe: publisher not identified.

——— (1758b), *Praktische Philosophie für alle Stände*, 2 vols., Copenhagen and Leipzig: Ackermann. (2nd ed., 1777.)

——— (1756), *Lehrbuch prosaischer und poetischer Wohlredenheit in verschiedenen Schreibarten und Werken, zu akademischen Vorlesungen eingerichtet von M. J. B. Basedow*, Copenhagen: Roth.

——— (1754), *Von der Glückseligkeit des Königsreiches Dänemark und der Regierung Friedrichs V.*, Copenhagen: publisher not identified.

——— (1753a), *Dissertatio de philosophiae studio a procerum filiis prudenter moderando*, Copenhagen: Havniae.

——— (1753b), *Versuch, wiefern die Philosophie zur Feigeisterei verführe*, Copenhagen: publisher not identified.

——— (1752a), *Inusitata et optima honestioris iuventutis erudiendae methodus*. Kiel: publisher not identified.

——— (1752b), *Nachricht, inwiefern besagte Methode wirklich ausgeübt sei und was sie gewirket*, Hamburg: publisher not identified.

——— (1750), *Epistolae ad Michaelem Richeium, P. P. Virum Praennobilissimum, Celeberrimum, II. J. Bernh. Basedovi: Additis Pueri Nobilis Octavum Annum Agentis Epistolis III. Non Emandatisi*, Hamburg: typis Jo. Grorgii Piscatoris et filii.

────── (1746), *Die Notwendigkeit der Geschichtskunde, dem hochedelgeboren und hochgelahrten Hernn Michael Richey, berühmten Lehrer der Geschichte am hamburgischen Gymnasium, zur Bezeugung seiner dankbegierigen Ehrfurcht gewidmet von dem Verfasser Joh. Bernh. Bassedau*, Hamburg: Conrad König.

Secondary Sources

Aquinas, Thomas ([1265] 1945), *The Basic Writings of Saint Thomas Aquinas*, ed. Anton C. Pegis, 2 vols., New York: Random House.

Bach, Adolf (1923), *Goethes Rheinreise mit Lavater und Basedow im Sommer 1774*, Zurich: Verlag Seldwyla.

Barnard, Henry (1863), *Memoirs of Eminent Teachers and Educators in Germany; with Contributions to the History of Education from the Fourteenth to the Nineteenth Century*, Philadelphia: J. P. Lippincott & Co.

Basedow, Armin (1924), *Johann Bernhard Basedow (1724–1790): Neue Beiträge, Ergänzungen und Berichtungen, zu seiner Lebensgeschichte*, Langensalza: Hermann Beyer & Söhne. [= AB]

Baumgarten, Alexander ([1757] 2014), *Metaphysics: A Critical Translation with Kant's Elucidations, Selected Notes, and Related Materials*, trans. and ed. Courtney D. Fugate and John Hymers, London: Bloomsbury.

Beiser, Frederick (1987), *The Fate of Reason: German Philosophy from Kant to Fichte*, Cambridge: Harvard University Press.

Benner, Dietrich and Herwart Kemper (2009), *Theorie und Geschichte der Reformpädagogik. Teil 1: Die pädagogische Bewegung von der Aufklärung bis zum Neuhumanismus*, 3rd ed., Weinheim: Beltz Verlag.

Benner, Dietrich and Herward Kemper (eds.) (2000), *Quellentexte zur Theorie und Geschichte der Reformpädagogik. Teil 1: Die pädagogische Bewegung von der Aufklärung bis zum Neuhumanismus*, Weinheim: Deutscher Studien Verlag.

Berlin, Isaiah (1993), *The Magus of the North: J. G. Hamann and the Origins of Modern Irrationalism*, London: John Murray.

Bessler, Johannes Ferdinand (1900), *Unterricht und Übung in der Religion: am Philanthropin zu Dessau*, Niederlössnitz: Adolph Adam.

Blankertz, Herwig (1982), *Die Geschichte der Pädagogik: Von der Aufklärung bis zur Gegenwart*, Wetzlar: Büchse der Pandora.

Bollnow, Otto Friedrich (1952), "Basedow, Johann Friedrich," in Historische Kommission bei der Bayerischen Akademie der Wissenschaften (ed.), *Neue deutsche Biographie*, I: 618–19. Berlin: Duncker & Humblot.

Borkman, Kurt Jonathan (1993), "Enlightenment and Enervation: the Philanthropic Program of Physical Training and Perceptions of Cultural Decadence in Late Eighteenth Century Germany," PhD diss., University of Michigan, Ann Arbor.

Cavallar, Georg (2015), *Kant's Embedded Cosmopolitanism: History, Philosophy, and Education for World Citizens*, Berlin: De Gruyter.

Chance, Brian A. (2019), "Kantian Non-Evidentialism and its German Antecedents: Crusius, Meier, and Basedow," *Kantian Review* 24 (3): 359–84.

Church, Forrest (1989), "The Gospel According to Thomas Jefferson," in Thomas Jefferson, *The Jefferson Bible: The Life and Morals of Jesus of Nazareth*, 1–32, Boston: Beacon Press.

Comenius, Johann Amos ([1657] 1887), *Orbis Pictus*, trans. Charles Hoole, Syracuse: C. W. Bardeen.

Dahlstrom, Daniel O. (2018), "Reason within the Limits of Religion Alone: Hamann's Onto-Christology," in Daniel O. Dahlstrom (ed.), *Kant and His German Contemporaries*, vol. II: *Aesthetics, History, Politics, and Religion*, 238–56, Cambridge: Cambridge University Press

Descartes, René (1984), *The Philosophical Writings of Descartes*, trans. John Cottingham, Robert Stoothoff, and Dugald Murdoch, 3 vols., Cambridge: Cambridge University Press.

Dewey, John (1987), *The Middle Works*, vol. 3, ed. Jo Ann Boydston, Carbondale: Southern Illinois University Press.

—— (1946), *Problems of Men*, New York: Philosophical Library.

—— (1900a), *The School and Society*, Chicago: University of Chicago Press.

—— (1900b), "Froebel's Educational Principles," *The Elementary School Record*, 5: 143–51.

Diestelmann, Richard (1897), *Johann Bernhard Basedow*, in *Größe Erzieher*, vol. 2, ed. R. Voigtländer, Leipzig: R. Voigtländer's Verlag.

Egerland, Herbert (1994), "Basedow und das Schulbuch," in Erhard Hirsch, Thomas Höhle, and Jürgen Gebhardt (eds), *Zwischen Wörlitz und Mosigkau*, 27–33, Dessau: City of Dessau.

"Fragmente über Basedow" (1790), *Deutsche Monatsschrift* 1(12): 281–316.

Frankena, William K. (1965), *Three Historical Philosophies of Education: Aristotle, Kant, Dewey*, Glenview, IL: Scott, Foresman and Company.

Fritzsch, Theodor ([1909] 1972), "Einleitung des Herausgebers," in Johann Bernhard Basedow, *Elementarwerk mit den Kupfertafeln Chodowieckis u. a.*, ed. Theodor Fritzsch, 3 vols., I: V-XXXVIII, Hildesheim: Georg Olms Verlag. [= E]

—— (1901), "Einleitung," in Johann Bernhard Basedow, *Vorstellung an Menschenfreunde*, ed. Theodor Fritsch, 1–8. Leipzig: Reclam.

Garve, Christian (1771), Review of Basedow's *Methodenbuch* and *Elementarbuch*, in *Neuen Bibliothek der schönen Wissenschaften und der freien Künste* 12.1: 282–324.

Gilow, Hermann ([1909] 1972), "Einleitung. Basedow und Chodowiecki," in Johann Bernhard Basedow, *Elementarwerk mit den Kupfertafeln Chodowieckis u.a*, ed. Theodor Fritzsch, 3 vols., III: 1–17. Hildesheim: Georg Olms Verlag.

Goethe, Johann Wolfgang von ([1814] 1890), *Dichtung und Wahrheit* (Book XIV), in *J. W. von Goethes Werke, Historisch-kritische Gesammtausgabe*, ed. im Auftrage der

Großherzigen Sophie von Sachsen, 133 vols., 1: 271–81. Weimar: Verlag Hermann Böhlau.
Göring, Hugo (1880), "Basedow's Leben und Wirken," in *J. B. Basedow's Ausgewählte Schriften*, ed. Hugo Göring, I-CXII, Langensalza: Hermann Beyer & Söhne. [= G]
Graves, Frank Pierrepont (1914), *A History of Education in Modern Times*, New York: Macmillan.
—— (1912), *Great Educators of three Centuries: Their Work and its Influence on Modern Education*, New York: Macmillan.
Hamann, Johann Georg (1957), *Briefwechsel*, eds. Walther Ziesemer and Arthur Henkel, 6 vols. Wiesbaden: Insel.
Herrmann, Ulrich (1979), "Die Pädagogik der Philanthropen," in Hans Scheuerl (ed.), *Klassiker der Pädagogik*, Munich: C. H. Beck.
Hertz, Frederick (1962), *The Development of the German Public Mind: A Social History of German Political Sentiments, Aspirations, and Ideas*, 2 vols., London: Allen & Unwin.
Hinske, Norbert (1990), "Die Tragenden Grundideen der deutschen Aufklärung: Versuch einer Tyopologie," in Raffael Ciafardone (ed.), *Die Philosophie der deutschen Aufklärung: Texte und Darstellung*, 406–58. Stuttgart: Reclam.
Hirsch, Erhard (2008), "'Das meiste neue pädagogische Licht ist von Dessau ausgegangen'. Zum 275. Geburtstag Basedows und 225. Gründungstag des Dessauer Philanthropins," in Jörn Garber (ed.), *"Die Stammmutter aller guten Schulen:" Das Dessauer Philanthropinum und der deutsche Philanthropinismus*, 23–82, Tübingen: Max Niemeyer Verlag.
Holst, Amalia ([1802] 1984), *Über die Bestimmung des Weibes zur höhern Geistesbildung*, ed. Berta Rahm. Zurich: ALA.
James, William (1897), *The Will to Believe and Other Essays in Popular Philosophy*, New York: Longmans Green and Co.
Jefferson, Thomas (1984), *Writings*, ed. Merrill D. Peterson, New York: The Library of America.
Johnston, James Scott (2013), *Kant's Philosophy: A Study for Educators*, London: Bloomsbury.
Kant, Immanuel (1900–), *Kant's gesammelte Schriften*, ed. Berlin-Brandenburg Academy of Sciences, 29 vols., Berlin: de Gruyter.
Kegler, Frank (1994), "Briefe an das Dessauer Philanthropin 1774 bis 1776. Ein Beitrag zur zeitgenössischen Rezeption des pädagogischen Werkes Joh. Bernhard Basedows," in Erhard Hirsch, Thomas Höhle, and Jürgen Gebhardt (eds), *Zwischen Wörlitz und Mosigkau*, 17–21, Dessau: City of Dessau.
Kilpatrick, William H. (1943), "Progressive Education," in Harry N. Rivlin (ed.), *The Encyclopedia of Modern Education*, 612–14. New York: Philosophical Library.
Kowalewski, Arnold, ed. (1924), *Die philosophischen Hauptvorlesungen Immanuel Kants. Nach den neu aufgefunden Kolleghesten des Grafen Heinrich zu Dohna-Wundlacken.* Munich and Leipzig: Rösl & Cie.

Krause, Horst M. P. (1994), "Joh. Bernhard Basedow – Abstand und Nähe. Versuch zur Annäherung an Person und Werk angesichts der neuen historischen Situation," in Erhard Hirsch, Thomas Höhle, and Jürgen Gebhardt (eds), *Zwischen Wörlitz und Mosigkau*, 2–10, Dessau: City of Dessau.

——— (1979), "Einleitung," in Johann Bernhard Basedow, *Das Methodenbuch für Väter und Mütter der Familien und Völker*, VII-LXXVI. Vaduz: Topos Verlag.

Landschoof, Joseph Aubrey (1933), "The Life and Work of Johann Bernhard Basedow," PhD diss., New York University.

Lang, Ossian Herbert (1892), *Basedow: His Educational Work and Principles*, New York: Kellogg.

Lauchkard, C. J. (1848), "J. B. Basedow," in Eduard Duller (ed.), *Die Männer des Volks, dargestellet von Freunden des Volks*, 6: 69–100. Frankfurt: Meidinger.

Locke, John ([1693] 1996), *Some Thoughts Concerning Education* and *Of the Conduct of the Understanding*, eds. Ruth W. Grant and Nathan Tarcov, Indianapolis: Hackett.

Louden, Robert B. (forthcoming), "A Mere Skeleton of the Sciences? Amalia Holst's Critique of Basedow and Campe," in Corey W. Dyck (ed.), *Women and Philosophy in Eighteenth-Century Germany*, Oxford: Oxford University Press.

——— (2017), "Becoming Human: Kant's Philosophy of Education and Human Nature," in Matthew C. Altman (ed.), *The Palgrave Kant Handbook*, 705–27. London: Palgrave Macmillan.

——— (2016a), "'Total Transformation': Why Kant did Not Give Up on Education," *Kantian Review*, 21 (3): 393–414.

——— (2016b), "Argue But Obey? Questioning Kant's Enlightenment," in R. Jiménez, R. Hanna, R. Louden, N. Madrid, and J. Rosales (eds), *Critical Paths outside the Critiques: Kant's Shorter Writings*, 284–300. Cambridge: Cambridge Scholars Publishing.

——— (2012), "'Not a Slow *Reform*, but a Swift *Revolution*': Basedow and Kant on the Need to Transform Education," in Klas Roth and Chris Suprenant (eds.), *Kant and Education: Interpretations and Commentary*, 39–54. New York: Routledge.

——— (2007a), *The World We Want: How and Why the Ideals of the Enlightenment Still Elude Us*, New York: Oxford University Press.

——— (2007b) Translation of Immanuel Kant, *Essays Concerning the Philanthropinum*, In Immanuel Kant, *Anthropology, History, and Education, The Cambridge Edition of the Works of Immanuel Kant*, Robert B. Louden and Günter Zöller (eds.), 98–104, Cambridge: Cambridge University Press.

——— (2000), *Kant's Impure Ethics: From Rational Beings to Human Beings*, New York: Oxford University Press.

Luther, Martin (1999), *Luther's Works*, eds. Jaroslav Jan Pelikan, Hilton C. P. Oswald, and Helmut T. Lehmann, 54 vols., Philadelphia: Fortress Press.

Meier, Johann Christian (1791–2), *Johann Bernhard Basedows Leben, Charakter und Schriften unparteisch deargestellt und beurtheilt*, 2 vols., Hamburg: Benj. Gottlob Hoffmann. [= M]

Mendelssohn, Moses (2011), *Morning Hours: Lectures on God's Existence*, trans. Daniel O. Dahlstrom and Corey Dyck, Dordrecht: Springer.
Mill, John Stuart (1961), *Essential Works of John Stuart Mill*, ed. Max Lerner, New York: Bantam Books.
Mönckeberg, Carl (1867), *Hermann Samuel Reimarus und Johann Christian Edelmann*, Hamburg: G. Ed. Notle.
Monroe, Paul (1907), *A Text-Book in the History of Education*, New York: The Macmillan Company.
Mozart, Leopold (1756), *Versuch einer gründlichen Violinschule*, Augsburg: published by the author.
Müller, Friedrich Max ([1875] 1967), "Basedow, Johann Bernhard," in Königliche Akademie der Wissenschaften (ed.), *Allgemeine Deutsche Biographie*, II: 113–24, Berlin: Duncker & Humblot.
—— ([1881] 1922). "Translator's Preface," in Kant, Immanuel, *Immanuel Kant's Critique of Pure Reason. In Commemoration of the Centenary of its First Publication*, trans. F. Max Müller, 2nd ed., rev., xxvii–lxxix, New York: Macmillan.
Neill, A. S. (1960), *Summerhill: A Radical Approach to Child Rearing*, New York: Hart Publishing Company.
Niethammer, Immanuel ([1808] 1968), *Der Streit des Philanthropinismus und Humanismus in der Theorie des Erziehungs-Unterrichts unsrer Zeit*, Weinheim: Belz.
Overhoff, Jürgen (2020), *Johann Bernhard Basedow (1724-1790): Aufklärer, Pädagoge, Menschenfreund. Eine Biographie*, Göttingen, Wallstein.
—— (2015), "Zum Titelbild," *Philanthropinum*, 33: 7–10.
—— (2010), "Basedow, Johann Bernhard," in Heiner Klemme and Manfred Kuehn (eds), *Dictionary of Eighteenth-Century German Philosophers*, 2 vols., 1: 59–63. London: Continuum.
—— (2007), "Franklin's Philadelphia Academy and Basedow's Dessau Philanthropine: Two Models of Non-denominational Schooling in Eighteenth-Century America and Germany," *Paedagogica Historica*, 43.6: 801–18.
—— (2004), *Die Frühgeschichte dees Philanthropinismus (1715–1771). Konstitutionsbedingungen, Praxisfelder und Wirkung eines pädagogischen Reformprogramms im Zeitaler der Aufklärung*, Tübingen: Max Niemeyer Verlag.
Parker, Chester (1912), "Experimental Schools in Germany in the Eighteenth-Century," *The Elementary School Teacher*, 12.5: 215–24.
Paulsen, Friedrich (1908), *German Education: Past and Present*, trans. T. Lorenz, New York: Charles Scribner's Sons.
Pinloche, Albert (1896), *Geschichte des Philanthropinismus*, trans. J. Rauschenfels and A. Pinloche. Leipzig: Friedrich Branstetter.
Priestley, Joseph ([1778] 2013), *Miscellaneous Observations Relating to Education. More Especially, as it respects the Conduct of the Mind. To which is added, An Essay on a Course of Liberal Education for Civil and Active Life*, Cambridge: Cambridge University Press.

"Progressive Education" (2002), in *the New Encyclopedia Britannica*, 15th ed., 9: 722. Chicago: Encyclopedia Britannica, Inc.

Quick, Robert Herbert (1896), *Essays on Educational Reformers*, New York: D. Appleton and Company.

Rammelt, Johannes (1929), *Johann Bernhard Basedow, der Philanthropismus und das Dessauer Philanthropin*, Dessau: Verlag Walther Schwalbe.

Rathmann, Heinrich (1791), *Beiträge zur Lebensgeschichte Joh. Bernh. Basedows: aus seinen Schriften und anderen ächten Quellen gesammelt*, Magdeburg: Verlag der Pansaischen Buchdruckerey. [= Ra]

Raumer, Karl von (1857), *Geschichte der Pädagogik vom Wiederaufblühen klassicher Studien bis auf unsere Zeit*, 2nd Part, 3rd rev. and expanded ed., Stuttgart: Verlag von Samuel Gottlieb Liesching.

—— (1843), *Geschichte der Pädagogik vom Wiederaufblühen klassicher Studien bis auf unsere Zeit*, 2nd Part, Stuttgart: Verlag von Samuel Gottlieb Liesching.

Raupp, Werner (2016), "Reimarus, Hermann Samuel," in Heiner F. Klemme and Manfred Kuehn (eds.), *The Bloomsbury Dictionary of Eighteenth-Century Philosophy*, 611–14, London: Bloomsbury.

Ravitch, Diane (2000), *Left Back: A Century of Failed School Reforms*, New York: Simon & Schuster.

Reble, Albert (1999), *Geschichte der Pädagogik*, 19th rev. ed. Stuttgart: Klett-Cotta.

—— (1965), "Leben und Werk Johann Bernhard Basedows," in Johann Bernhard Basedow, *Johann Bernhard Basedow: Ausgewählte pädagogische Schriften*, ed. Alfred Reble, 253–64, Paderborn: Ferdinand Schöningh. [= R]

Reimarus, Hermann Samuel (1970), *Reimarus: Fragments*, ed. Charles H. Talbert, trans. Ralph S. Fraser, London: SCM Press.

Rogers, Richard and Oscar Hammerstein (1949), *South Pacific*, [Musical], USA.

Rousseau, Jean-Jacques ([1762] 1979), *Émile, or On Education*, trans. Allan Bloom, New York: Basic Books.

Rudolph, Frederick (1962), *The American College and University: A History*, New York: Vintage Books.

Rutschky, Katharina, ed. (1977), *Schwarze Pädagogik: Quellen zur Naturgeschichte der bürgerlichen Erziehung*, Frankfurt: Ullstein.

Sahlberg, Pasi and William Doyle (2019), *Let the Children Play: How More Play Will Save Our Schools and Help Children Thrive*, New York: Oxford University Press.

Salzmann, Christian Gotthilf (1784), *Noch etwas über die Erziehung nebst Ankündigung einer Erziehungsanstalt*, Leipzig: Siegfried Lebrecht Crusius.

Schiller, Friedrich ([1795] 1967), *On the Aesthetic Education of Man in a Series of Letters*, ed. and trans. Elizabeth M. Wilkinson and L. A. Willoughby, Oxford: Clarendon Press.

Schlosser, Friedrich Christoph (1844), *History of the Eighteenth Century and of the Nineteenth till the Overthrow of the French Empire*, trans. D. Davidson, London: Chapman and Hall.

Schmid, Karl A. (1898), *Geschichte der Erziehung vom Anfang an bis unsere Zeit*, 5 vols. Stuttgart: J. G. Cotta'schen Buchhandlung.

Schmidt, Karl (1861), *Die Geschichte der Pädagogik*, vol. 3: *Die Geschichte der Pädagogik von Luther bis Pestalozzi*, Cöthen: Paul Schettler.

Schmitt, Hanno (2008), "Versuchschule vor zweihundert Jahren. Ein Besuch am Dessauer Philanthropin," in Jörn Garber (ed.), *"Die Stammmuter aller guten Schulen:" Das Dessauer Philanthropinum und der deutsche Philanthropinismus*, 169–77, Tübingen: Max Niemeyer Verlag.

Schummel, Johann Gottlieb (1776), *Fritzens Reise nach Dessau*, Leipzig: Siegfried Lebrecht Crusius.

Seeley, Levi (1899), *History of Education*, New York: American Book Company.

Spazier, Karl (1792), *Carl Pilger's Roman seines Lebens: von ihm selbst geschrieben; Ein Beitrag zur Erziehung und Kultur des Menschen*, vol. 3, Berlin: Verlag der Konigl. Preus. Akadem. Kunst- und Buchhandlung.

Specht, Joachim (1999), *Ich, Johann Bernhard Basedow*, Dessau: Anhaltische Verlagsgesellschaft.

Steinhauben, Jan (2008), "Geschlechteranthropologie und Erziehung der Töchter im Philanthropismus," in Jörn Garber (ed.), *"Die Stammutter aller guten Schulen:" Das Dessauer Philanthropinum und der deutsche Philanthropismus 1774–1793*, 179–208. Tübingen: Max Niemeyer Verlag.

Stern, David (1912), *Johann Bernhard Basedow und seine philosophischen und theologischen Anschauungen*, Königsberg: Buchdruckerei R. Leopold.

Sumalvico, Thea (2018), "Baptism and Basedow: A Debate of the 1760s," unpublished manuscript.

Swet, Curt (1898), *Beiträge zur Lebensgeshichte und Pädagogik Joh. Bernh. Basedow*, Zwickau: Druck von C. A. Günther Nachfolger.

Swrakoff, Konstantin D. (1898), *Der Einfluss der zeitgenösischen Philosophie auf Basedows Pädagogik*, Giessen: Brühl'sche Univ.-Buch und Steindruckerei.

Talbert, Charles H. (1970), "Introduction," in Hermann Samuel Reimarus, *Reimarus: Fragments*, ed. Charles H. Talbert, trans. Ralph S. Fraser, 1–43, London: SCM Press.

Thalhofer, Franz Xaver (1907), *Die sexuelle Pädagogik bei den Philanthropen*, Munich: Verlag der Jos. Kösel'schen Buchhandlung.

Tonelli, Giorgio (1967), "Basedow, Johann Bernhard," in Paul Edwards (ed.), *The Encyclopedia of Philosophy*, 8 vols., 1: 251, New York: Macmillan.

Vorbrodt, Walter (1920), *Basedows Leben und Werke*, Halle: Pädagogsicher Verlag von Hermann Schroedel.

Weisskopf, Traugott (1970), *Immanuel Kant und die Pädagogik. Beiträge zu einer Monographie*, Zurich: Editio Academica.

Wilcker, Johann and Joachim Ernst Scheidhauer (1790), *Ueber Basedow's Begräbnis. Ein Abendgespräch zweier Freunde, allenfalls auch ein Pendant zur Kirchen- und Ketzergeschichte des achzehnten Jahrhunderts*, Magdeburg: im Scheidhauerschen Verlag.

Wokler, Robert (2001), *Rousseau: A Very Short Introduction*, Oxford: Oxford University Press.
Wolf, Ursula (2004), *Christian Heinrich Wolke: Ein Pädagoge der Aufklärungszeit*, Dessau: Manuela Kinzel Verlag.

Websites

Gymnasium Philanthropinum Dessau – Schule der Menschenfreundschaft (2019), "Schulprogramm," http://philan.de/schulprogramm/ (accessed November 19, 2019).
Magdeburgischen Gesellschaft von 1990 e.V. (n.d.), https://www.mg-90.de (accessed November 11, 2019).
Salzmannschule Schnepfenthal (n.d.), http://salzmannschule.de/ (accessed November 11, 2019).
Taylor, Kate (2019), "Fallout From College Admissions Scandal: Arrests, Damage Control and a Scramble for Answers," *New York Times*, March 13, https://www.nytimes.com/2019/03/13/us/college-admissions-probe.html (accessed November 11, 2019).

Index

Aquinas, St. Thomas 136, 202 n.4

Bahrdt, Karl Friedrich 85, 164, 208 n.51
Basedow, Carl Adolph von (grandson of Johann Bernhard Basedow) 208 n.8
Basedow, Emilie (daughter of Johann Bernhard Basedow) 173
   birth 5, 92, 149
   star pupil at Philanthropin 19–21, 122, 182
Basedow, Emilie (née Dumas – Johann Bernhard Basedow's first wife) 4–5, 53, 61–2, 67, 70
Basedow, Franz (first son of Johann Bernhard and Gertrude Elisabeth Basedow) 92
Basedow, Friedrich ("Fritz" – second son of Johann Bernhard and Gertrude Elisabeth Basedow) 149, 203 n.1
Basedow, Gertrude Elisabeth (neé Hammer – Johann Bernhard Basedow's second wife) 5, 62, 92, 173
Basedow, Heinrich Josias (Johann Bernhard and Emile Basedow's son) 62, 70
Basedow, Johann Bernhard
   alcoholism 1, 79–80, 164
   alleged German Rousseau 2, 25, 110, 185 n.4, 198. 27, 203 n.8
   birth and early years 3–4, 29–43
   character flaws 1, 3, 29, 33, 43, 144
   civil rights for Jews 73, 139
   copper plates 114, 146
   cosmopolitanism 10, 72
   criticism of universities 50, 96–7, 123
   death and burial 173–4
   discipline and conformity 102, 107
   excommunication from Lutheran Church 5, 80–1
   father of progressive education 2–3, 6, 13, 177–83
   final years in Magdeburg 6, 171–4
   foreign-language instruction 14, 63–6, 114–16
   girls' education 119–22, 187–8 n.17
   Glaubenspflicht doctrine 86–7, 119, 136–7
   health problems 3, 34, 43, 50, 75, 79–80
   Kiel dissertation 4, 14, 57, 61, 63–7, 172
   learning through play 36, 54–5, 63–4, 107–8, 111, 122, 134, 150, 153
   memorials for 174, 176–7
   moral education and 74, 105, 110–13, 134, 137
   moral education council 122–3
   naturalism 63, 101, 179–80
   need for public education 123–4
   need for teacher-training institutes 115
   opposition to memorization 64, 84, 111
   philosophy and 68–9, 71, 73, 141
   professor at Gymnasium Christaneum 5, 76–7, 79–92
   professor at *Ritterakademie* 5, 62, 67–76
   physical education 65–6, 104
   realia 112
   religious persecution of 5, 80–1
   religious tolerance 86, 133–4
   religious views 9–11, 42, 48–9, 59, 64, 69, 71, 76, 117–19, 135–7, 182–7
   resigns from Philanthropin directorship 28, 160–2
   reward and punishment 102–3, 105, 111, 150–1
   sex education 74–5, 105–7
   runs away from home at sixteen 4, 36–7
   school library project 87–9, 124–7
   student at Johanneum 35–8
   student at Hamburg Gymnasium 38–42, 45
   student at University of Kiel, 3, 50–1

student at University of Leipzig 3,
    45–50
transformation of schools 2, 90
tutor in Borhorst 4, 53–62, 172
vocational education 140
see also Philanthropin
Basedow, Ludwig von (third son of Johann Bernhard and Gertrude Emilie Basedow) 6, 173, 208 n.8, 209 n.9
Bassedau, Anna Maria (née Jungbluth – Johann Bernhard Basedow's mother) 4, 32–3
Bassedau, Hinrich (Johann Bernhard Basedow's father) 4, 32–3, 45
Baumgarten, Alexander 47, 119, 192 n.9
Benzler, Friedrich August 149, 203 n.3
Bernstorf, Johann Hartwig Ernst von 75–6, 80, 89, 196 n.9
Boessel, Georg Daniel 37
Büsching, Anton Friedrich 157, 206 n.34

Campe, Joachim Heinrich 21, 22, 26, 156
    directorship of Philanthropin 162–3, 188 n.27, 206 n.29
Catherine the Great 164–5, 187–8 n.17, 200 n.3
Cautius, Emmanuel (Emilie Basedow's husband) 173
Chodowiecki, Daniel Nikolaus 6, 17, 130, 134–6, 144–7
Comenius, Johann Amos 17–18, 147
Cramer, Johann Andreas 80, 196 n.5
Crichton, Wilhelm 6, 164
Crusius, Christian August 4, 47–9, 192 n.5, 195 n.16

Danneskiold-Samsøe, Friedrich 75–6
Descartes, René 197 n.17
Dewey, John 13, 178, 209 n.5, 210 n.8
Dohm, Christian Wilhelm von 130–1, 202 n.1

Feder, Christoph Friedrich 154, 157, 204 n.12
Friese, Martin 51
Ferdinand, Karl Wilhelm von Braunschweig-Wolfenbüttel 174
Funk, Gottfried Benedikt 80, 156, 173–4, 196 n.7, 208 n.5

Garve, Christian 28, 130, 181, 183
Goethe, Johann Wolfgang 3–4, 17, 29–30, 95, 145–6, 183
Goeze, Johann Melchoir 80, 82, 85–6, 89, 195 n.1
    urges parishioners to stone Basedow 196 n.10, 197–8 n.19

Hamann, Johann Georg 30, 189 n.4
Harboe, Ludwig 76, 80, 196 n.4
Hauber, Christoph Immanuel 154, 204 n.13
Herder, Johann Gottfried 30, 189 n.4
Holst, Amalia 21

Iselin, Isaac 131, 141, 160, 162

Jahn, Friedrich Georg Wilhelm 156, 160, 206 n.27
James, William 87, 198 n.24
Jasperson, Johann 157, 160, 206 n.36
Jefferson, Thomas 83
Joseph II 97, 133, 200 n.3

Kalisky, Anna Maria Dorothea 6, 171–2, 176, 182
Kant, Immanuel
    anticipation of Dewey 210 n.8
    borrows Basedow's advice on child care 200 n.5
    central importance of education 181
    Copernican revolution 18, 187 n.15
    cosmopolitan education 72, 182
    criticism of Basedow's drinking 30
    criticism of Basedow's syncretism 84
    definition of enlightenment 84–5, 197 n.17
    disappointment over Campe's departure from Philanthropin 162–4
    Essays Regarding the Philanthropinum 2
    ethical theory 138, 201 nn.12–13, 202 nn.5–6
    fund-raiser for Philanthropin 27, 163–4
    higher and lower faculties 186 n.9
    naturalism in education 188 n.20
    opposition to fables in education 200 n.8

physical education 104, 187 n.13, 200 n.6
postulates 87, 119
Philanthropin as experimental school 179–80
Philanthropin as "mother of all good schools in the world" 164, 179–83
Philanthropin as teacher-training institute 22, 180–1
praise for Philanthropin 2, 7, 150, 164, 179–83
Robert Mothersby and 207 n.44
sex education 200 n.7
transformation of schools 2
unity of world religions 182
use of *Methodenbuch* in pedagogy seminar 187 n.12, 189 n.34, 200 n.5
Klopstock, Friedrich Gottlieb 46, 67, 80, 91, 196 n.6, 203 n.1

Lavater, Johann Kaspar 4, 29, 189 n.3
Leopold III, Friedrich Franz, Prince of Anhalt-Dessau 29, 98, 131, 133, 149, 185 n.1
  intervention in quarrel between Wolke and Basedow 164
  and Palais Dietrich 162
Lessing, Gotthold Ephraim 40, 46
Locke, John 58, 66, 194 n.14, 191 n.24, 194 n.14, 210 n.10
Luther, Martin 197 n.16

Mangelsdorf, Carl Ehregott 132, 141, 202 n.3
Meier, Johann Christian
  bias against Basedow 34, 187 n.11, 191 n.19
Mendelsson, Moses 11, 91, 119, 139, 186 n.5, 201 n.15
Mill, John Stuart 20, 187 n.16
Moltke, Adam Gottlob von 67, 68
Mozart, Leopold 26
Müller, Friedrich Max (Johann Bernhard Basedow's great-grandson) 31, 73, 173, 190 n.6
Müller, Johann Samuel 36, 37, 190 n.13

Neil, Alexander Sutherland 186–7 n.10
Neuendorf, Carl Gottfried 156, 157, 160, 165, 206 n.33

Niethammer, Friedrich Immanuel 59–60

Oberlin, Johann Friedrich 27, 28, 189 nn.32–3
Overhoff, Jürgen 191 n.24, 196 n.12

Pechlin, Johann von 63, 67
Philanthropin(um)
  administrative changes 6, 160–5
  clothing of students 18
  curriculum 6, 154–60
  daily life for students 6, 15–16, 150–3
  de-emphasis on memorization and punishment 11–12, 153
  foreign-language instruction 13–14
  gender 19–21, 182
  learning through play 3, 11–13, 36, 54–5, 63, 153
  merit board 152–3, 200 n.9
  naturalism 24–6, 63
  original building destroyed in World War II 148, 175
  Palais Dietrich 154–5, 162, 175, 204 n.14
  Pensionisten and *Famulanten* 19, 151, 154, 158–9, 204 nn.5, 7
  present-day Gymnasium Philanthropinum 175–6
  public examination of 3, 9–28, 149–50
  realia 16–18
  religious tolerance 3, 9–11, 153, 182–3
  rich and poor students 18–19
  sex education 3, 22–4
  teacher-training institute 21–2, 180–1
  vocational and physical education 14–16, 155
  see also Basedow, Johann Friedrich
Platner, Ernst 26, 188 n.23
Priestley, Joseph 193–4 n.13

Qualen, Josias von (father) 26, 53, 67, 193 n.1
  Basedow in family home of 4, 13–14, 26, 110, 114, 172
Qualen, Josias von (son) 53, 55, 60, 115
  Basedow's tutoring of 55–7

Reimarus, Hermann Samuel 4, 38, 40–2, 49, 119

Richey, Michael 52, 57–8, 60, 66, 191–2 n.3
    Basedow's favorite teacher 39–40, 81
Rochow, Friedrich Eberhard von 26, 188 n.30
Rousseau, Jean-Jacques 120, 178, 194 n.16
    alleged source of Basedow's ideas 2, 25–6, 60–1, 110, 185 n.4, 194 nn.14–15

Salis-Marschlins, Karl Ulysses von 22, 164, 208 n.51
Salzmann, Christian Gotthilf 22, 167, 169–70, 188 n.8
Samson, Peter 156, 160, 205 n.25
Schiller, Friedrich 193 n.2
Schlözer, August Ludwig von 127, 130–1, 144
Schummel, Johann Gottlieb 12, 23–4, 26, 106–7, 188 n.26
Schütz, Christian Gottfried 154, 204 n.10
Schwarz, Abel Anton 149, 203 n.2

Spalding, Johann Joachim 91, 199 n.32
Spazier, Johann Gottlieb Karl 163, 207 n.50
Sulzer, Johann Georg 91, 154, 199 n.33

Telemann, Georg Philipp 174
Trapp, Ernst Christian 21, 132, 154, 156, 159, 168

Vogel, Friedrich Erdmann 156, 157, 160, 206 n.32

Wilckens, Matthäus Arnold 47, 191–2 n.3
Wolke, Heinrich Christian 106, 130, 131, 140, 149
    administrator at Philanthropin 163–5, 169
    Basedow's first assistant 19–20, 186 n.8
    teacher at Philanthropin 24, 157, 159
    tutor of Emilie Basedow 92, 122

Zedlitz, Karl Abraham von 17, 145, 203 n.9

www.ingramcontent.com/pod-product-compliance
Lightning Source LLC
Chambersburg PA
CBHW072107010526
44111CB00037B/2026